HOW I BOUGHT THREE LONDON PROPERTIES FOR A FOOTBALL TICKET

Laurence Lameche

Copyright

Powerhouse Publications

Suite 124
94 London Road
Headington
Oxford
OX3 9FN

Cover design and formatting: Oxford Literary Consultancy
www.oxfordwriters.com

Testimonials

"Laurence started out sleeping in a car in London, then through sheer determination and hard work built up his own property portfolio. No matter what obstacles came along, he always found a way around them. His story is incredibly inspiring for anyone wondering if they can do it too."

Stephanie J. Hale
Author of "Millionaire Property Author"
and "Property Trendsetters"

"Laurence Lameche persuades the reader in a simple way to buy property with little money. He gives you all the pieces of the puzzle that many people want to know how to buy property with no money and no mortgage. No matter how hard some people work it seems almost impossible to get on the property ladder however Laurence's book shows you how to do this. Be prepared to be inspired by this book."

Joel Bauer
Author of "How To Persuade People
Who Don't Want To Be Persuaded"
www.joelbauer.com

"I like the common sense approach this book gives you on "How I Bought 3 London Properties For A Football Ticket" for no money. You are guided through Laurence's simple processes so you can do this too."

Simon Zutshi
Author of 'Property Magic'

"I have known Laurence for over 10 years now and I have seen by first-hand experience how he bought "3 London Properties For A Football Ticket". Laurence has also bought many other properties in London and Brighton for just £1. His determination, hard work and dogged persis-tence, coupled with his respectful and sincere approach towards people, has enabled him to do the kind of deals that many can only dream of! In his book, he explains how you can also acquire property which generates great cash flow and equity growth. I thoroughly recommend this book to anyone who wants to learn how to own properties without the need to invest large deposits."

Heath Williams
Millionaire Property Investor & Business Owner

With over 12 years' experience in the banking and asset finance industry, I really thought that no one and especially no book could alter my opinion on how I buy property. But after reading this book my perspective has completely changed and I have realized that it's skill and innovation that creates the right deals not large deposits. This book is a great tool that will guide you step by step to change your life though property and Laurence's unique ideas and concepts really set him apart in the industry as a real innovator and mentor who has created strategies for the masses and not just for the Rich.

Paul Fletcher

Managing Director, Affinity Funding

Millionaire Investor

"I think the Million Dollar business card is a fantastic promotional idea, it caught my attention – well done Laurence I think you're awesome."

Mary-Clare Carlyle

Author of "How To Be A Money Magnet"

"When I first met Laurence and he told me that he buys properties in London for £1, I have to admit I didn't believe it was possible but after getting to know him I have seen for myself first-hand all the properties that he has bought because he showed me all of them. His clever marketing techniques work as I can tell you that he does 'Network Without Talking To People' and he has a 'Million Dollar Business Card' so all the principles he talks about in this book he has done and continues to do them. This book is a go-to bible on how to buy property with No Money and No Mortgage, I just pray that you buy it because it could change your life."

Sandra Apan

"I am full of admiration for your Approach, Ethics and Sincerity. It is rare indeed that we come across people who stand up against the massive tide of self-centredness and selfishness. It was an eye-opening experience to see you go about your task of helping people find tickets, and the interaction with the people who were looking to sell their tickets. I am glad that I was able to meet you at Wembley Stadium, and see what you do. The World needs many more Laurence Lumeches."

Bharat Patel

"I met someone who really stands out at an event with 7,000 people: I saw Laurence holding his sign 'One Million Dollars For Your Business Card'. That's just a genius idea. I think it is one of the most brilliant business cards I have ever seen. I thought: what an absolutely great strategy, making a difference with intelligent marketing."

Paul Preston
Author of "How To Get Houses For Free"

"I really thoroughly recommend you Laurence as a person to transform the lives of people who are maybe in great need of help. I think you're an agent for good and you perform great tasks and achieve great things for a great many people given the opportunity.

I got the impression that from the moment when we first spoke that you were on my wavelength and that you were committed in assisting me in the best way you could which is exactly what you have done and I respect you for that.

Any person you contact in the future in a similar situation to me, who has financial problems or meeting their commitments is a big problem for them, I think you're got the ultimate solution. Your services are 100% superior to anyone else in this particular area that you operate in and they are the best. You have got the solution to anyone's problems and I will be enterally grateful to you Laurence and I wish you the best of luck and thank you personally from my heart for all you have done for me.

It's fantastic meeting you Laurence and you have solved all my problems."

Michael Mclean
Property owner who sold his two Brighton flats to
Laurence for £1 each

"Amazingly unique business card, and I'm so impressed, I know I will never forget him. It is absolutely awesome and he is very memorable."

Nur Ines

"Thanks to Laurence and The London Property Buyers, I actually got a deal with my flat that is actually higher for the going rate at the moment, so I did pretty well. As it stands I've got a debt out of the way and that's the best thing, I don't have to worry about it and it's a big burden off my shoulders. Laurence helped me out immensely, he is very easy to deal with: the best thing about it is I don't have to deal with a tenant, I'm not a lundlord anymore. Anyone wanting to get rid of their property quick and hassle free whether you've got tenants or it's empty or whether you've got equity or not, as long as you're happy, they're happy, everyone's happy.

If you want to get rid of your property for any reason get in touch with Laurence and The London Property Buyers and I am sure they can help you. I recommend him."

Wayne Swords
Property owner who sold his London Flat to
Laurence for £1 each

"Laurence thank you very much– because of you I got a free ticket to go and watch the play off final at Wembley Stadium. You proved to me that you should never pay more than face value and sometimes you get lucky and people just give you a free ticket, thank you once again."

Sneider Gomez

"Selling my property to Laurence has allowed me to move on, I have been in financial trouble for a while and I was glad when Laurence came along when things started to go a bit bad. Laurence helped me get out of this mess because I was in arrears with my mortgage company, service charge payments. When Laurence spoke to me, he came across as genuinely wanting to help rather than to take advantage of my situation, whereas estate agents or other investors they were looking to make a quick buck regardless of how badly that affects me.

It's very rare to come across that and compared to other people I think that's what sets him apart. Laurence agreed to pay me £60,000 more for one of my properties; I don't think I would ever be able to achieve that in today's market, certainly not in the next few years. The service that Laurence offered was absolutely fantastic; I would highly recommend Laurence and The London Property Buyers to help solve all your problems.

From what I have experienced, they are the best that I have come across. Anyone who wants to sell their property fast and effectively, contact The London Property Buyers today."

Joynal Hussain
Property owner who sold his '3 London Properties to Laurence For A Football Ticket'

Thank You

To my wonderful son Harrison – Daddy loves you very much. I am very proud of you and I wrote this book for you so that you can learn more about me and my journey in life.

I would like to thank my Mum and Papa, who have always been an inspiration to me in my life.

This book would not have been possible without Stephanie Hale, my amazing book coach. Thank you for doing such a great job of interviewing me and helping me put my ideas onto paper. I am very grateful for your kind help, advice, and assistance in helping me write my book.

Special thank you goes to Keith Badman, Darren Hassle, Robert Key, Heath Williams, Paul Fletcher and Doreen Banura, all of whom helped to inspire me to write this book. Thank you all for your advice, guidance, help, support and kind words of encouragement that have always meant the world to me.

Thank you to all my heroes: Paul McCartney, John Lennon, George Harrison and Ringo Star. I have always been a massive Beatles fan, and I have grown up loving your music. You have made the world a better place with your beautiful songs. Thank you for inspiring me to be a Paperback Writer!

Thank you to Michael Jackson, Muhammad Ali, Steve Davis (the greatest snooker player of all time).

Thank you to Ian Wright, Dennis Bergkamp, and Thierry Henry, my Arsenal heroes, and to every player who has ever played for Arsenal. Thank you on behalf of all Arsenal fans everywhere — I have had so many happy memories over the years watching Arsenal at Highbury and at the Emirates Stadium and watching games on TV.

Thanks to Mo Farah and Usain Bolt and to all Team GB athletes for representing your country and for all the wonderful memories. Watching you on TV and being inside the London Stadium to watch those live events have been some of the greatest events of my life: the atmosphere was incredible at the London 2012 Olympic Games and World Championships in 2017.

Thanks to Watt Nicoll, the best motivational speaker I have ever seen. Thank you for spending time motivating me when I was a young boy with your words of wisdom; you have always been an inspiration to me.

Thanks to Tony Robbins, Brian Tracy, and Joel Bauer. I have learned a lot from your seminars, books, and CDs.

This book is also dedicated to you, the reader. I wish you every success in the future.

Foreword

I have known Laurence Lameche for almost twenty years now. What started as a mutual love for both The Beatles and Arsenal Football Club has developed into, I'm pleased to say, a most rewarding friendship.

Back in 2001, I interviewed him for my book *The Beatles: "The Dream Is Over"* (about his part in getting Sir Paul McCartney his knighthood). Since then, I have seen his business grow from being a London tour bus guide, to becoming a night club ticket seller (in a small booth situated in Piccadilly Circus) to a highly successful property magnate.

In hindsight, it was obvious he would dip his hand into buying and selling houses. With his charming, most relaxed persona, he is well equipped (and most capable) of dealing with (and solving) many people's property problems that arise from this already, most pressurized industry. As others have quite rightly verified, he has been, quite simply, a breath of fresh air to the London property scene.

Remaining humble throughout, and with his ascendency in this endeavour showing no signs of faltering, you cannot help but admire how much he has achieved in such a relatively short space of time. I often joke with Laurence that, at the rate he is going, he will, one day, own half of the Capital. And I believe he will.

So how did he do it? Well, you are about to find out. Sitting here, within the pages of this book you are about to read, are the secrets of his success. The book presents you with the information of how you, yourself, can buy "Three London Properties For A Football Ticket."

And the fact he is willing to divulge all this with you is the mark of a thoroughly decent man, I think you will agree. He deserves his success, and now you can share in it too.

Keith Badman,
Best-Selling Author of "Marilyn Monroe: The Final Years" and
The Beatles books, "After The Break-Up",
"Off The Record", and "The Dream Is Over"

London, England
November 2017

Contents

Chapter 1
A Secret in This Book

The purpose of writing this book is to show you how I bought three London properties for a football ticket and how you can do it, too. The great news is that anyone can invest in property.

What I am explaining is not rocket science; it's straightforward and my simple processes will explain how I did this.

Property investment is quite simple if you know what to do. All the information you need is in this book, and I will help you along the way by explaining exactly what I did so that you can buy properties this way as well.

In this book, I talk about Money-Making Secrets that I have used in my life and the Famous Success Formula. You, too, can apply these strategies to your life and become even more successful if you follow these simple principles. Those who are searching for it and open to these ideas may pick it up. If you're ready to use it in your life, you will recognise this Secret.

Humble beginnings

I was raised in a single-parent family, so we never had any money and we couldn't afford to go on holiday. I was never good at school and I didn't get any qualifications. As a child, I always dreamed of moving to London one day, where I imagined the streets were paved with gold. I would love to watch films like *Mary Poppins* because they inspired me to live on a street like Cherry Tree Lane, with its beautiful Georgian properties, and to think that hopefully one day I could move to London and buy a property there. It was always my dream as a child to be successful and have my own business, but I had no idea how to do that.

My mum didn't have any money, and she had different jobs to try to make ends meet. My grandmother lived through the Second World War, and even in her later life she couldn't afford to buy a television or even a washing machine—she would wash all her clothes by hand. She never went on any holidays and lived off a state pension.

I just remember thinking as a child that there must be more to life than this, only to retire on pennies and not be able to afford or enjoy life to the fullest. Reflecting on my grandmother's situation made me want to have something better and to try to achieve more with my life.

I never liked school. I was never good at it and struggled. I found it difficult to even read and write. I found it very difficult to learn. I just was not good at school whatsoever.

I grew up in the countryside, so even as a very young child, I made a decision to not make friends at school because I didn't want anything to tie me down to that area (since my dream was always to move to London). It was easy because I didn't have many friends. I was quite bad at school and struggled to read anything.

What Stephen Hendry taught me

I loved snooker and played it a lot as a child. My hero was Steve Davis—to me, he is the greatest snooker player of all time. During the 90s, Stephen Hendry came onto the scene, and people classed him as the greatest, which annoyed me. A few months before, I was lucky enough to meet Steve Davis for the very first time. I had a great photograph with me and Steve Davis and so I had that printed on the front and back of my t-shirt which also stated "Steve Davis: Snooker's Greatest World Champion."

A few weeks later I found out that Stephen Hendry was going to be signing autographs at a John Lewis store near where we lived in Norwich and I thought, "Well there's going to be loads of people, it's going to be packed," but no one turned up except me! So I went up and asked Stephen Hendry to hold my t-shirt – so he held it up and got someone to take a photo. All the passers-by in the shop were walking past laughing. I just wanted to prove to the kids at school and people that I knew who told me that Stephen Hendry was the greatest that he was not, as Steve Davis was and will always be, the greatest snooker player of all time.

I'm not a fan of Stephen Hendry as you may tell, but when no one turned up to his autograph-signing event he kind of got a little annoyed and he saw people laughing at him holding my t-shirt. Then, he read it and looked at me and said, "You know what this is good for? Cleaning windows." I replied, "No Stephen, if I had your face and name on the front of the t-shirt, that's what I would use to clean windows." I began to walk off – I was just a little boy at the time – and then his manager actually said to me, "Well, if you think you're so good at snooker, why don't you play him?" Stephen Hendry started taking off his leather jacket and said, "Yeah, come on then, if you think you're so good I'll give you a game." The thought of losing against him wasn't an option, so I politely turned him down, saying, "No thanks, I think I'm busy tonight Stephen, I'm thinking about washing my hair, or something like that, so can't play." I was maybe twelve or thirteen years old at the time!

The power of dreaming big

I supported Arsenal as a young boy after watching them on television. Back then, they would show games every Saturday; the first match they played was probably against Norwich. I went there to watch them, and then I would go with the Arsenal supporters' club, and every other weekend I would travel to London by myself as a teenager to watch Arsenal play. I remember watching them play Liverpool on 25th May 1989 to win the League in the last minute when Michael Thomas scored the winner; it was just amazing.

I liked the atmosphere at Arsenal. I liked the uncertainty around whether they were going to win or lose, and I liked the celebrations. The greatest thing is when they score and the whole crowd goes crazy—there is nothing quite like it for me.

I originally picked Arsenal to support when I saw them on TV. In fact, the very first time I ever saw football on TV was Arsenal, and they won. A few weekends later, I saw them on TV and they won again, so I thought, "Wow, they're good." The third time—I think a few months later—they played and won again. I just thought it was fate; I thought that they were the team for me.

Ian Wright was my hero along with Dennis Bergkamp and Thierry Henry—they were all my heroes. I just thought they were in a different class. At the time, Ian Wright was the all-time leading scorer in Arsenal's history. Dennis Bergkamp was an absolute genius and

Thierry Henry then became Arsenal's leading goal scorer of all time. I just thought the way they played football was just out of this world.

I wanted to be a footballer myself, but I had asthma and struggled. I always like to win at whatever I do. I would have loved to have played for them but was sad that I couldn't. I used to play football at school and then would play in the street or in the park. I remember I just used to imagine the crowds and that I was playing at Highbury and scoring the winning goal or I was playing in the World Cup final and had scored the winning goal for England.

I think every schoolboy imagines one day playing for the team he supports and that his team would eventually play for their country. I use to envision myself playing in the World Cup, holding up the trophy, and also holding up the FA Cup at Wembley and winning the Premiership.

If you couldn't tell by now, I'm a dreamer. I would listen to The Beatles and collect Beatles records when I was younger. My whole room was covered with photos, newspaper cuttings, and posters of The Beatles and Arsenal. I loved their songs and would enter my own world when I listened to them. In terms of my formative years, my ideas were mainly coming from television programmes and films I watched as a kid. It began to get my imagination running wild watching films like *Superman, Rocky, James Bond, Indiana Jones, Back to the Future, The Great Escape, Willy Wonka & the Chocolate Factory, Forrest Gump,* and *The King of Comedy* as well as TV shows like *Lovejoy, Antiques Roadshow, Only Fools and Horses.*

I had a little TV in my bedroom, so I would do some schoolwork and watch TV. I also had a record player, so I'd put on Beatle vinyl records or cassettes and listen to them. I would listen to them so much that the records and cassettes would wear out.

It was magical. As I said, I heard The Beatles on the radio and then my mum bought me *Yellow Submarine* as my first-ever album. I use to play it repeatedly, and every night it would take my mind away, how they sang the songs. It was as if I entered a fantasy world, I had just never heard music like that and it was so incredible. I loved listening to The Beatles every single day. From that age, I decided that one day I wanted to have the largest Beatles collection on earth. Collecting memorabilia was my dream, and I would go every weekend to record fairs and buy new albums and singles from the pocket money I saved up.

I'd collect antiques, art and memorabilia, coins and stamps, pocket watches, and Toby Jugs. I would go to antique fairs and charity shops and really spend all my time collecting things. My hobbies went in stages: maybe one year I would be collecting coins, and then the next few years stamps, and the next year pocket watches, and the year after Toby Jugs. (I found some rare Toby Jugs at a charity shop once.) I'd travel all around to find these things.

I was always interested in making money and thought that if I could buy these items as a kid, then maybe in the future they might be worth something. I was always collecting things to hold onto and maybe sell later for profit. I eventually began collecting war medals from the First and Second World War. I would read books and magazines on antiques and Beatles memorabilia to learn about them and try to help me discover that rare find.

I always wanted to be successful and do well in life, and I just thought that since I was always buying and selling antiques, I could maybe one day open up an antique shop. I was fascinated by old things and loved collecting them; I was excited by the idea of buying something for a few pounds that years later would be worth hundreds (if not thousands) of pounds.

I was always looking for antiques at these collectors' fairs and car boot sales. I was always on the lookout for the George Cross or the Victoria Cross, which are extremely rare medals. I don't know why, but for some reason I always had hope that one day I would come across them. People sometimes get lucky at car boot sales, charity shops, and art fairs, but if you know what you're looking for, then you're ahead of the majority of people. (Of course, I also bought things because I liked them).

Shows like *Lovejoy* and *Only Fools and Horses* inspired me as a kid. They would buy these antiques and they would be worth a lot more, or as Del Boy would say, "this time next year, we'll be millionaires". I know these were just TV shows, but I was always inspired by the idea that these people were working-class men who just kept on working with that dream that one day they would be rich. I love the *Antiques Roadshow* and used to watch it every Sunday just to try and understand where people bought things from and their history. I went to the Roadshow a couple of times to show them some of the pocket watches and medals that I bought; I had them reappraised, and they told me they were worth more than I paid.

Watching the pennies

My mum had to work several jobs to make ends meet. She couldn't afford a cooked meal for me at school, so she'd always make me sandwiches, reminding me not to throw away the foil that she'd wrapped the sandwiches in. I'd have to unwrap my sandwich nicely and then fold it back nicely and bring back the foil each day so she could reuse it for the next week.

She wouldn't have any money to buy clothes, so I'd just have to be very careful. I wasn't one of those kids that would scuff their shoes; I'd really look after them and always try to make all of my clothes last as long as possible. I'd stretch my socks and jumpers so that she wouldn't have to buy them again and would reuse all of my clothes until I couldn't use them any longer.

When there would be school trips away, I would never ask my mum if I could attend because I knew she couldn't afford to send me. There were times at school where you used to pay a little money and you could come in without your school uniform. Now, for all of the other kids, it was a joy since they didn't like wearing their uniform (but who does?). But I didn't want my mum to have to pay that because I knew she couldn't afford it. I would be the only kid in the whole school that would go that day in my school uniform. Yes, everyone gets bullied at school, but I didn't care—they could tease me, they could call me names, it didn't matter. I was just looking out for my mother who didn't have any money and I thought it would be irresponsible of me as her child to ask her to pay for something I didn't really need.

As you can see, I was always conscious of the value of money from very early on. My mum would treat me now and again, taking me to restaurants on very rare occasions. I love dessert, but because I knew sometimes she couldn't really afford it, I would say,

"Oh no, I'm full, thank you. I don't want dessert," or I would try to choose the cheapest meal on the menu to help her save a little money.

This even reflected in my holiday gifts: I wouldn't be interested in designer or brand name clothes, but I would always look out for the cheapest thing instead. Even at Christmas, I would say to her, "Please just buy me one present." She would always try to treat me with presents, but I just would ask for maybe one and would be happy with that. I knew it cost too much money buying things, and I didn't really need anything I didn't ask for and just wanted to save her money.

As a child, I often thought there must be a better way to life than this and I made myself a promise not to retire poor, but to retire a millionaire.

I used to mow the grass, wash cars, and bring cookies into school to sell them. On hot sunny days, I would take fruit juices into school and I would sell them to the other kids for a profit. Sometimes I would share my cookies and the kids would say, "Oh wow, these are amazing cookies, where did you get them from?" I'd reply, "If you want, I can bring some back tomorrow and you can pay for them." I would give things away freely, and then other kids would hear about them and would want to buy from me, so I would then sell them for double the price my mum paid.

I ended up giving my mum back the money that she spent on them and keeping some pocket money of my own to re-invest in buying more. Every weekend, I'd go and buy sweets and cookies and stock up on them and would just go into school on a Monday and sell them all throughout the week.

From childhood, I always wanted to be a millionaire; that was the dream. I would tell my mum that and she would always encourage me, "Oh yes, you can do anything." She'd tell me that Richard Branson, Albert Einstein, Henry Ford, and Steve Jobs were all dyslexic: "They didn't know how to read and write." She would always put it in a way to mean, *"Look, you're no different from them, they failed at school, they didn't get any qualifications."* She would always try to inspire me to be like these brilliant people who left school with no qualifications: *"Don't worry about it,"* *she would say*. I found school very tough. She would always look to encourage me to think that the most successful people in life didn't always do well at school.

She would always try to turn it around, telling me not to worry. She knew I struggled at school and wanted me to do my best. She would always be very positive and try to encourage me, so I used to sell things at school, which gave me the pocket money to buy stamps, medals, Toby Jugs, Beatles memorabilia, and all the other antiques I was buying.

I would tell my classmates at school and also my mum's friends about what I wanted to do when I grew up, when they asked, "What do you want to do when you grow up?" Most kids are asked that question, and I would normally say, "A millionaire." Some of them would laugh at me and say, "Come on, how are you going to do that?" And I would say, "I don't know, but I'm going to try and find a way." I didn't know how, but my mum would say to me, "Look, if other people can do it, so can you. They're no different from you: they have a brain, you have a brain. You'll work it out."

It Doesn't Matter Whether You Are The Smartest Or Bravest Person – But If You Are Courageous To Take Bold Risks, Challenge Yourself And Dream Big, Mixed With An Attitude Of Let's Do It, You Can Accomplish Anything

Laurence Lameche

Inspirational heroes

I was quite inspired by Richard Branson and other famous businessmen at the time. The stories of people that came from nothing to achieve greatness really inspired me. He started his student magazine and would call from a telephone box to get advertising, but he would have to be quick to speak as he would run out of money. Then he went on to develop a mail order record company, which went onto become Virgin Records. Then he started the Virgin Atlantic airline and many other different businesses.

For example, someone that jumps out in my mind, (I don't know if I want to say this because I'm a vegetarian now), was Bernard Matthews, with his chickens and turkeys. I think the story was that he started with two chickens and bred them in his back garden. He would sit there all night to stop the foxes from getting them. It would be inspirational stories like this I would read about in the newspaper or watch on TV that made me start to think, "Well, if they can do it so can I." I would think, "But how?"

I would always look up at the stars at night when I was young and think *I needed to aim for the stars.*

As a child, I was always inspired by stories of people who, no matter what happened to them in life, never gave up. Stories like those about:

Sylvester Stallone

People told him he talked funny and he couldn't act. He was broke, and he was rejected 1,500 times by agents, talent scouts, and everyone in the film industry. Nevertheless, he never gave up, and he thought if no one would hire him as an actor that he would need to write a movie and star in it. He was so poor that he even had to sell his dog for $25. He was once homeless, and he was broke when he wrote the script for Rocky. At first, he was offered $125,000 but was told he couldn't star in the movie, so he said, "no". Then a few weeks later they offered him $250,000 but he still could not star in the movie so he said, "no". The third offer was for $350,000 but he still rejected that offer because he really wanted to be an actor. He turned down the offers and eventually accepted $35,000 for the script and starring in the movie, as well as a percentage of the films sales. That movie grossed $200 million at the box office. The first thing he did was to buy his dog back for $15,000, and he gave the man a walk on role in the first Rocky movie along with his dog.

The Beatles

The Fab Four were turned down by almost every record label until George Martin signed them to Parlophone. Even Decca Records said, "guitar groups are on the way out," but The Beatles didn't give up. As John Lennon often used to say to the other members of the group, "Where are we going, fellas?" and they would reply "To the top, Jonny," and he would say "Where's that fellas?" and they say, "To the topper-most of the popper-most" and then he would say "Right." This would cheer them up. Even their manager, Brian Epstein, believed in them so much that he told them they were going to be bigger than Elvis – and they were. The Beatles are the most successful group of all time.

Michael Jordan

Jordan was cut from his high school team, but the good thing about failure is that it only inspired him to work harder. He said about failure, "I missed more than 9,000 shots in my career. I have lost almost 300 games. On 26 occasions I have been entrusted to take the game winning shot, and I missed. I have failed over and over again in my life. And that is why I succeed." He then went on to become the greatest player in NBA history.

Walt Disney

Disney was sacked by a newspaper editor for a "lack of creativity and because he had no good ideas." No one would employ him as an artist, so he founded his first animation studio called Laugh-O-Gram, which later went bankrupt. More than 300 banks rejected his application for a loan to start Disney World. However, today more than 116 million people visit the Disney theme parks every year. He went on to create Micky Mouse and he won 22 Academy Awards.

Colonel Sanders

The colonel was a school drop-out and at the ripe old age of sixty-five, he began to sell his secret fried chicken recipe and franchise idea. He was rejected over 1000 times before building KFC into over 15,000 restaurants worldwide.

Thomas Edison

The famous scientist was the brains behind many inventions, including the light bulb. He said, "I have not failed once. I have succeeded in proving that those 10,000 ways will not work. When I have eliminated the ways that will not work, I will find the way that will work." He went on to hold 1,093 patents. He suffered many failures on many occasions, but where others quit, he 'never gave up'.

Albert Einstein

Einstein was one of the most brilliant minds that ever lived, but he didn't speak a word until he was four years old. He couldn't read until he was eight years old. His teachers and parents thought he was mentally handicapped, anti-social, and slow. This resulted in his expulsion from school. He later went on to win a Noble Peace Prize and changed the face of modern physics.

J. K. Rowling

The author, divorced at 38 years old, moved back to her sister's home in Scotland. At this time, she was suicidal and diagnosed with clinical depression. She thought of the idea of Harry Potter and it took her five years to write the book. After one year of trying to get it published, all the major publishing houses turned her down and rejected the book. Eight years after first publishing the book, J.K. Rowling became the first author to become a billionaire.

Vincent Van Gogh

The painter created over 2,100 pieces of art, but he only sold one painting during his lifetime to a friend.

He considered himself a failure and committed suicide when he was 37 years old.

Winston Churchill

The British Prime Minister during the Second World War failed twice to get into college. He lost five elections and he had clinical depression. He had a severe lisp and he had trouble making speeches and speaking. However Churchill went on to become one of the most successful politicians to have ever lived. He was known for saying that, "Success is not final, failure is not fatal: it is the courage to continue that counts," and "Success consists of going from failure to failure without loss of enthusiasm."

There is no success without failure. What did these people teach us? Nothing of value ever comes easy. Stories like these are what kept me going. They made me think that I, too, should never give up on my dreams. I hope they inspire you too.

Sleeping in my car

Though Frank Sinatra sang, "If I can make it here, I can make it anywhere," I always thought he was singing about London! I had always dreamed of moving to London. As a little boy, my favourite game was Monopoly. I absolutely love that game. I'd always win; I won so much no one else wanted to play with me. When playing I would think, "Wow, wouldn't it be amazing to one day own properties in real life in London in those areas."

I came to London. I would sleep in my car – it was a second-hand old Ford Fiesta. I managed to save up to buy it with the help of my mum and nanny. I use to drive everywhere in it, and it's what brought me to London. I would hang a shirt and a suit in the back of the car and would just dress casually unless I was going to an interview. I would go to hotels to wash from the sink in the toilets.

Once, a police officer knocked on the window and asked me to come out of the car in the freezing cold winter. I would sleep in my sleeping bag inside of my car so the windows were all steamed up. I asked, "What's the problem?" He said, "Sir, can you step out of your vehicle?" I just replied, "Yes, but I'm just trying to sleep in my car." He gave me a strange look, and then asked me, "Well, don't you have anywhere to live?" and I replied, "Yes officer, this is my home, would you like a guided tour of my car?"

The police would often move me on because I would be sleeping in hotel car parks. They would see me on the CCTV walking into the car and not getting out; I'd use a little torch, so maybe it did look a bit weird. When I'd come back really tired after interviewing all day, the car would be absolutely iced over and freezing cold inside. I would have to drive the car around for half an hour to warm it up and put the heaters on full blast before I would try to find another car park or quiet road to park on so I could sleep there for the night. I would just sleep on the backseat with my sleeping bag and pillow. I'd be all crumpled up and would try my best to get a little sleep.

Every morning, I would buy the *Loot* newspaper just to look up jobs and would call them up from a telephone box with the spare change I had. Sometimes I would run out of time on the phone so I had to learn to talk quickly: "Hi, I've seen your job advert in the Loot, when can I come in for an interview?" I got many interviews. I'd finally get offered a job and they would ask me where I lived. When I told them I lived in my car, they thought I was taking them for a ride. And they would tell me: "Well, get back to us when you have a permanent address."

When they said that, I changed my approach to look for somewhere to live first before I looked for a job. Then, every letting agent I met would ask if I worked, even before I could rent a flat. When I told them I needed somewhere to live before I could get a job, they would tell me that I should come back when I found a job. It was a vicious cycle. Luckily, I met a very kind Jewish man who had been a prisoner of war during the Second World War. He believed in me. I begged him for a chance, and luckily, he gave it to me. I've been living in London ever since.

Early days in London

When I managed to rent my first property in London, it was May 1998 and I was so excited that I packed my car with all my possessions and drove to London to collect the keys. Arsenal was playing that day. I didn't even unpack my car or go into 'my new room' in a shared house; I just wanted to go and watch

Arsenal play. At the time, I lived within walking to their stadium in Highbury.

That was one thing I wanted: to live near Arsenal so I could walk to games to see them play. I could hear the crowd cheer when they scored a goal. I wanted to be around it. Arsenal won the game that day against Everton, which meant they won the Premiership. I wrote on a piece of paper, "ONE TICKET WANTED, CASH PAID" and stood outside the stadium. Obviously, no Arsenal fan wanted to sell their ticket and I quickly decided it would be better to stand in the away section where the away fans were and I managed to buy a ticket from an Everton supporter.

I worked part-time at different places on temporary contracts. I also had full-time jobs, but nothing was working. In London, you work to live: all your money is going towards rent, travel and food. I was just going from job to job to job. Contracts were not being extended and I was sacked from many jobs. I was working in offices, banks, department stores. I would take whatever I could just to pay the rent.

It wasn't something I was happy doing, but you have to start somewhere and I didn't really know what I wanted to do, so I just really had to take any offer. I would go to temping agencies, but most of the jobs I got were mainly down to myself from looking in the *Loot newspaper* and applying for jobs that way, to going to job centres, to looking at postcards in newsagents' windows.

Every job that I took, I just always wanted to do the best that I could. I would work longer hours and bend over backwards to help the customer.

A helping hand led to my first home in London

My first landlord was a very kind, retired man with lots of properties in London. As a company policy, their tenants were all working people and they didn't accept people on benefit or the unemployed. He gave me a break as he rented me a room in a shared house. When his daughter (who ran the business) came back from maternity leave, she informed me that I was lucky I met her father because she wouldn't have given me a break.

It was a very small place, just a bit bigger than a shoebox but smaller than a telephone box. It did have its own kitchen and I had to share the toilet and shower with other housemates. I tried to make it cosy, and I did enjoy my time there. It was just down the road from Arsenal's Stadium, which is why I moved there.

Soon after moving in, I had about three different jobs, and I also applied to Arsenal to be a steward. Because I didn't have any money to go watch Arsenal play, I thought if I could work for them as a steward that at least I could watch them for free, so that's exactly what I did. I applied, got a job, and worked as a steward and in the turnstiles at Highbury. I got to watch my beloved team for free and I got paid for it. It was a great job.

I would also sell tickets on the street for an open top bus company in London at weekends. Because I liked sales and talking to people, I thought that seemed like a fun job, selling tickets to tourists. I wanted to be the best at it – and I was always competing with other ticket sales representatives from other companies. The company placed us in different locations all over London and my goal was always to get more sales than the competition.

One time when I was working in a bank, whenever I would go to the toilet and come back to work my manager would say, "Where have you been for three minutes?" I didn't know he was timing me. I really hated being told what I could and could not do and most of my bosses seemed to have an attitude, which I didn't like.

I then got sacked from different jobs and was quite unhappy; I didn't do anything wrong it's just that I guess I wasn't that good at the job and maybe I didn't fit in because I didn't go to the pub with them after work. I was stuck in a rut for almost three years, in and out of jobs.

The last straw was when I worked for a farmer and I had to carry hay... no, I'm only kidding, I was working for a well-known department store in London. The customers loved me – most of the times I served a customer on a till or around the store they would give me their business card. It was a very high-end department store, and the customers would tell me, "Wow, you are great, you're fantastic. Whenever you want to come visit my country you can come stay with me, give me a call."

I had contacts from people all over the world. Obviously, I was doing something right, despite it being quite unusual; when you go into a shop to buy something, you don't usually give the person selling the goods your business card.

However, I wasn't asking for it, I was just being polite and being myself. The customers responded well to me being nice. I wanted to do everything I could to help them and to make their experience enjoyable. I wanted to do my job to the best of my ability. I was transferred into another department and after the manager returned from holiday, I was sacked because for some reason she didn't like the fact that all these customers were so happy that they gave me their business cards.

I felt I was treated quite badly by the manager because she didn't like me and wanted to get rid of me because she said, "Your face doesn't fit in my team and I didn't sanction any more staff to be working in my department, so you have to leave."

I left and then thought to myself, "What am I doing? I came to London to be successful, but I've been here for three years in the rat race, I'm panicking. I'm trying my best and working hard, and I feel like a hamster running fast in a wheel yet getting nowhere and I'm just trying to keep up, to keep my head above water. I didn't come to London to just work in all these terrible jobs."

So I took about a month off. I then went back home to my mum, even though I still kept my little room in London. I still paid the rent, but I did have to get out of London to clear my mind in the countryside for one month to think about what I wanted to do, what my perfect job would be.

I kept asking myself that question and I thought I wanted to be a tour guide. I actually asked myself to think about what my greatest fear is – public speaking – and how I could overcome it. When I saw tour guides on the open-top buses, they all seemed to be having so much fun, loving their work as their own boss with no desk job and no 9 to 5, with no one really telling them what to do.

Fear Is Nothing But A State Of Mind

Laurence Lameche

Becoming a tour guide

I thought I would try to become a tour guide and overcome my fear of public speaking as I thought it seemed like a fun job to do. So I changed my approach and focused on doing something that I would enjoy if I could overcome my fear, rather than just working in a dead-end job which I had been doing for years, which I never enjoyed but I only did it so I could pay my rent.

I thought it over and decided I wanted to set up my own tour in London one day. I went on a two-week training course with an open-top bus company in London. There were 30 people on the course and we all got up to speak many times each day on the microphone. I would even practise in my bedroom when I got back home each night by standing on top of a chair and holding a pen as a pretend microphone and visualising the route and talking about the history and what I learnt that day.

We received information on the famous tourist attractions, the history, and the buildings, as well as what to say along the route. I took loads of notes and almost everyone passed the course, but two people failed and I was one of them. The other guy that failed didn't even speak English, which didn't make me feel too good. Everyone thought we had all passed and went to the pub to celebrate; I had to go knowing I failed, putting on a brave face to smile and be jolly with everyone else. I couldn't just leave because then they would have known that I didn't pass, so I had to do that, and I thought, "I'm not going to let that be a 'no'," because I didn't have another job at the time.

Rock Circus offered me a job; the place was a Madame Tussauds wax museum at Piccadilly Circus. They played music like *The Beatles*, and I thought it was a dream job, but it really didn't challenge or push me. It was an easy job to just guide people around and talk about music, which no doubt I do love, but I just kept thinking the tour bus company would challenge me to improve my public speaking skills which I thought would be useful later in life.

I went back the next day, spoke to the manager and said, "Look, you have got to give me a chance. I know I can be the best tour guide in London, I'm just nervous. I've never done this before, but I know I can be great, so please give me a chance. I'll not let you down, you'll have great reviews about my tour." He said, "Ok Laurence, we will give you a chance, and we were hoping you'd come back and say that." They put me on the bus the next day.

I did the job for a year and a half and I was the best tour guide they had. I had hundreds and hundreds of people from all over the world come on my tour that wrote to the company saying what an amazing job I did and that I was the best tour guide they'd ever come across. The comments were all very kind and positive because I really did try to make it fun and entertaining.

I thought about how I could make my tour different from everyone else's because we were all taught the same thing. I would not take any time off work and I would instead go back on tour to listen to what other tour guides were saying. I wanted to listen to my competitors and find out what they were saying and work out how I could do it better; what other things they would say, so I could pick up on different jokes, new ideas and interesting history.

I've always loved doing impressions and did lots of them as a kid, so on my tour I tried to do impressions of the Queen, (I'm sorry Your Majesty) and throw in fun jokes to make it interesting and not boring or dull, so I think that's why people liked me. I was enthusiastic about London, and it was an honour to be a tour guide.

I felt like an ambassador of London as I showed all the amazing historical monuments and history. London is like no other city on earth and I truly love it, so it was a pleasure to do.

What we covered was all Central London: Buckingham Palace, Big Ben, St. Paul's Cathedral, Tower of London, Tower Bridge, and London Bridge. I would tell them the history, trying to imagine myself as a tourist and what I might like to hear from my tour guide.

At that time, I'd have rather jumped out of a plane than speak in public. I was very, very scared. I'm a very shy person naturally. I don't even drink, but to get the courage to do my first tour I had to have something strong to try and give me the courage to just get up on the microphone because my hand was shaking, but I knew I had to overcome my fear. I thought it would be good for me to overcome and master this fear I had.

Still to this day, one of my dreams is to operate my own tour in London. I already have the route and script planned out for a two-hour tour. To make this happen I had to learn how to sell tickets on the street, how to market myself as a company with a website, what the tourists wanted, and logistics, such as how to organise the bus stops. I wanted to make this *my tour*; I wanted to learn everything about the business so I could train up others.

Back to Walt Disney's story – he was so passionate about his mouse, more passionate than anyone else about his Disney drawings because he was the one who created them. They had a TV show and they wanted Walt Disney to host it and talk about his cartoons but he didn't really want to do it. When he quit the show it was never the same because he was truly so passionate about what he loved. I wanted to emulate that passion; I truly loved my job as a tour guide in London. It shone through my personality and I wanted to constantly be so excited every single day,

I would say, "Ladies and gentlemen, coming up now on our left is Big Ben," every time I saw it and other great monuments in London I kept thinking "Wow!" It was exciting for me. I wanted to make it fun for all the people who came on my tour, whether they were children or adults or even people who didn't speak any English—I just wanted them all to have fun and to remember me when they thought of their time in London. I tried to make it the best tour of their lives.

As Samuel Johnson once said, "When a man is tired of London, he is tired of life."

Chapter 2
The Law of Attraction and Mindset

My mother worked for a company where she would have to hire different speakers to talk at events she would organise every few months, and business people would pay to go along to listen to them. I was a teenager at the time, and she would sneak me into the room along with all the business people so I could also learn. I started thinking about how amazing these people were and how differently they thought.

As a teenager, I would have to dress up in a suit for the day to go along with my mum to her events. I was so shy at the time that I really didn't talk to anyone, so I would just kind of sit at the back of the room, listening.

The best motivational speaker I have ever seen in my life was a Scottish man named Watt Nicoll MP (which he told me stands for 'Motivated Person'), truly a one-off character who was a folk singer during the sixties. He had so much energy and was so inspiring.

He was in his sixties and known as The Guru of Personal Reinvention and was voted The World's Best Motivational Speaker in 1997 in America.

I remember attending one event in particular where this guy was speaking with such a big, booming voice that it came through the walls. The event had separate rooms with other speakers, and I was in a different room listening to some dull speaker when suddenly, through the walls of the next room, you could hear someone shouting the words "Yes, Yes, Yes." He was saying things like, "You can have anything you want in life. Be anything you want, do anything you want", "Your dreams can become reality, once you know the secret", "Opportunities are all around us", "Visualise thinking as a winner." It made me curious to find out who this was because he was so inspiring and motivating, and I came to find out that it was Watt Nicoll.

Luckily, I had time to catch his talk, and he was fantastic. I told my mum about him and she hired him for quite a few events. I asked her if she could go pick him up from the airport, so I could at least spend some time in the car with him. I needed to talk to him so I could learn some of his secrets about life, motivation, and finding success. I got to ask him a question: "What would you do differently looking back on your life now?" I wanted to know how I could get started; I was just a kid at the time. He replied to me that he "would have done things a lot, lot sooner." He only became a motivational speaker once he reached the age of sixty, after having written his first book around the same time. I always found him so inspirational.

He had written this book called 'Twisted Knickers and Stolen Scones' and he wanted the book to be a number one best seller, but couldn't get it published. I believe he self-published it, and he stood outside the front of bookshops selling the book and pitching it to people walking by as "The greatest book ever written" and he would say things like, "This book will change your life" and "I personally know the author." (Of course, he was the author!)

He would sell many of his books outside the front of bookshops, and one day he was speaking on stage telling his story about how he wrote this book, and how it was his dream to have a number one best seller. Richard Branson was in the audience: he heard the story and was so inspired and impressed with him that he ordered his book for every single member of his staff that worked for Virgin around the world as a Christmas present. Thanks to Richard Branson and Virgin, Watt Nicoll's book became a number one best seller.

Watt Nicoll was always so amazing and kind to me, so I want to give thanks to him in this book because he really helped me as a young boy. He was so caring and helpful and he spent time with me trying to pass on his wisdom. He had time for me and always gave me advice and help and had some fantastic ideas. In one of his stories, he said that he really wanted to meet someone that was quite famous because he wanted to go into business with them.

Now, he never told me their name, but he said that he found out that this person liked fishing and liked using a particularly expensive fishing lure. He found out through a magazine interview that in his collection that the only thing that he was missing was this lure. Therefore, he researched, searching the world over to try and find it, and he bought it for him for his birthday and sent it to this guy with a happy birthday note saying: "I was just reading an article that you're missing this lure for your collection and I hope you like it." He didn't put his name or details, and a few years later he actually by coincidence met this person. He said how much of an honour it was to meet him and mentioned the gift and that he hoped he had liked it. The guy was so shocked and speechless that he took him out for lunch and they've been really good friends ever since.

Watt Nicoll is Scottish, so he was driven out of Scotland because his fellow countrymen didn't like the fact that a Scotsman was helping the English to win at football, especially since they started winning again thanks to him. He thought about how much he loved his country. People were walking down the street spitting at him and calling him a traitor, so he decided that it would be better to stop coaching England.

The power of persistence

Listening to many different motivational speakers who were very inspiring rubbed off on me and made me aspire to achieve great success in my life.

It made a real and positive impact on me because I often kept to myself as a child, not really having friends and instead spending most of my time at home. I would watch TV, but other than that, I would just always be thinking, dreaming and hoping that one day I could be successful, but I just had no clue how to do it.

These speakers had a huge impact on me growing up, and my mum hired many different speakers and it was very interesting watching them on stage and learning from them, especially when they offered to give away their books. I think one guy, got out fifty pounds from his wallet: "Would anyone in the room like fifty pounds?" I sprinted from the back of the room and grabbed the cash, and he asked the crowd, "What stopped the rest of you?"

He was quite interesting, but I was just a young boy and was just there to learn what I could even though some of the concepts were even too advanced for me at the time. Some kids on the weekend go and play football in the park, or they go out with friends or watch TV, but I would go with my mum to these events and try to learn about life and success. This was a change for me because I found school so completely dull and a waste of time.

Every Day I Am Better And I'm Growing Richer, In Every Way
Laurence Lameche

Getting started

When I moved to London, I started to read books about mindset and success. Even though I hated reading when I was at school, I knew I had to better myself and to learn how to become successful. I didn't have any money to buy any books, so I would go into Waterstones in Piccadilly (a large bookshop in London) to read. Each night, after I finished working whatever dead-end jobs I had at the time, I'd read, finding inspiration to become better and richer, and to learn how to be successful at making money.

This opened up my mind to the possibility that there was hope out there, because other people just like me had achieved success so I could too. I then went on different motivational courses and attended various events and seminars.

A lot of these courses were good – but they didn't really tell me, step by step, what it took to be successful, rich and a millionaire or to set up a business or how I could make money.

> **The books I read in the bookshops had a huge effect on me – one of the very first I read was _The Magic of Thinking Big_ by David J Schwartz. That was a fantastic book. I read many other books, like _How to Think Like a Millionaire_ by Charles-Albert Poissant, _Think and Grow Rich_ by Napoleon Hill, and _The Power of Positive Thinking_ by Norman Vincent Peale.**

I had no idea which books to read. I just walked into bookshops and went to the self-help or business sections, on the lookout for what positive-thinking books stood out to me. A few people I had met or gone onto courses with along the way had recommended some books, so I just went there and read them, cover to cover. I found it very inspirational. Every night after leaving work, I got quite excited to go to the bookshop until it closed and they literally had to kick me out as I was always the last person to leave. I'd put the book back on the shelf and then come back the next day to start reading again from the next chapter.

The Anthony Robbins effect on my life

I then heard about a guy called Anthony Robbins, and he was doing an event called *Unleash the Power Within,* where you could walk across burning hot coals barefooted and learn about finding motivation and making your dreams and goals come true. I really wanted to attend this course, but didn't have any money. I thought I would just go down there. I didn't know how I was going to get in, considering it was quite a lot of money at the time – I think it was about £500 for a weekend course.

It was held at Wembley Arena in London; you can't get in unless you had a ticket, so I was walking around trying to figure out how I could get in for FREE. I put it in my mind and I believed that someone would give me a FREE ticket to get into the event and this is exactly what happened – someone came up to me and gave me a FREE ticket and I walked straight into the arena. I found a spare seat and then went on the seminar.

Tony Robbins talks about limiting beliefs and taking that idea that you don't ever think it would be possible in your mind to decide to walk across burning hot coals barefooted. I did that and it was a life-changing event for me. In the seminar, he asked everyone in the audience to close their eyes and think where they would like to be one year from now. In my mind America popped up, and I didn't quite know why – I'd never been to America before, didn't know how it was possible to get there, or even what it would be like to work in America.

After going on this event, I thought how incredible it was that anyone could walk on burning hot coals barefooted, even myself, and so that was a very positive event for me. After thinking that something that I once believed was once impossible is now possible, I began every day to visualise and believe that I would be traveling and learning about business in America within one year, I achieved my goal and it actually happened.

Here's how I did it:

> The next day I thought to myself, *I'm going to give myself one year from today to meet someone on my tour bus who will give me an opportunity to travel and learn about business in America*. I almost didn't want to sleep that night because I was so excited to go into work the next day, knowing it could be the day I would meet someone who could give me this opportunity in America.

Eight months later, on a very cold, wet, and windy February day, I wasn't even planning to go to work, but my tour schedule was changed at the last minute to another time.

Three Americans walked on my tour bus, and I started talking to them. After five minutes, one of the people said, "Do you want to learn about business? I live in Florida – do you want to gain experience? I'll pay for your travel over there; here's my business card. What are your details?" We exchanged details; I was thinking that I didn't just want to visit America and stay in one place but I wanted to travel, to see the different states. I wanted someone to buy my plane ticket and to receive free accommodation, and he offered me all of that. He helped train and coached me in how to run a business and this was a great opportunity to learn from a successful business owner.

Your Dreams Can Become Reality, Once You Know The Secret

Laurence Lameche

The American dream I didn't know I had

He was a middle-aged man and was just looking for help over the summer because he had a business in Florida and would tour up and down the East Coast of America going to different events. He would have a stand in a field and would travel to different areas of the country selling goods, so he needed some help to do that and he wanted me to help him.

At first, the people I worked with in London thought I was crazy because they didn't believe it was possible – no one had ever offered anyone, out of all the hundreds of tour guides working for the company, an opportunity to learn business in a foreign country. It was just unheard of, but I truly, with all my heart, knew and believed that someone would offer me this to me and everything that I thought of and visualised for my summer came true.

I think it was because of the power of my thinking that it happened. It was not a question of hope. I also wanted to have a free return plane ticket bought for me, I wanted free accommodation, I wanted to travel to different parts of America, going to different states and seeing different things. I did not want to be stuck in an office. Everything that I visualised and wanted became a reality.

But I was scared about going to America since I had become comfortable living in my little room I had been renting for three years in a shared house. I had my job working as a tour guide that I absolutely loved. Every other weekend I was stewarding at Arsenal as well and I had a part-time job volunteering at Radio Gosh as a DJ, which was part of The Great Ormond Street Hospital for Children. It was a lot to give up because after giving notice for my room I would be back at square one again living back home with my mum when I came back to England because I could only stay in America for three months.

One of the questions I asked myself before I decided to go or not was, "When I'm in my rocking chair at 80, looking back on my life, would I regret not going?" I think it's an important question to ask yourself from time to time when you make important decisions in life. The answer was "Yes I would regret not going," so my mind was made up I had to go.

I like to push myself. In life, I've always enjoyed testing my limits. At that moment I thought, "I'm 24. I can come back and get it again." I thought I just had to go for it because if I didn't I would always end up regretting it. The idea at the time was that when I got to America I was to find a business there that I could bring back to Britain that wasn't done in London. That was my intention for three months – I kept thinking to myself, *I'm going to find something here and bring it back to London.*

I was staying just outside of Tampa, Florida in a retirement resort. You could only live or own a property there if you were over fifty, so this guy could play golf for free whenever he wanted. It's sunny and warm every day. It was incredible and I really loved it. I learnt to play golf for the first time and found the people there very friendly so I really had the time of my life. I really loved the country and the people.

The birth of my business idea

Before going to America, I worked at many jobs in London that involved working for other people, and I wasn't happy with them, so I decided I needed to work for myself. Still, I really didn't know what I wanted to do. When I went to America, I set a three-month goal to find a new business idea that I could bring back to London that was not happening in the capital at the time. I went to America with a certain mindset.

I was determined to find a business idea in America and bring it back to London, but I didn't have any idea what that would be. I was just open to finding it, and that focused my mind to consider every single opportunity that presented itself.

I travelled up and down the East Coast of America. Never before had I been there in my life. America is a fantastic country. On 11th September 2001, I was actually in New York during the World Trade Centre attack on 9/11. I was there by myself for a few weeks holiday. I then travelled down to Washington, and then Disney World in Florida. It seemed like I was the only person in Disney World at the time; it was like a ghost town. I went on every different ride many times and then I met some people that worked in Disney who took me out and became friends with me.

They took me to a Disney World Resort called Pleasure Island, which had many different nightclubs inside it. It was a nightclub theme park for adults, which was fantastic – you pay $20 to get in and get to experience eight different nightclubs. There was one nightclub with a revolving disco dance floor with 70s music, there was a jazz bar, a piano bar, a comedy club and an R&B Club, all different kinds of music. Every night at midnight, they celebrated as if it was New Year's Eve with fireworks and balloons. I thought in that very moment: "Wouldn't this be a great idea to try and bring to London?"

I imagined that maybe I could approach all the nightclub owners in Leicester Square, join them all together, and bring people on a sort of nightclub tour of the area. Bear in mind I had never gone to a nightclub before in my entire life—I don't drink, smoke, or even enjoy that kind of music, so the whole atmosphere was very alien to me.

I really didn't know how I could do it, but I knew it was a great idea. I could set up an information point or business shop where I could give people impartial advice on which nightclub plays what music and hopefully save them money. They could jump the queue and get a free drink as well. That's what I developed when I came back to London.

After coming back from America, I had to move back into my mother's home again. I'd given up the little room I was renting before, so I had to go back to live with my mum again and then try to figure out a way back to London. I devised a sort of plan to approach the different nightclubs in London and I tried to think how I could do it but had no idea, really.

I even got a job working on a party bus; they took people around different nightclubs in London. It was mostly hen nights, stag nights, and birthday parties on this double decker bus. We went to four different nightclubs in one night, and I worked as a sort of usher guiding the people from one club to another and back onto the bus. I thought that the nightclub owners were probably open to the idea of wanting to get more customers into their clubs, so I approached all of those nightclubs.

One of the nightclubs I approached told the people that I was working for at the time on the party bus, which got me sacked because they thought I was trying to set up a competing business, but I wasn't. I had just wanted to arrange for tourists and couples to attend clubs which was not the kind of events they were pre-booking. All of the nightclubs said "no" to me, which was quite frustrating. I would keep trying to call up and ask if I could speak with the owners. No matter how good my idea was, it wasn't really working because I could never get through to the decision maker.

A friend of mine used to work for Elton John. He was very influential in my life. When I was a tour guide on the open-top buses, Elton John was trying to sell some of his clothes and every few years he would sell a lot of his clothes for the Elton John AIDS Foundation to raise money, and so I used to see it on TV and even as a teenager, I would come from the countryside all the way to London. I remember buying a green suit, which I thought was so cool at the time (looking back now, I can see that it was hideous – I looked more like The Riddler). Yes, I actually went to a job interview in this green Versace suit. They just laughed at me and asked, "What are you here for?" When I answered, "For a job interview," the response was: "There's the door, leave now or I'll call Batman."

They didn't even want to know. So when I was a tour guide on the open-top buses, I went into the last day of one of the sales thinking, "I'm not going to be really able to afford anything in here." It was all Versace, designer, one-offs; many of the clothes were what Elton John wore on stage. They were just the most amazing clothes ever: suits and shirts and jackets and belts and sunglasses and shoes, like a treasure trove. I felt like Aladdin – it was just unbelievable.

They hired this shop in Central London each time for a week to sell everything. The last day I went there, I tried on this jacket and just felt like a million dollars. The jacket was unbelievable – all the staff in the shop told me it fitted like a glove, it was made for me, it fitted me better than Elton, and he had worn it on stage. But there was no way I could afford it because I think it was about £1,500, and I was just a tour guide earning maybe £200 pounds a week. The staff in the shop told me to speak to a man by the tills. Everyone in there was wearing t-shirts so they all looked the same. I talked to this guy and said, *"Look I really love this jacket but I don't think I can afford it, but the staff said I should come over and talk to you."*

When he had me try it on and saw how good it fitted me, he said, "You know what, I'll reduce it to £100 for you if you want it – it's the last day." I couldn't say no to that so I took it. Which then led me on to help the Elton John AIDS Foundation afterwards for many years to repay his act of kindness. So I called up his office a week later just to thank him. I didn't know who he was but finally after calling a few times got through to his secretary who remembered me in the shop and said she was sure he'd love to talk to me, so she put me straight through to him.

He was very kind to me and we became friends for many years. He was really one of the kindest men I've ever met. He always had time for me and he always made me feel special.

A few years later, over dinner in London, I was talking to him about my nightclub idea and he kind of warned me against it because he thought I was too nice and he said I wouldn't want to get involved in that world as people in the nightclub industry are not always the nicest. He said to me, "Look, think of your poor mother. She's going to be worried sick, you working in that kind of industry." I didn't really know what he meant and said all I was looking to do was to try and help people get into the nightclubs. That's all I was looking to do, but none of them had given me a chance. Anyways, he called a friend of his who owned one of the nightclubs in Leicester Square. He got me a number to call the next day.

The man who answered said he would try to set up a meeting with his managing director, but if he said, "no", to not bother calling him back. I said, *"Oh thank you so much,"* and that led me to then get a meeting with this guy who is one of the fiercest guys in the industry—but, he gave me my first contract. He said it was a brilliant idea and asked me when I could start. I went all the way back to my mum's just to fax him over my first contract.

He was such a hard negotiator. I've never been so nervous in front of anyone and I must have lost two stone after the meeting because I sweated so much, because he was that terrifying – but he actually ended up being a very nice person and I worked with him for many years, always bringing many people to his nightclub.

That developed my business because I was then able to refer to him and the other nightclub owners couldn't believe he had agreed to work with me because he was the one that never gave anyone a chance and never did business with that many people. When they found out he was doing it they would say, "Yes, you can bring people to our club as well." This is how my business started.

Believe That You Can And You're Almost There

Laurence Lameche

My nightclub business

My idea was to get people into three nightclubs in one night with a free drink for £10. It was an unbelievable idea because most nightclubs alone charge £10 entry, and you don't get free drinks. I negotiated that with the clubs to bring specifically what they were wanting: groups of girls or couples over eighteen years old who dressed a certain way. I had a few hundred pounds that I had saved, so I thought I would print up these flyers that I could leave in all the hotels in London so that the tourists could see them when they checked in.

I thought I could split the ticket commission with the concierge. In the daytime, I was going to all these different hotels to pitch the idea. Some of them seemed quite interested. I had a little book of fifty tickets that I'd printed to give to each concierge, and to make the ticket books look legitimate I printed them with a barcode, but the barcode was the same on every single ticket. The first night I launched it, after one week's preparation I got six people to turn up from the hotels.

I had this big sign made on a pole, like a property "for sale" sign with a luminous yellow background and black writing: "Three nightclubs in one night, plus a free drink for £10." I had loads of people come over as I stood outside Piccadilly Circus Tube station with this sign from nine o'clock in the evening. I took the six people that turned up and walked them to the first nightclub and told them I'd meet them in a couple of hours to take them to the next nightclub, that we were going to be here all night

Then, there came many other people reading it and coming up to the sign to talk to me, but because the sign was so big and it was windy, it was very difficult to walk and talk with people. I sold a few more tickets that night and the next week. After a couple of weeks, I kind of thought that I really needed to hire someone to hold the sign.

After I did this, I was able to use my time much better just talking to people for four hours each night, which brought me loads of people rather than spending a whole week going around to hotels to market my nightclub tour. The business worked and started to make money after a few weeks. All the flyers I had printed I just threw in the bin because the original idea didn't work. From that point on, I changed my strategy to just talk to people on the street at night.

Still, I was very scared talking to people as a guy who never used to approach women. I was never brave enough to approach women on the street, in a nightclub, or anywhere really – I was very, very shy. To approach beautiful women who are going out was not easy for me, but I had to kind of think that I wasn't there to chat them up—I was there to try to help them get into the right nightclubs. I felt like it was my responsibility to try to help them go to the right place because sometimes the bouncers at these venues would really tell you anything to get you through the door.

Every business comes with challenges

I started to do that, and then on the second weekend I had my biggest group yet – twenty people – and I took them into one nightclub, collected them, took them into another, everything was fine. When they came to the last nightclub, the birthday girl was the last person to be allowed in. It was her 21st birthday. Everyone had ID – either driver licences or passports – but for some reason some bouncers can be a bit funny (I don't mean that in a good way).

For whatever reason, the bouncer didn't let her in. She was not drunk, she was a nice girl, he just wouldn't let her in. All her friends were inside and I tried to help, but he just wanted to be difficult. Anyway, I had about twenty people surround me demanding their money back and I told them not to worry, that I was very sorry and would get them back into one of the other nightclubs. They weren't having any of it and almost wanted to attack me, but luckily, a couple of the girls in their group said, "Look, it's not his fault, he's only trying to be helpful. It's the bouncer." They still weren't having it.

I did get them back into the other nightclub and gave them back all their money and they still chased me and I ran into the nightclub. Some of them were big guys. I'm not a big guy but just like Michael Jackson would say, 'I'm a lover not a fighter.' Hehe. So I just had to run for my life. I was thinking, "I've given all their money back, free entry to another night club, a free drink... What the hell do these people want: the shirt off my back as well?"

Luckily, I snuck out of the back entrance of the nightclub, very scared, and hailed down a taxi. I was lying on the floor because they were circling around the building and the thought crossed my mind, that did I really want to do this every single week. Then I thought that what I had learned was that persistent people didn't give up. I could not let this obstacle get in the way. It's not in me to give up and not get what I want in life.

Some of the people working for the nightclubs were making it quite difficult because they saw me as a young guy and thought I was making all this money, which really was not the case. The bouncers were dealing with people fighting in the clubs, and to them I was just bringing them many people.

A few of them actually, said, "Look, we can play it two ways. I know you have the deal with the owner, but he's not here at night or over the weekend so your deal with him is not valid. You have to now deal with me because I'm the head of the security and I look after all the bouncers. I can turn away every single one of your customers and you can go crying back to the owner saying it's not fair, but at the end of the day, it's my decision because he's not here. I can ruin your business or help it succeed but I want a cut."

I had a lot of pressure from the bouncers to give them something in return, but I guess that's sometimes how things work. On top of that, I was selling tickets on the street like most walking tours do in London, so I didn't know that there was anything wrong with that. Westminster Council didn't like the fact that I was talking to people on the street and getting them into the nightclubs and they wanted to stop me doing this.

So then I approached one of the nightclubs to ask if I could sell the tickets from inside the club. I offered to even pay them for it, but they said they didn't want any money but in return all they wanted was for me to bring all the people to their club first. I was doing that for many months – about six months I believe – and then the council kind of approached the club owner and said I was violating the street trading law.

They warned the nightclub owner that unless he terminated my agreement immediately, they would terminate his licence and therefore close down his nightclub.

I had a team of people by then working for me and literally had to let go of everyone. I took some time off to rethink what I could do to overcome this challenge. I knew I needed a ticket office. I approached every single shop that was closed at night in Leicester Square. "No, no, no, we're not interested," was the only response I heard.

At that point, I was bringing so many people in by myself and needed to hire staff. I didn't know the first thing about recruiting or staff and had no money to pay staff. Then I thought, "If I could get another ten people like me, I could at least double or triple the amount of people I get every night." In the end, I did hire more people and had to convince them to work on a commission-only basis that was quite hard, but some nights the people working under me would earn more than me.

I believed in the business. I believed we would do well eventually and would make money. I just persevered and eventually got a ticket office.

Straw hats

When I went to America to work with the businessman, he would buy loads of different items to sell at his stall. When I went in the summertime it was quite hot, so people wanted something to put on their heads to protect them against the sun. He'd buy these cheap straw hats for a dollar and would then sell them on his stand for $7.50 or $10. His mark-up would be quite good and he would sell about 200 or 300 of them over the weekend.

It was unbelievable. He would also sell these replica swords from movies like *Braveheart*, *The Lord of the Rings* and other great movies. People would love that, but they would cost around $100 to buy and then he'd sell them for $125 to $150, so not many people bought them. From a very early age, I learned that volume sales were better: if you can make a few pounds over hundreds or thousands of items, it's much better than making even a larger amount on a single item or a few items.

That's what I saw in London with the nightclubs. When I sold tickets individually to all the different nightclubs, I specifically targeted the clubs that were not for the celebrities, the rich, the famous. Instead, I targeted the nightclubs that were more touristy, student-like clubs that many people might not even go in. In that industry, a lot of people almost laughed at me – "Oh look at him, selling all these cheap nightclubs that no one wants to go in."

But that wasn't the reality. I had so many people every weekend wanting to go to these nightclubs. I used to look at other promoters dressed up nicely on the street walking around who would say, "I take people to the best nightclubs in London." When I'd ask how many people they took into the nightclub, they would say about ten. Ten people over a whole night? I would take fifty people a night just by myself. One or two high-end clubs would possibly make more profit, but Piccadilly Circus doesn't really cater to the high-end people that want the top nightclubs; those people go to places like Mayfair or Chelsea – they are not coming to Leicester Square.

It's about knowing your marketplace. With the help of other staff I trained, I was able to take thousands of people into these nightclubs. We only had to make a few pounds margin on each of them to make a real profit, and that's what we did. What I learned from the businessman in America was an invaluable lesson to bring back with me.

Threats to my nightclub business

I rented a ticket office from some very interesting characters who took a real interest in my business because what I was doing was so different to what everyone else in the industry was doing. As my business got more successful, the rent started to increase and I decided to move elsewhere.

The new shop that I rented was on a six-month contract. I said to them, "Look, obviously if you're happy with me, then I'd like to know if my contract will be renewed." I said that because in this industry, someone might have wanted to take over the business or copy what I was doing, so I wanted to be sure that I would not be kicked out if they were offered more money.

Of course, I was being naïve. This was business – and in business, cash is King. So, it turned out that the new landlord wouldn't sign the contract with me. I kept on asking them to extend my contract during the last few months that I was there, but they made it clear they were not going to rent to me, giving the reason that someone else had made a better offer. This other company rented quite a lot of buildings from the landlord and it felt like they were like a massive shark and I was a little tadpole.

I didn't know what to do and went to three of the nightclubs that I worked with, who actually rented from the same landlord. I thought that if I could tell the owner that their competitor wanted me out, so all the people I was bringing to them every single week were going to go to a rival nightclub, then maybe they might be on my side and approach the landlord because they would have more power than me.

Perhaps, I thought, the three of them together were more powerful than this one company. They were like a whale compared to a shark—that's how I saw it. Then, they all talked to the owner and said, "Look,

don't kick him out because we rely on his business."
In the end, the landlord reconsidered and said to me
"*Okay, well you can continue renting, but instead of
paying the same rent, I now want you to pay more
rent each week.*"

"Take it or leave it," they told me. Did I really have a
choice? There was no other place I could rent; I
wanted to rather establish the business there and to
sell day-time tickets like theatre tickets, sightseeing
tours and attraction tickets as well. So I just signed it.

Many of the nightclubs over the years were closing
down and it just wasn't the same people as before. I
began to think, "What the hell am I doing? I'm
wasting my time. I don't even enjoy this industry." I
didn't like talking to the other people that I had to
deal with. It felt like there were sharks everywhere. I
just wanted to end it and take some time off and
then work on trying to buy properties in London,
which would be much better for my future.

I had signed a five-year contract for my shop. (As
general business advice to anyone, always try to sign
as your limited company. I signed it all in my name – I
was new in business, and didn't know better then.) I

had hoped to get exclusivity in my contract for renting the shop, as I didn't want any competitors to rent another ticket office next door to me and poach my business. Because I was agreeing to a five-year contract, it was a large commitment. .

Unfortunately two weeks after I signed the contract, guess what happened? A competitor moved into the shop next door! Fortunately, the competitor didn't last long and closed down after about six months. It was quite painful during that time – as I felt as if they were trying to take my staff and all the nightclubs that I worked with.

At that point, I just went to the nightclubs and said, "Look, I've been very loyal to you all these years and I want you to show me the same loyalty. If you start working with my competitor, I'm not going to work with you anymore and I'll work with *your* competitor." That bought me time and a lot of the nightclubs stayed loyal to me, and my competitor lost out.

What I've learnt the hard way is that you need to carefully vet your employees to ensure that there is loyalty and trust. Remember the saying: you are only as strong as your weakest link. Your staff are the links that make a business strong enough to overcome challenges in the long term.

Sometimes other promoters would offer my staff double or triple the money I was paying them. Thankfully, the majority of my staff stayed quite loyal to me because they knew that I would pay them – every single pound that they would earn they would get, unlike when working with other promoters.

The grass is not always greener on the other side, and some people that did leave me actually came back. I'd never employ them again, but they came back and told all the other staff, "Oh yeah, they're all crooks out there, you should stay with Laurence and we're sorry that we left him." That was quite nice, but I did try and warn them.

A little like Rocky

I felt like Rocky every week: I had to always come and fight. I always had to fight and fight to try and get anywhere. It always felt like an uphill battle, like I couldn't really concentrate on growing the business as much as I would have liked.

I am usually a pretty calm and laid back person, but I had a competitor who seemed to be attacking me and undermining my business in many underhand ways repeatedly over time. I'd had enough of being treated like this, so I thought maybe it was time to stand up for myself.

So I just approached the owner of the shop he was renting and asked how much he was paying and then offered more money. It took about four months convincing the landlord, taking him out to nice restaurants, buying him bottles of champagne, saying, "Look, I am long term; the longer that you wait the more chance it is that he will not be here next week, but I will be here for many years to come." Luckily, he liked me and we did a deal which kind of closed out my competitor. As I say, this is not really me or how I usually behave or like to operate, but I felt like had been walked over too many times and I needed to take a stand.

I never had a website, never did any advertising, didn't have an office. We just kind of approached people on the street that were going out, and in the end, sold individual tickets to all the different nightclubs in the area. We just undercut all the nightclubs with their permission so they got in cheaper if they bought a ticket with us, jumped the queue, and we would guarantee that the music that they wanted was what was actually played in the nightclub.

If they didn't like it for any reason they could come back to us and we would just give them a full refund. It worked quite well. I gave away free lollies that cost me a lot of money to buy. The customers would just love them.

That was our unique selling point at that time. We tried to just be honest with the customer and we let the good people in so kept good relations with the nightclubs. Obviously, they didn't want drunk people. I even employed two bouncers on the ticket shop to just check the IDs of all the customers to make sure that we were sending the right people to the right nightclubs.

Borat Night

One of the general managers of one of the nightclubs I used to work with contacted me one day and said that the owner of the nightclub – he's a Manchester United fan – really wanted to go see them play against Arsenal. She knew I was a football fan and that I support Arsenal, so she asked me if I could get him a ticket for the game. I got him a ticket and I thought: "Let me just give it away to him for free." I had never met him before.

I gave him the ticket, and it was the last home game that Thierry Henry scored for Arsenal before he left to go to Barcelona, and Arsenal beat Manchester United 1-0. But the nightclub owner still had a nice time and was very thankful for the free ticket and after that we got to know each other.

That New Year's Eve, at one of his nightclubs a promoter let him down last minute, so he thought of me and told his general manager to contact me to see if I'd like to hire it. He allowed me to hire the club for only £500 in total.

Bear in mind, I had never done this before. I was scared. I didn't want to let him down, especially in his business where New Year's Eve was the most important night to make money. I was scared that I wouldn't be able to fill the club, that no one would buy any drinks.

We'd have staff that would walk the people into the nightclub to make sure they got in safely and they got to jump the queue. I took it on. I thought most New Year's Eve parties were somewhat boring – all the nightclubs usually advertise certain styles: bow tie, dinner jacket, Casino night, you know. To me those were all a bit dull, and I thought I needed to plan something different.

That was the year the movie *Borat* came out. If the club was called Jerusalem, I'd say, "I predict a riot in Jerusalem with special guest Borat." I hired a Borat impersonator that looked like him, dressed like him, talked like him and he even bought his sister along as well and she was 'very nice'.

I paid him for the night, dressed up the nightclub in balloons, and hired a DJ. I had never done anything like that before and it was a great success. We completely packed the nightclub. We did such an amazing job that the owner invited me back the next year for the same price of £500 to hire the whole nightclub again, so I took all the ticket money and the door money, and he kept all the bar money. That's not bad going: £500 for a venue in London. It was unbelievable.

And this whole success was because of the Arsenal ticket I gave to him.

Problems popping up

I bought my first property in London. When I saw how much my property went up in value each year compared to what I was earning, I thought that I wasn't setting myself up for long-term wealth. I was spending all of my income.

I thought if I could just buy one property a year in London or acquire it somehow, and if I could get three more properties, then I would be far better off than I was then. I thought, "Well, I think I can do that." But I couldn't do it working full-time with the nightclubs business and dealing with all these people.

I realized that the only way to be in control of my own destiny was to own property myself and be a landlord. That's when I thought, "I don't really want to do this nightclub business anymore – to pay astronomical rent to landlords so I'm working for them."

Because the nightclub industry is a very competitive market place, the cost of operations started to increase and I was working so many hours that I really thought that it was not worth it for me to continue. I was trading my time for money and I realized that my time is valuable. I have always been interested in property and this thing called passive income that landlords talk about is something that I wanted to pursue.

The whole point was for me to work for myself, but I felt like I was again an employee working for the landlord. Everything I earned went to paying them, I thought I should just find a way to get into property, and that was to be my next journey. I ended the nightclub business soon after. Many people probably thought I was crazy to give all that up because it was a good business. However, I knew I needed to make a change.

To See The Light You Must First Go
Through Darkness, If It Continues Then
Go See An Optician

Laurence Lameche

Chapter 3
My Property Journey

I was thinking of residential property. I didn't know how I could get into commercial property and I thought, *"I just need to be a landlord; this is something I think I could do."* I think it was just the fact that I loved playing Monopoly as a kid, I just thought it was fascinating. Moreover, London has so many great properties: Georgian, Victorian, newly-built properties.

Traditionally, property prices in the UK double in value every ten years.

I was very specific in my mind that I wanted to buy a flat in London – that was my dream— so I bought a flat in Islington for around £200,000 – this was in 2003 / 2004. I also wanted it to be on a quiet, tree-lined street; I didn't want it to be on a main road or above a shop. I wanted it to have tall ceilings and facing a garden. I wanted it to be within a five-minute walk to the nearest tube station and in Zone

1: Central London. In addition, I wanted a lease over one-hundred years.

Literally, almost every estate agent I went to all around London laughed at me and said, "Good luck finding it. You're not going to find anything for that budget." Nevertheless, I was determined that I would, and I wouldn't take "no" for an answer. I thought that even though they wouldn't help me, someone would and I would find the right property and it would be exactly what I was looking for. I must have gone to view fifty different flats; none was quite right. Some flats I viewed had almost everything that I wanted but would be on a busy road, have a short lease, or be above a shop.

I met with an agent one day and he drove me down a street, and as soon as he parked his car opposite where the property was, I knew that I was going to live there. I just knew I was going to buy the property, even though I hadn't even seen it yet. It was this feeling that I got inside.

He took me into the building – fantastic. He took me into the property – brilliant. I thought, *"Yes! This is going to be where I live, this is where I'm going to put the bed."* It was completely empty and I was there imagining where I'd put my desk. I thanked him and walked back home, taking a good amount of time.

I went back to the property over the weekend when it was dark; I wanted to make sure that I felt safe walking the streets at night and that it was in a nice neighbourhood with no noisy neighbours. I came back a few times and on Monday called up the agent to make my offer, but he said he was sorry, but it was off the market because someone else had already made an offer.

I told him, "But you can't, this is my property. Maybe there's some confusion – I haven't put the offer in, but it's mine."

He said, "No, sorry. Someone else has made an offer and it's been accepted."

I asked, "What if I offer more money?"

"Well, you can't," he said, "it's been accepted."

I responded, "Please. I've searched long and hard for this property and I'm going to be living there, this is my home – you need to help me."

He wasn't having any of it. No matter what I said, he answered, "Look, go find somewhere else, don't waste my time," and just hung up on me.

I thought that wouldn't stop me because, in my mind, it was my property, so it didn't matter what he said to me. I thought, *"This is my property, I'm living here, and I'm moving in."*

Worthwhile shenanigans

I really tried to figure out how to do that. I went back to the property, knocked on the door, and spoke to all the neighbours. They knew the person who used to live there, but he wasn't living there anymore as the property was empty, and they didn't have any contact number when I asked. I then went back home, typed up a letter, and hand-delivered it and posted it under his flat door but I didn't get a reply. There were two For Sale signs outside the property, so there was another agent. I went to the other agent one day and thought, *"I've got to make up a story so I can meet the owner."*

I went to the other estate agent's office and said I was a repair person—I even wore clothes that looked like I was a handyman. I said, "Oh hi, I'm just here to do some work for this property." I asked if they could call the owner because I'd lost his number.

They said, "We're an estate agency, what do you expect us to do?"

"Well, can you call him for me, please? I replied.

The agent took a deep breath, called him, and then looked at me funnily over the desk like I was some kind of weirdo coming into their office.

The agent put down the phone and said, "I'm sorry, but he doesn't know who you are."

I said, "Oh look, this guy—he's a joker. I am here to do some work for him because he hired me; I'm not here to waste anyone's time. I've come from the other side of London and I do need to do some work, so can you please give me his number?"

They wouldn't, so I asked if he could call again and I could talk to him. I don't take no for an answer. I said I wasn't going anywhere and was going to sit there all day. I asked to call him and tell him to come round because I was just trying to do some work on his property, that's all. They called him back again and said he's not in London but would come to the office in two or three hours. I said, "OK I'll wait." I waited in their office and was so determined to get this property.

The guy eventually came with a big guy next to him and said, "Who are you?"

I said, "Oh hello, nice to meet you," and put out my hand to shake his hand.

He refused to shake it and said, "Who the hell are you? Why have you called me here?"

I said, "Let me talk to you outside."

I went outside and told him, "Listen, I'm sorry for calling you like this, but I really like your property and I want to buy it, and I didn't know how else to get a hold of you."

He let his guard down and blew a sigh of relief, telling this big giant friend to go away, and said, "Oh, no problem. Let's go to the pub and I'll buy you a drink."

I told him that I wanted to make an offer for his property. We talked about it and then he told me that the other people had gone on holiday for three weeks and he wasn't impressed with them. I reiterated that I really wanted to buy it, I loved the property, and I could complete the purchase quickly, putting forth my offer and asking him to please give me a chance. He said, "Sure, no problem." We agreed a price and I went ahead and bought the property!

I saved up all the money that I could to put down for a deposit and got a mortgage. When I moved into the property, all I had was a cardboard box in the middle of my living room and that's what I put my computer on. I didn't even have any chairs – I sat on the floor. I couldn't afford to buy any furniture. I had friends that came around but they had to all sit on the floor. I didn't have anything. I couldn't even afford to buy curtains for myself for a full year, so I had to put up black bin liner bags in the bedroom and stick them to the big windows to block out the light.

It was scary and I thought, "Oh, I've got a 25-year mortgage, what if something goes wrong? What if I can't pay it?" All these negative thoughts and worries came to test me and I just thought that I would cross those bridges if they happened. I always wanted to get onto the property ladder and to buy a property first, so the rest was left to figure out. I decided I could just save up again, and when the time was right I could buy these other things, and that's what I did.

The Law Of Attraction Is Visualizing What You Want, Believing It's Possible And Taking Action To Get It

Laurence Lameche

Islington One-Bedroom Flat in London

Price of the property bought at the time in 2004: £213,000
Today's value (price in 2017): £600,000

Equity: £342,000
(£30,000 per year property increases in value)

Mortgage: £258,000
Mortgage: £835 per month
Rent: £1,750 per month

Profit: £915 per month

My aha moment

In the few years that I had this property, it went up in value each year. I hadn't painted it. I hadn't changed the kitchen, the bathroom—I didn't do anything at all, but its value kept going up each year. That's what made me realize that I really had to jump on board and buy more properties in London.

I couldn't do it with the business that I was in. I was working seven days a week and had no time to look for properties, but I thought I was making a major mistake by not doing it. If I had bought one property a year, I'd be in a much better position than I was in. That was because I felt I wasn't really building long-term wealth. I felt I was on a hamster wheel, constantly running to keep up but knowing I couldn't retire this way and had to have other assets around me. I needed to buy property that I could rent out.

Any person who wins in life must be willing to burn his ships and so there is no retreat. This will help you to have a burning desire to win. That's how I felt with the nightclub business: it was a good income, and the people who knew me thought I was crazy to give that up, but I knew that property was the best route for me to build long-term wealth. Thus, I closed the business, which was a huge risk, and then said "OK, how do I get into property?" I had no idea.

I know it may sound very strange that I didn't want to keep my business, but I'm not like that as a person. I have to put all of my eggs in one basket to make it work, and whatever happens, I'll make it work. It took me just over six months to then be able to buy another property, and I only did that by remortgaging my property to give me the deposit on the next.

I went on some property courses because I didn't know what to do and thought I was taking a big risk, and so I needed some education. I would spend £300, £500, £1,000+ on a one- or two-day weekend course to try and educate myself to learn from the mistakes of other more experienced property investors so that I didn't make them myself. That's what I did for the next several years: I tried to attend as many different property courses, seminars and events as possible.

The way that I had bought my flat was to visit every single estate agent and talk to them about what property I wanted to buy. There was one guy I had a good feeling about, and I kept on asking if I could take him out for a drink, but he was not interested and didn't have time. I was looking to make a business relationship and learn more about him and have him offer me the best deals first; that's all I wanted to do.

I'd found out a bit about him, including the fact that he liked football, so I'd call him out of the blue and say, "I have a spare ticket to Arsenal's Champions League game tonight because I can't go that night as I'm working." He was like "Oh, wow, really? Fantastic! Yes! Oh, I'll drop everything, when can I pick up the ticket?" So I bought him a ticket and I said I would meet him to give him the ticket any time. He went to the game and had an amazing time and then I knew that was my foot in the door, because he'd have to meet me for a coffee outside his office and then I could talk to him more.

I bought him a coffee and when he sat down, he said, "Laurence, I've got to tell you this. In all the years I've been an estate agent, no one has ever given me anything." He said one of the investors he used to give the best property deals to was retired now (as he bought over £10 million worth of property in

London). He had never even bought him a coffee or said thank you.

The next guy he worked with who bought properties from him was now retired, and he bought £20 million of properties from him; he didn't give him a coffee either, let alone a football ticket. He said, "I haven't done anything for you and you've done this for me. This is unbelievable." I said, "I would really like to be the third person that you work with – you give me all the great deals and I can try and make it worth your while as well." I offered him a finder's fee of 1% cash on completion of whatever price that I paid for the property or for any future properties and he would obviously get paid commission as well, as an agent, but I could give him that as an extra if he gave me a good deal.

He said, "Let me see what I can do."

I said to him, "If you have a good deal for me, then I could get there with in one hour's notice. If the deal is that good, call me and you don't have to waste your time showing it to 10, 20, 30, 40, 50 people before it's sold. If you find me what I'm looking for, I will make you an offer there and then, or within the next few hours." He said it sounded great.

He found this one-bedroom flat in Camden near to Kings Cross station, and when I walked into the flat I couldn't tell if the floor was wooden or if it had carpet on it because it was so dirty: there was so much mess, newspapers, and magazines thrown all over the floor of the whole flat. An older man had been living there since the 1970s.

The bathroom was in a terrible condition, the kitchen was smaller than a telephone box, honestly. It was just unbelievable, a real dump of a property. I still saw potential, but I would have to renovate and redecorate the whole property. I'd need to install a brand new kitchen, refigure the walls like an open plan, and possibly make a separate bedroom to add value to the property. After considering the possibilities of what I could do with the place, I thought it was great, and I made an offer that the owner accepted.

I paid £165,000 for it in 2008 and then spent about three months renovating the property. I took out a loan from the bank for about £25,000, which was the price for a new bathroom, kitchen, flooring, lights, and cost to pay the builder. The builder's wife – she was from Bulgaria – wanted to use the toilet, but it was so disgusting that she decided she'd rather use the public toilets. *That's* the condition the property was in when I bought it.

When my mother came around and saw the property, she thought I'd gone mad and wasted my money. She was telling me off, saying "What were you thinking? This is terrible! You're never going to get your money back." She couldn't believe it. I said, "Don't worry. I know what I'm doing. I've been on a property course!"

Three months after renovating the property, I got the mortgage company to come back to revalue it and they then valued it at £275,000. Therefore, in three months it had gone up £110,000. I only spent £25,000 on refurbishing it, and then the beauty of it was that I could then remortgage and pull out my original deposit, which was £20,000 and the £25,000 that I paid to the builder, so I remortgaged the property and I got back £75,000. All the money I used came back and then I was up £30,000. I felt like going to Vegas. (As of writing this book in 2017, this same one bedroom flat is now worth £500,000. You read correctly: in less than 10 years, this property has gone up 300%).

I thought "Great, what's next?" That was around the time the recession hit – in 2008 – and I didn't really have enough money to try to buy another property; plus, it was difficult to get a mortgage. I had to make a decision. At the time, I didn't really know anyone in property or any investors with money, which was a shame because I was offered many great deals.

I found another property on the next street from there and even approached my mum, showing her all the figures, and saying, *"This is what I've made and this is the rental income."* I turned it straight into a holiday let. If this flat was rented on a long-term contract, then the tenant would pay a rental of about £1,000 per month, but on a holiday let I was renting it for a lot more.

Because of my tour guide background, I saw that it was near to Kings Cross station, and I thought tourists would like to stay there. I put in four single beds from Ikea and bought a big mattress topper so I could push them together and make them into a super king-sized bed in one bedroom. The other room could have single beds for the kids. The flat was renting for £1000 pounds per week and it was fully booked, but on average, I was generating about £3,000 a month, and would make about £4,000 per month during the summer. The mortgage was only £500 a month. I was on average making about £2,250 per month profit after paying the bills like the council tax, gas, electric, water, TV, and internet.

What's Great About Property Is You Can Work Once And Get Paid Forever

Laurence Lameche

Camden One-Bedroom Flat in London

Price of the property bought at the time in 2008: £165,000
Today's value (price in 2017): £500,000

Equity: £307,000

(£37,000 per year property increases in value)

Mortgage: £193,000
Mortgage: £508 per month + £175 bills
Rent: £2,300 per month

Profit: £1,617 per month

The path to more properties

I was desperate to do this again and acquire more properties. I even approached my mother to tell her I needed to do it again. I would do all the work and we could split the profits because I found another property literally a one-minute walk away from the previous property. I already had the money for half the deposit, and I asked my mum if she wanted to go into this deal with me and pay the other half of the deposit. She didn't want to – for whatever reason, she thought it was too big a risk, and she was older now and didn't like taking risks. I couldn't do this deal by myself because I didn't have enough money for a deposit. I considered what I could do and how I could get more leads.

I put the little money that I had left into a building a website because I thought maybe I would get more leads this way. I used Google AdWords and SEO (Search Engine Optimization). Now, I don't know the first thing about websites. I knew I wasn't going to build it, so I asked another company that builds websites to do this for me. After that, I had no more money left. I couldn't buy property the traditional way anymore, and I kept on thinking to myself, *"How can I help more people in London sell their property, and how can I buy it without a mortgage and no deposit?"* I was sure there must be a way to do this, because I knew that there were some people who bought investment properties and were behind on their mortgage payments.

"Maybe I could help those people," I thought. *"Rather than they lose the property, I could be there to help them. Maybe I could agree a price with them, maybe I could pay off the debt outstanding and buy it in the future when I have more money or when the property has gone up in value."*

I thought about people who were going to move abroad and didn't want the hassle of having a property anymore. I thought I would be a property problem solver for people in London.

If a landlord has a problem tenant who doesn't pay them, it's going to take at least six to eight months to go to court for those people to evict the tenant, but during this time a lot of people couldn't afford to pay their mortgages and were going to end up losing their properties. *Maybe I could get those people to contact me and I could help deal with that problem for them and take care of the whole process.* I thought it might work but wondered how I could let people know what I was doing.

The website was built and now online and I started to get leads and call people. Again I thought, "How can I talk to someone, and what could I give them?" I didn't really have anything. But I looked into this in depth and found the right solicitors who said that I could legally do this. That's what I did and that's how I started to then find properties in London and buy them for £1 or a football ticket.

How I found great property deals, and how to create a win-win deal

You have to do different things to generate leads so that people call you:

- hand out your business card.
- print lots of flyers and post them through people's doors in areas you want to buy properties.
- figure out the streets to flyer (either do this yourself or speak to someone who already

does this for a living) and offer to pay them some extra money if they could post your flyers along with the companies they work for.

I did all of that. I printed tens of thousands of leaflets, I hand delivered all of them with a friend, because I couldn't afford to pay someone to do it for me, and it got me several enquiries. I know you're meant to keep it up over a long period, because people may not be looking to sell now, but they might be looking to sell in six months or at some point in the future.

I did that and then I went to visit a woman in Camden because I was new to this and I wanted to try to buy her home creatively. I said, "Look, how much do you want for your property?" I think at the time she wanted about £300,000 and I said "OK, no problem, why are you selling?" She said she was moving to the countryside; she wanted to have a bigger home and for her kids to have a garden. I said, *"Ok great. I can give you that, but I can't give it to you now – maybe in a few years."* She looked at me like, "Why can't you give it to me now?"

I said, *"I'm looking for the market to go up a little bit and that's how I buy property, so you don't have to get an estate agent but I just need a few years to do that."* It didn't work for her, so I went to a few other people that called me to go visit them in different parts of London. I was dressed up in a suit and said, "Look, I can buy your property in a few years." This idea doesn't work for everyone – like for people who were looking to buy somewhere else and who needed the money now.

I met with many other people who weren't interested, so I thought I was wasting a lot of my time. I had been to different parts of London, sitting down, meeting people, and they were not interested. The property courses I had attended said you couldn't negotiate a whole deal over the telephone, but I thought, *"Well, they can't, but I will. Just because they can't, they can't tell me I can't do it. I can and will negotiate over the phone, and I will find a win-win solution for the seller and for myself."*

Rather than waste my time going to all different parts of London to people who weren't interested, I changed my approach and put postcards in newsagents' shop windows and different local shops in different areas. I would have special business cards made with illuminating colors, bright orange backgrounds, bright fluorescent yellow workman's jacket, glow in the dark and great for Halloween, but those didn't really get me any leads.

I'd hand them out to different people, put them on the Tube, and put them on bus seats. When I went to buy groceries at the supermarket I'd give them to the checkout person. I would give my card to everyone and would get a few calls, but nothing really. I even had a jacket made with my website name and number on the back of it that glowed in the dark and I walked around London with it on whenever I needed to go out, which meant I was a walking, talking advertising sign for my business. I even had an umbrella made with reflective words written on it that says: We Buy Property and then my 0800 number on it.

The Best Time To Buy A Property Was 10 Years Ago.
The Next Best Time Is Now

Laurence Lameche

How can you buy a £1 property deal in London?

I spoke to the owner over the phone and started asking him why he wanted to sell his property. He told me that he needed to raise money because he wanted to start a business. He was also a bit behind on his mortgage and service charge payments. He owed a few thousand pounds and I went to meet him and to see his property.

The first time I met him, I could only offer him about £5,000 which was basically all the money I had in my bank account together with some credit cards that I could also use, but he wanted £15,000. I said, "I can't give you that amount right now. You have my card – if you change your mind and want to discuss anything in the future, feel free to contact me any time." A couple of months went by, and he called me again and asked if I could do it for £10,000. I said I could manage about £6,000 and would pay all his legal fees as well, and he agreed to that.

So I got my second investment property near the Tower of London for only £6,000. I thought I'd just won the Crown Jewels. He was very happy with this deal; he was tired of dealing with tenants and was a bit behind on the mortgage and service charges payments, so he just wanted to get rid of it. I asked him how much he wanted for the property. He said the mortgage was £115,000 and he had a £20,000 secured loan on the property as well. In total, it was £135,000 for the property.

I did this deal by agreeing to babysit his mortgage and loan payments every month for his property, so there was no risk to him. In the legal paperwork that we drew up, there was a clause that said if I missed one of his mortgage or loan payments then the property went back to him. Obviously, this gave him peace of mind (that I would pay his mortgage and loan payments). I agreed to look after his property and to take care of it for him just like it was my own home, and I would look after the tenant. The tenant would pay me the rent money and I would use that money to pay the mortgage and loan payments. I'd have the right to renovate, decorate, and sell it as well. That was the first deal that I did in this creative way in London.

Shadwell One-Bedroom Flat in London (near to The Tower of London)

Option to buy the property in 2011: £135,000
Today's value (price in 2017): £300,000

Equity: £165,000
(£27,500 per year property increases in value)

Mortgage: £292 per month + loan: £240 per month
+ £200 bills
Rent: £2,500 per month

Profit: £1,768 per month

I believe that to approach a deal ethically, you must try to find a win-win solution for the seller that will help them. I am a property problem solver, and I help people who want to sell their property quickly by providing a solution. I always do my best to put myself in the sellers' shoes.

When you meet a motivated seller, ask yourself how you can help them. Before I buy any property from a seller, I always do my best to consider if selling the property to me is really in their best interest. If you come from this thought of trying to help people then you'll stand ahead of your competitors.

> **You could even say this when talking to sellers:** *"Maybe selling your property to me may not be the best thing for you and if it's not I will tell you and I will offer you the best advice I can to try and help you!"*

Bouncing back from setbacks

I have spoken to hundreds, possibly even thousands of people wanting to sell their property and I just keep going and going and going. It doesn't matter if most of them say, "no" because I only need a few to say, "yes". What I've learned is to draw on the experience of others, such as Walt Disney. Remember what happened to Walt: his dream to create Disney World was rejected by more than three hundred banks. Yes, that's right: he was turned down by many banks and they told him that no one would want to go to his theme park. Who would keep going after 10, 20, 50, 100 banks said "no"? The guy kept going. I've learned from this (and from other life experiences) to keep going no matter how many rejections I encounter.

I knew that I could genuinely help people. I knew that there were people out there with problem properties who just wanted a way out and who couldn't sell for many different reasons. *Maybe I could even offer them more money than what their property was currently worth, but pay them in the future.* I just kept going and it didn't matter how many times I was told "no". I was quite scared at first – I will admit to that. I was nervous and didn't know what to say to people. I would get laughed at, sure, but it's really about trying to build the relationship with someone over the phone and talking to them and finding out the reason they wanted to sell so that you can make a deal that worked for everyone.

That's what I did.

Don't Worry What Other People Think About You Because It Does Not Matter
Laurence Lameche

Practise and take action

I did a lot of practicing. I was very scared to make the first phone call. I used to put off doing things. I know many people perhaps may suffer from this, but like many times in my life, I procrastinated. Many times I'd put things off for later. Later never comes – I thought I would call people in the afternoon, or in the evening, then it became the next day. I thought, "I'll do it tomorrow, I'll do it next week, I'll start next month." I even bought this book written by Brian Tracy called *'Eat That Frog!'* to help me end procrastination...but I put off reading it for two years. (It's honestly a great book and I do recommend it, I just wish I'd read it sooner).

Later never comes. You have to do it now.

It didn't come easy for me. I had challenges and I had to get through them and do the best that I could. I don't like rejection either – no one does – but I knew I didn't want to spoil the deal of the century and mess up because I don't know how to talk to people on the phone. I was putting off calling people and getting back to them and leaving messages. It's just not professional.

I was quite scared and nervous. I didn't want to give up the deal of the century, so I thought about how I could overcome that. People would say, "What's the worst thing that could happen? They hang up, say 'no', go away, scream or shout, but they don't know you. Try to blank that out, don't take it personally, and just call. It's a numbers game." I thought, *"Instead of calling people in London who have property for sale, I will call people outside London in areas that I'm not interested in buying properties."* I called people in different parts of the country because then I had no fear. I didn't care if they screamed, shouted or swore at me, because it didn't matter. I called them to try to build up my confidence and to understand what it was important to be saying.

Finally, I got an English call centre to answer my calls 24/7. They would answer the phone like this: "Hello, good morning. The London Property Buyers, how can I help you?" The caller would say they were interested in selling their property. The call centre would take the person's name, property address, phone number, and email address, along with how much they wanted to sell the property for and what reason they wanted to sell the property. They would also find out if there was a mortgage on the property and how much was outstanding— there was a list of questions I would have them ask every single caller.

Then the call centre member of staff would say to the caller, "Let me check if someone is available," and they would put the caller on hold and wait a few seconds and say, "I'm sorry, no one is available right now, but I will get someone to call you back." Then they would immediately email me all the details they took down straight away. This works quite well because it means that I can call back the seller in my own time.

The call centre was quite cheap and reasonable to arrange – I'd highly recommend using one.

You need to be quick when a motivated seller contacts you. I wrote a script to help you because I had to write questions down to know what to say to people who called me, just like my call centre.

Questions for Sellers:
A Handy Guide

Their Name:

Telephone Number:

Email:

Property Address For Sale:

Description of Property:

PROPERTY DETAILS:
FREEHOLD /LEASEHOLD (tick appropriate)
Lease term? ....
Maintenance/Ground rent?...............
Service Charge? ....

TYPE:

Flat/House	[ ]	Age/Build date	[ ]
Bathrooms	[ ]	Gardens	[ ]
Receptions	[ ]	Parking	[ ]
Construction Type	[ ]	Ex-Council	[ ]

Next to commercial Premises?.....................................

CONDITION:

Poor / Average / Good / Excellent

Any works needed to make '*Good*'?.............................

Any structural problems? ....

1. What is the main reason why you are selling the property?

2. Is the property for sale with an agent, who & value?   Y/N

AGENT...................... VALUE ....
(What do you think it's worth) ....

How long has it been on the market? ....
How many visits have you had? ....
Has it always been on at that price? ....
Have you dropped it? ....

1. If currently For Sale, why don't you think the property has sold?

2. Do you live at the property? ....

3. Is it tenanted? ..... (Why not?)

4. How much rent is tenant paying per month?

5. How quickly are you looking to sell?

6. Anyone else involved? Have you spoken to other people like me?

7. How have you found them? When you speak to them? What do you like and dislike about them?

8. What is the Outstanding Mortgage?
Mortgage/s: ……………………………
Secured Loans: or (Credit Card debts) ……………………..
Monthly Payments: …………………..
Unsecured Loans: …………………

9. What mortgage is it? (fixed rate): …………..
Interest Only or Repayment? …………….………………..
(Any redemption penalties, Any arrears? Why)

WHAT IS THE MINIMUM PRICE YOU COULD TAKE FOR THE PROPERTY? £…………………
How much do you need? ………………………………..

1. What time would be a covenant for you so I come and view the property?
(Before agreeing to this I would normally do some research and prepare myself to look at what other comparable properties are in the area or view the property and then research afterwards)

2. Do you have any questions?

Now write down the answer to these questions

What offer you made: ....

Their reaction: ....

(Put in diary to speak to the seller or agent and call them in one month's time to say is that property sold yet.) Has their situation changed?

Make 3 offers depending on their situation

1. Offer Price verbally (based on 80% to 75% discount of valuation based on your own research)

2. Make a Lease Option Offer (i.e. offer them the full asking price or even more, but agree to do this in maybe 3 to 5 years or a time frame that is suitable for both you and the seller. I usually like to agree over a 10-year period as most of my deals I have agreed for 15 years.)

3. Full Market value now, where we can offer you 75% of the property's current market value today, and then pay you the remaining 25% in 3 to 10 years!

Setting the rules

- **Explain how you buy property.** (I do buy property and I can do it very quickly, I buy it for less than it's worth, I will give you a low offer, I can do it really quickly. For some people that really doesn't work, but for others it's a great solution because they need to sell quickly).

- **Describe the benefits** (i.e. no chains, cash buyers, FAST completion, there are no Estate Agency fees to pay, there are no survey fees to pay, no cost at all, I will pick up all the costs, the price we agree is what you get, I will do it within a certain timescale, you don't have lots of people walking through your property, your neighbours will never know, there are no for sale signs).

- **We need to conduct our own valuation** (Once we will come and see your property to make sure it's what we want, and then when we go ahead we will get a valuation done).

- **Visit only on the understanding that the sale would be at a specific discounted price** (Look if the property is what you told me, it's the kind of thing we buy, and if we can help you and we can do it in the time you want, the ball park figure I will be looking at is around

...£250,000 to £300,000... depending on the condition of the property, if everything else is ok, would that work for you?).

- **We will pay all the costs** (we pay all your costs the solicitors, so the price we agree is what you will actually receive).
- **If they pull out, they will meet the costs** (Look if anything goes wrong with the sale and it doesn't go forward obviously, because you have changed your mind, we would of course bill you for the costs involved for surveys and solicitors etc.)

Explain the Process

- We will make an initial visit and provisional offer.
- One of our surveyors will visit the property.
- We will make a formal offer.
- We will instruct the solicitors.
- We buy cash so that we can complete quickly.

RESEARCH INTO ENQUIRY

VALUATION	
DATE LAST SOLD	
SOLD FOR	
VALUATION OF OTHER SIMILAR PROPERTIES ON MARKET	
ACTUAL VALUATION	
MORTGAGE REPAYMENTS	
DEPOSIT	
RENTAL VALUE	
ADDITIONAL INFO	

Sometimes I would use this phase below when talking to sellers:

Q: What are you trying to sell your property for?
....

A: "Ok, I think I can help you and buy it for that price, but I buy property in a completely different way than most people do, and I need a little bit of time to buy it. How would you feel if I agreed the price you want, but bought the property in a few years?"

I'd pause and let them think about it, and some people would say "no", as they really wanted to sell the property now because they were buying another property or they needed the money for their business, and that's ok because this won't work for everyone who is trying to sell.

These are the type of property owners below who may say "yes" to the similar deals I have done, if they are in any of these situations:

1. Financial difficulty / debt

2. About to get repossessed

3. Moving abroad

4. Don't want to be a landlord anymore

5. Has a bad tenant

6. Negative equity (which means the mortgage is more than the value of the property)

Another question to ask:

Q: "What if you can't sell your property right now?"

And most people would say they would just have to rent it out.

I would ask:

Q: "What if I just rented it from you on a fixed term contract for like three years? Within those three years I would buy the property. I just need a bit of time to buy. How does that sound?"

I'd just talk to people normally and some people would say it sounded interesting and to let them think about it. Others weren't interested. Some people would ask more questions about it, but it's really as simple as that. Finding the right seller that you can help and creating a win-win situation that works for everyone.

This is how I started to buy property in London for no money.

Don't Try To Fit In
When You're Born
To Stand Out

Laurence Lameche

Chapter 4
How I Bought Three Properties In London For A Football Ticket

I spoke to this guy who had three flats for sale in East London. After talking to him, he wanted £600,000 for all the flats, but after doing my research, I found out that they were only worth £500,000. I asked him, "Do you want £100,000 more than what they are truly worth today?" he said, "Yes, that's what I want." I asked how long they had been for sale now; the answer was about one year. He said he couldn't sell them, and I said I wasn't surprised – no one was going to give him £100,000 more than what they are truly worth.

I asked him why he wanted to sell; he told me that he didn't want to be a landlord anymore. He was a single guy when he bought the properties but had since married with two kids and a third one on the way. I was speaking to him and said I could offer him the full asking price (over market value) and came up with a solution to give him exactly what he wanted. I offered to babysit his mortgage payments every month until I bought all three properties. I explained that I would need a few years to do this and to complete the purchase. He looked at me funny and said he was not interested.

I called him back the next month and he still refused, saying he was still looking for a cash buyer. I said, "No problem. Well, my offer's still there." I called him again three months in and got the same answer. I told him my offer was still good and to call me back if he wanted to go ahead; this went on for months. By the sixth month, I called him and it was on a Monday. Like you do with most people, I asked him "Oh, hello, how are you? How was your weekend?" He said it was terrible. "Oh no what happened? Are you okay?" I wondered. He said, "Yes, but Arsenal lost."

I said, "Oh no, that's terrible. Sorry to hear that." We got talking about Arsenal and I said, "Oh, have you been to watch them play?" He said a few times, but he had always wanted to go and watch Arsenal play at the Emirates Stadium – it was his dream to go and watch Arsenal play there one day. I told him that I would buy him a ticket to watch Arsenal play at a game of his choice if he agreed to go ahead and do this deal with me. "Great, where do I sign?" was his response.

That's *exactly* how I actually bought three London flats for one Arsenal ticket!

I did this by talking to the seller and understanding his problem, by relating to him and finding out what he liked, and by understanding that the pain of these properties was too much for him. He didn't want them any longer. He wanted to get rid of them.

I agreed to buy these properties over the next 15 years. All the tenants would then pay me and I would then pay his mortgages. I thought that I could increase the rent by renting them all as serviced accommodation / holiday-lets. All three properties were new builds, so they were all nicely decorated and in good condition with nice furniture, so I didn't have to spend any money on improving them. They were easy to rent out and he was happy with the situation.

You obviously don't need to support Arsenal (but it helps). In all seriousness, the point I am trying to make is this: when you want to get to know someone or do business with someone, I have found that by giving them something they want for free, they will feel the need to return the favour.

This could be anything from

- Football tickets
- Concert tickets
- Other sporting events
- Theatre tickets
- Flowers
- Nice bottle of wine or champagne
- A nice meal at their favourite restaurant
- Something nice for their children

You could do many different things for someone. Just try to understand the person who you are looking to do this for and what they like.

Structuring the deal

He had two one-bedroom flats and wanted £190,000 for each one. The third flat was a two-bedroom flat that he wanted £230,000 for. I was happy to give him that; I just couldn't give him that money right now, but I could at some point in the future. We came to a mutual agreement that I would give him the money in 15 years.

Now, that does sound like quite a way into the future; it sounds like a long, long time. So you may be wondering who would agree to a deal like that where I could fix the price now but pay him that price 15 years in the future? Traditionally, property doubles in value in the UK every 10 years, so who would agree to that?

Well, I am a property problem solver. I'm always trying to think about working out a win-win situation for everyone, and especially to make the seller happy. When I first talked to him, I asked why he didn't just sell it through an estate agent. He said he had tried, but it had been on the market for a year and no one would buy them because he wanted £100,000 more than they are currently worth.

I thought they may not be worth what he wanted today, but they would be in the future, and if I could rent them out as holiday-lets, I would get double or even triple the normal monthly rental income. I was trying to figure out a way that works for him and for me as well. I made detailed notes of the agreed upon purchase price: the value of it and the rental income.

Putting yourself in their shoes

With this deal, for example, I found out that a tenant in one of the flats was not paying his rent. That was an enormous problem for the landlord because if he let the tenant stay, he wouldn't be paying his mortgage and would eventually lose the property because he didn't have any money to pay it. I agreed to take on the burden of the issue and agreed that I would continue to pay his mortgage and I would deal with his problem tenant. It was just too painful and too much of a hassle for the owner, who didn't know how to take the tenant to court.

I agreed to act on his behalf and handle the eviction process. It was a very long, hard process: the tenant wasn't paying and was giving every excuse under the sun why he couldn't pay. I started legal proceedings and I didn't know what to do because I had never done this before, but I learnt quickly and did all the paperwork myself and took the tenant to court.

I had to pay the mortgage which was £411 a month for eight months, and also the service charge payment of £125 per month as well, so the total amount for both payments was £536 per month x 8 months = £4,288 (which is the total amount I had to continue to pay). I didn't get any rent during this time. It was not easy. This was one of the reasons why he wanted to deal with me.

East London One-Bedroom Flat (1)

Option to buy the property in 2011: £190,000
Today's value (price in 2017): £240,000

Equity: £50,000
(£8,000 per year property increases in value)

Mortgage: £693 per month + £300 bills and service charge
Rent: £3,000 per month

Profit: £2,007 per month

East London One-Bedroom Flat (2)

Option to buy the property in 2011: £190,000
Today's value (price in 2017): £240,000

Equity: £50,000
(£8,000 per year property increases in value)

Mortgage: £683 per month + £300 bills and service charge
Rent: £3,000 per month

Profit: £2,017 per month

East London Two-Bedroom Flat

Option to buy the property in 2011: £230,000
Today's value (price in 2017): £330,000

Equity: £100,000
(£16,500 per year property increases in value)

Mortgage: £411 per month + £300 bills and service charge
Rent: £3,750 per month

Profit: £3,039 per month

Evicting a tenant in one day without taking them to court

The owner had a few properties repossessed a few years before he met me and he said he wished he had met me sooner, because he would have given me more properties. Unfortunately, he had other tenants that didn't pay him, and he didn't know what to do and couldn't pay his mortgages. The bank just repossessed the properties and took them back, which is a real shame because I could have helped him and I can help many people in this situation. I can make sure that doesn't happen by paying the outstanding unpaid mortgage arrears and I can help save the property from being repossessed and everyone wins.

I did all of that and then rented some of the properties out with an increase in the rent because I was renting them as serviced apartments / holiday lets. The eviction experience is still very painful to me. The law in England is on the side of the tenant, and it's not fair from a landlord's point of view to have someone in your property that doesn't pay rent. At the end of the day, you can lose your property unless you can supplement the mortgage payments another way and continue to do so, and most landlords rely on the tenants to pay, which enables the property owner to continue to pay the mortgage.

I kept thinking *there must be a better way for me to figure it out*, and that's why I thought of doing holiday-lets. These protect landlords against tenants who don't pay rent or want to stay in the property because a holiday-let agreement means the tenant has no rights; and they have to leave the property straight away without going to court, all within 24 hours.

From the very first property that I bought, I was always worried in the back of my mind that I might have a problem tenant that wouldn't pay rent and that it would take me forever to try to get them out. It would put this tremendous stress and pressure on me to pay the mortgage. The solution is to never give a tenant an AST, which is an Assured Shorthand Tenancy Agreement, because then they have a legal right to stay in the property.

I thought, "What do I do?" I came up with a great idea after speaking with the best solicitors and barristers in London who specialise in property law. I spent £5000 to find a clever way that essentially ensures landlords never have to worry if they do the right paperwork and sign a holiday-let agreement with the people who want to rent their property.

For every person that moves into their property, it protects the landlord so now the tenants have no rights, and you can get them out of your property within 24 hours. No Court. No Bailiff. No Problem.

With a holiday-let agreement, you can evict someone legally within 24 hours. Many landlords don't know about this clever loophole. This is something I learned from the school of hard knocks. I couldn't let that eviction nightmare happen to me again. Over the course of several years, I had about five different holidaymakers that have tried to be clever and they would say and think: "I'm a tenant, I know my rights, I'm not paying any more rent and I'm not moving out, you have to take me to court."

Sometimes they pay me one month's rent and one month's deposit, but other times I don't even get a deposit from them and they just don't pay again. They act very technical, asserting their "rights," but then hope they can stay there for at least six to eight months rent-free.

In addition, when they leave some of them are not from this country and so there's no way of sometimes getting any money back. However, with a holiday-let agreement you can effectively not have to deal with all the painful hassles that are involved in taking half a year to complete an eviction.

Other property deals – how to buy property in London for £1

This guy from Australia contacted me because he wanted to sell his one-bedroom flat in Islington, London. He needed to sell because he was behind on a secured loan against the property. I asked how much he was behind. He said £2,000. The secured loan was for £25,000, so the bank wanted to take him to court to repossess the property next month. All he owed them was £2,000.

I said to him, "Well how much do you want to sell your property for?" He explained he wanted £250,000; the mortgage outstanding was £200,000. He wanted to make £50,000 profit, so he was quite happy with £250,000, plus the secured loan for £25,000 on top. In total, I'd have to pay him £275,000. I said, "No problem, I can do that. But I think I can do it within the next 15 years."

The reason that I say to people 15 years is that it just gives me peace of mind. Because when I first started doing these deals I thought that it might take me that amount of time to save up for a deposit to buy the property. What I have learnt recently from speaking with different mortgage brokers is that the deposit is already in the deal, because after a period of years the properties have all gone up significantly in value from where they were. I don't actually need a deposit. I can use the equity that has already built up in the property and then I can buy it in my own name, which is what I'm planning to do with the properties right now.

Alternatively, I would look for an investor to lend me the money for the deposit so I can then buy the property and then after six months to one year, I can re-mortgage and then give back the investor the money with interest. That's what I was looking to do as well. This particular deal with the guy we agreed over a 15-year period. I paid off the £2,000 immediately to the loan company, which stopped the court action and repossession. Then I just continued paying the loan payments; every month, I would pay his loan. Every month I would babysit his mortgage payments. The property would be taken care of, and I would ask the tenant to leave when I took over the property so I could rent it as a holiday let.

This property was a student-type one-bedroom council flat in London. The bedroom walls were painted blue and the living room was painted grey. I just replaced the furniture; the kitchen and bathroom were newly decorated. All I did was add a tumble dryer in the kitchen and buy brand new furniture for the living room like a double sofa bed, glass table, four chairs, TV and stand and some pictures of London on the walls. The bed was quite good that was there already, but I have since replaced it with a nice bed and bedroom furniture, and the flat just looks amazing now. I've rented it out and it's done well. It's gone up constantly in value and has been a very good property investment. Again, I bought it for only £1 – a one-bedroom flat, in central London.

Islington One-Bedroom Flat in London

Option to buy the property in 2013: £275,000
Today's value (price in 2017): £450,000

Equity: £175,000
(£43,750 per year property increases in value)

Mortgage: £900 per month +
Loan: £248 per month
+ £250 bills
Rent: £2,750 per month

Profit: £1,352 per month

Owning property

Think about it: if you buy a property, but you have a mortgage, you don't actually own the property because the bank does. If you stop paying the mortgage then the bank will repossess the property and you will lose it. Even if your name is on the Land Registry or Title Deeds the bank technically still owns the property because they have a first charge on it.

You have the right to sell the property and after paying off the mortgage you keep the profit or you can rent it out.

What I have done is to control these property deals in London through something called a lease option, which gives me the right (but not obligation) to buy the property in the future. This means that I don't have the hassle of a mortgage or ownership of the property I just control the asset and it allows me to benefit from the rental income and allows me to either buy the property one day myself for an agreed price or to sell it to an investor or through an estate agent. For me, it's the perfect way to get into property and to control large assets without a mortgage or deposit.

Solicitors

Most solicitors do not understand this type of transaction and they don't know how to do it.

Some of the solicitors that you speak to may even claim it's illegal, but they simply do not know what they are talking about. There is no point trying to educate them. Instead, find a solicitor who has already done these type of deals and knows how to do them properly.

You need to make sure the deal goes through quickly and finding the right solicitor to help you do this is important. I have worked with many different firms of solicitors over the years and some are better than others. Because I find that solicitors can be quite slow at getting things done, they need a gentle reminder from you to see what is happening and what they are waiting for. Sometimes you will need to work closely with the seller to help them get the paperwork signed and sent to their solicitor as these things can slow down the process.

Your solicitor should also be able to help recommend another solicitor that they have worked well with before to help represent the seller if they don't have a solicitor. They are duty bound to protect the seller and to look after them with the sale of their property. I will recommend to the seller to use this solicitor and sometimes it might be worth considering to offer to pay for their legal fees if they use this solicitor because it will help speed up the process; it also benefits the seller because they don't have to pay the solicitor's fees.

Agree on a timeframe with the seller, and do your best to stick to it. Let the solicitors know that you are working towards a deadline and that this deal may fall through and you could possibly lose it if they don't act quickly (even if the deal falls through you will still be liable to pay all the solicitor's fees). Sometimes solicitors can take up to eight to twelve weeks to complete a property purchase, but it can possibly happen faster than that. A more efficient solicitor should be able to do the paperwork within three to four weeks if they work well together with the other solicitor. In my experience, you will need to regularly call them or email them to chase them up to get the deal done and ask them what else needs to be done and what can you do to speed things up.

Million dollar business card

During the years, I have printed loads of business cards myself. I have collected literally thousands of business cards from people all over the world that I've met at different events. Many people make the mistake with a business card of never putting their photo on the card. It doesn't matter whether you're the most charismatic, wonderful, amazing person that I've ever met in my life, but when I get back home and have about 30 to 50 business cards in my pocket, I can't remember who I actually met if there is no photo on the business card.

I put them on my desk and sometimes won't look at them until the next day or maybe a few days later. I used to regularly meet lots of people from going to property events and different networking events. It would be very difficult to remember who I actually met, which is unfortunate because sometimes I meet amazing people that I would like to get to know better and invite them out for a drink or do business with, but I can't remember their business card because it doesn't have a photo on it.

At one point, I'd step up my game by doing certain things to try to get every single business card in the room from people. At that point, you just cannot remember everyone you meet. I would recommend that you should always put your photo on your business card so that people can remember you. Otherwise, no one ever will. I always have a double-sided business card, where on the back of the business card, I would tell people what I'm looking for and what I do.

When I got home and looked at the business cards after the events, I would have no idea what company someone belonged to. I recommend putting bullet points on the back, including what you do at that particular company. When you're giving out your business card that you've printed and spent money on, you might as well go that extra mile, because the person you're giving it to may actually need your help. If you haven't clearly explained what you do, they will have no idea.

At the end of the day, many people throw business cards away. Most business cards end up in the bin. But I've come up with what I believe is the greatest business card in the world which no one ever throws away when I give it to them, and this is my million-dollar business card; I think it's the greatest business card ever.

The million dollar business card

Are you ready for this?

I've actually printed a one million dollar bill that looks like an actual dollar bill. I remember someone on-stage at one of these events I went to who asked the whole audience, "Who wants to be a millionaire? Does anyone want to be a millionaire?" Most people's hands in the audience went up. The speaker on stage would have a million dollars in their hand, and they'd say, you know, "If I was to say to you right now, who would like a million dollars, would anyone like a million dollars? Who'd want a million dollars?"

This would go on until someone from the audience would run up and grab the million dollars from the guy's hand standing on the stage.

Then he'd say, "Well, what's wrong with the rest of you? Didn't you all come here to make a million dollars? How come only one person came up and grabbed it? I'm waving a million dollars here." Sometimes in life, opportunity is right in front of you. Then, he said, "I'll do it again. Who wants a million dollars?" A few people ran up and another person grabbed it. He just repeated it again, "Okay, who wants a million dollars?" He kept on doing this until the whole audience grabbed their million dollars. I even sprinted up, and again, you don't want to feel like a fool running up and then not being able to get what he's giving you. I grabbed it, and I remember the feeling that I got a million dollars; I was so excited with a million dollars in my hand, thinking, *"This is amazing!"* I felt like a millionaire and I had a big smile on my face. I saw the reaction of everyone else that grabbed it; they were all so genuinely happy.

What this guy on the stage didn't do was to put his face on the front of the million dollars and on the back of it was no information about him whatsoever.

I thought what I should do is put my face on the front of the million dollars and on the back my name, my website, and my telephone number. Every time that I've given it to people, they all burst out laughing.

They will say to me, "This is the greatest business card I've ever seen!" I've given this business card away for many years now and people always remember me. Try it yourself; it works.

Years later, people still come up to me and hug me; some people I can remember, but I have forgotten most of them. Still, they always remember me because of that business card, and they'll always ask if I do the same thing. Some people even say to me, "Laurence, I wake up every morning, and the first thing that I think of is you because I can see you on my vision board every day or you're on my desk next to my computer or I keep you in my wallet for good luck. You've got the greatest business card ever."

Many people tell me, "It's the only business card I've never thrown away in the bin." I just say to people, "That's great. You're welcome. You know, if you ever do want to spend it, then please ask for the change." It's very, very memorable, and I would encourage you to get something like that. I had to go to America to get the million dollars made, but the impact is unbelievable. You want people to remember you and you must stand out from the crowd and be different.

I've put my photo on my business cards over the years, but now I've taken it to another level by giving people a million dollars. Someone I met recently said that my business card made him feel special, and that's the secret: to make people feel special because they will always remember you.

I'm Not The Next
Richard Branson
Because
I Am The First
Laurence Lameche

The power of visualisation

You can do anything you put your mind to, so visualise anything you want and go out and make it happen. You must also believe it is possible and have faith that what you are visualising will come true.

Think about this: when you order something online, you don't have any doubt in your mind that the item you ordered will arrive – and that is exactly what you need to do when you visualise something, just know that it will arrive because the universe will bring it to you.

Visualise something now. For example, see yourself buying a property in London or anywhere you want for £1. Believe you can do it—it doesn't matter how, but you will find a way if you practise and put into place the teachings of this book. This is exactly what I did.

You need to gain the right knowledge to make this happen, but you are on the right track by reading this book and learning from other people who have actually done this. Read other books about this subject and invest in going on a course that teaches you, or find a mentor to show you how to do this and buy properties for no money.

Just take action and start to do something—even if you think you may not be ready, it doesn't matter because you will never be officially "ready." This is what I thought—I kept waiting to learn more because I never thought I was ready, and then one day I thought, *"Well, I may never be ready and I may not know all the answers, but I must begin at once whether I think I am ready or not and I can learn, practise, and grow along the way."* The time has come to take action, which is exactly what I did, and this is how I bought the majority of the properties I did in London with no money—and you can, too.

I never liked school, mainly because I was never good at it and I made the mistake to think that as soon as I left school I would stop learning. I soon realised that in order to be successful in what you do, you must continue to learn and gain knowledge relating to your chosen purpose, profession, or business.

How to deal with worry

Death: Accept it as a fact of life. It will one day happen to all of us, so what's the point of spending your life worrying about it?

Poverty: Do not worry about what you have in regards to wealth.

Fear of criticism: Don't worry about what other people think of you because their opinion doesn't matter.

Old Age: None of us are getting any younger, so just embrace it and don't see it as a handicap but as a blessing of wisdom that youth cannot understand.

Loss of Love: Get along without love. It's better to be single than in an unhappy relationship.

Destroy the thoughts of worry by deciding that 'nothing in life is worth worrying about.' If it's not a problem, don't create one. When you decide this, you'll experience calmness of thought and peace of mind, which will bring you more happiness.

Do One Thing Each Day
That Will Take You One Step
Closer To Your Goal.

Laurence Lameche

Chapter 5
An Interview with the Author

Tell us about your experience getting started in property. What advice would you give someone just getting started?

Well, I went on lots of property courses and seminars over the years, but I put off getting into property or doing anything for years before I finally got started. I always thought that you needed money to invest in property. These speakers were talking onstage and I remember thinking, *"Oh, it's all right for them."* They were standing and showing photographs of the different properties they bought across the country but no one that spoke on stage ever bought any properties in London. They would say things like, "This property I bought here and it cost me X amount, and I had to put down a deposit of this amount." I remember sitting in the audience thinking, *"Well, what if you don't have any money to invest?"* because I didn't have any savings or a deposit and I couldn't get a mortgage, so how could I possibly buy a property in London?

At the end of these property courses, I used to go up and talk to the people who had spoken onstage and say, "That all sounds fantastic – I'd love to get into property, but I don't know how to get started because I don't have any money." They would always say to me, "Well, that shouldn't be a reason for you to not start investing in property." I would reply, "But how can I get started if I don't have any money?" They wouldn't ever give me an answer.

I found it very, very frustrating that I'd spent a lot of money on a course only to hear them say, "Well, you don't need money to invest in property." I remember one guy said he bought property with his credit card. At the time, I didn't even have a credit card, so to get started on this journey, I made myself a business card.

I think there's nothing worse than going to a seminar, course or networking event and running out of business cards. If you've met someone, and you say, "Well, let's swap business cards. And their reply is "Oh… I don't have any," and then you ask them to write it on piece of paper—they are never going to stand out this way or be remembered. Most people will just throw away that piece of paper in the bin, so it's time to get serious and the first step is to get some business cards made up that say you're a property investor.

When you go to an event you're meeting so many new people, you want to network with as many people as quickly as possible. When I got started, I just went to a company that printed free business cards. They were quite cheap looking and a bit tacky because they had their logo on the back of the card, but if that's all you can really do, it will work. Just put your name, a mobile number, and an email address on a business card. Get an email address that sounds property related and start from there.

Then start going to property events. There are many different events once a month all over the country, especially in London. They're quite reasonable, and they give you an insight into people's journeys and what they're doing in property and how the market is at the moment. Start talking to people in the room to find out what they're up to. I tried to make friends with as many people as possible that I thought were on a similar journey and that were trying to do things similar to me. I tried to exchange ideas with them and ask for their help, guidance, and advice.

A key piece of advice: whenever you go to events, you need to start telling people you're a property investor and that you buy property in whatever area you plan to get started in or want to invest in.

I suggest putting postcards in your local shops / newsagents in the area where you want to start investing – you know, something like "I buy houses for cash." Put your number and then see the response. I also did leaflets. I printed tens of thousands of leaflets and posted them through people's doors. I would also consider putting in a newspaper advert or maybe even get a website built. I looked at all the competitor websites online and I saw what made the websites that looked good to me stand out.

Then I approached some website designers to try to build an improved replica of the competitor's website. Start trying to speak with estate agents so you can assess the current market for buying rundown properties. Always try to look to increase the value. Many rundown properties need refurbishment. You can buy them cheaper and do the work that's needed to increase the value.

If you're starting without any money, can't get a mortgage, or have bad credit, work on your credit score. Go to Experian to find out your credit score and it will show you ways to improve it. I went from a credit score of about 400 to 986 in a matter of eight months (the maximum score is 999). You can try to do the same thing by learning how the credit score works. This knowledge is useful because you need to have a high credit score in order to get a mortgage.

If at the moment you cannot get a mortgage and have bad credit, then I would recommend going down the route of Rent to Rent, which means speaking to landlords or letting agents and renting out their properties. To do this, you will need to pay one month's rent and at least one month's deposit or sometimes 6 weeks' deposit. You will normally need to sign a 6 to 12 month contract and then sub-let the property out as holiday-let /serviced accommodation,

In many scenarios, you can double or even triple the rental income. This works all year round in London and this is something I do. I have properties that I don't even own that I rent. The landlords are tired and a bit fed up of renting to tenants and students that don't look after their property. Every year they have to get new tenants / students to rent their property because they always leave; sometimes they rent each room individually. I just come along and say, "Look, I can rent your property. How much do you want?" We agree upon the rental price. I pay all the bills and sometimes I decorate their property as well, which means I get it painted – it's amazing what a little paint can do. Sometimes I have to paint the whole property and decorate it to make it look like a hotel room with nice sheets, pillows, and cushions. These sorts of improvements can really make a world of difference. Take nice professional photos and start advertising it as a holiday-let. Go online and start that way – that's what I do with all of my properties.

If you can't afford to pay any rent, then still contact the landlords and letting agents and ask them if you could rent their property and turn it into a holiday let where you take care of the property and book it out to holiday makers. You will do all the work and pay them a high commission; that way, you are not guaranteeing a rent or a deposit and there are no up-front costs and you therefore cut your overheads, which is what I do as well to have a balanced portfolio and to spread the risk.

In a way, you would kind of be doing a joint venture with the landlord on a trial basis and you could even say to them, *"Give me one month to show you how much money I can make you."* Then, as soon as you take over the property, take professional photos and start to market it on websites like Airbnb for free (as they only charge a commission if people book the property on their website) and you will get paid 24 hours after the guests check in.

If those are the first steps, what other things if you had to take somebody through a process, what would you say that would be the things they need to do?

I would say to find a buddy. I met a guy ten years ago on a property course and I thought he was one of the most interesting people I met there. I had exchanged many business cards with other people on the event, but there was something about him. He was determined and successful.

He said to me that in ten years – he was forty at the time – that he wanted to retire. He had a corporate job and was looking to buy houses in his spare time and wanted to build up his property portfolio. However, I remember him mentioning to me: "Well, property can be quite a lonely journey."

It's an experience you go through alone. He is married and has a daughter, and they didn't go on any property courses. All of his friends and work colleagues had corporate jobs and had nothing to do with property. No one that he knew bought any property. I said to him, "Well, what are you doing to buy more properties?" He said, "Oh, well, you know, next week, I'm going to get some leaflets printed and I'm going to put them through letter boxes in my local area with my wife and daughter. I'm also speaking to estate agents and I'm going on another property course and reading a property book."

Then he said, "Well, what are you doing?" I said, "Oh, I'm going to put adverts in local newspapers." From there we compared notes every few weeks or once a month and through the years I've tried to do this with different people I've met on different courses along the way: I would say to them, "Look, do you want to buddy up so we can kind of help inspire each other?" When you've got no one else around, it's sometimes can be challenging to motivate yourself to get the things done that need to be done in order to further yourself and grow.

I have had many different buddies over the years. I have always initiated it and said, "Look, we could speak once a month, and try to inspire each other and try to help each other on this property journey." You need to find people who are serious because many people go to these courses or events and on average only probably about ten percent of the people in the room actually take any action at all after the event has finished.

I do know how it feels: it is quite challenging because after the seminar or course finishes the next day you get back to work, or you have your family and other commitments and life gets in the way again. These things sometimes prevent you from furthering yourself and progressing. It can be quite challenging. I would really recommend finding a buddy, and if you're like me and have few friends, then I suggest going to property events to try to make them. Try to find the right person.

Sometimes you might meet someone you get on with and – it happens to me, too – you schedule the call and they keep changing it and rescheduling. I always try to stick to the first date. If you start moving it around, it then becomes the next week, and then the next week becomes the next month, and you never accomplish anything.

Then I've had buddies that have never done anything over the last week or month but I have done a lot of work, then I said, "Oh, well what are you up?" "Oh, this month, I couldn't really do anything." There are always excuses. Life is full of them, but still, action taken is action taken, that particular person may not be right for you. You may need to keep on looking – if you feel you're not on the same path then find a new buddy.

You need to be motivated. This guy that I often used to talk to once a month would always tell me, "Oh yeah, I just bought another house this month." Even if I didn't do anything, it would inspire me to think I needed to compete with him and step up my game because he's got a busy full-time corporate job, he is married, has a daughter, but he always finds the time for property because he has a ten-year goal.

When I spoke to him recently he told me that he has now retired at age 50 and he is a property millionaire, but it took him ten years to do it. Now he is living off the rental income of his property portfolio of eighteen houses. Sometimes it's not about getting rich quick, but having a plan and taking action. It can take time, but with hard work and determination, anything is possible.

To start to do deals like this and attract motivated sellers you need to do some of the following from the list below:

- Get a business card
- Go to networking events and speak to people
- Print some flyers / leaflets to post through doors
- Print postcards and put them up in local newsagents
- Newspaper adverts

- Visit and speak to estate agents
- Visit and speak to letting agents
- Build A website

Your Power Team

Create your power team of people that can help you:

- Call answering service like a 24/7 call centre
- Builder
- Handyman, Plumber, Electrician, Boiler Repair
- Cleaner
- Mortgage Broker
- Solicitor
- Accountant
- Buddy
- Mentor

So far, you have recommended improving your credit score, finding a buddy, and attending property courses. What other steps would you take in the early days?

I would read books, on property in the areas I want to specialize in or get into, or that I think I can do. A lot of courses will teach property, how to find property at auctions, how to do HMOs (which are houses of multiple occupancy) and none of that really interests me.

People then started talking about lease-options, I didn't get it at first, and it took me about six months to understand that it is a fantastic strategy. I thought if I could try to understand it better, then I could try to make it work in London. Then I thought, *"How can I do even better than that?"*

I rented out the first investment property I bought in London as a holiday let. I did this because I was a tour guide in London, so I thought that I could make it work because London is one of the most popular cities in the world where millions of tourists visit every year. So I thought if I could rent out a flat as a holiday let and make it cheaper than a hotel, then I was sure it would work –and it does and it is almost fully booked all year round.

You have to research your area with other properties to compare if it's priced correctly. Research your competitors: find out if there are any holiday lets in that area as well as how much they charge. Go to have a look at them, view them, and see how much they are charging and think about if you can do the same thing or make it better.

In the beginning I was reading quite a lot. Again, it was quite difficult for me, but I have to try to change my life. What I thought would be the best thing to do is to try to learn about mind-set, to try to learn and read personal development books, read about property books that were in the subject that would interest me, listening to what other great books people have read.

Or I'd go into a bookshop and read for free. Go to a library, read for free. Buy audiobooks if it's challenging to read – if you're driving, listen to it in the car rather than your radio. Try to spend an hour listening every day. The first thing I would do each morning is listen to a great audio book – I'd call it "power hour."

Go to seminars, read, listen to audio books, go online, and learn. I also pay a lot of money to go on seminars and courses to learn about my industry and I also pay to have coaching sessions with people who are more experienced than me to help me.

My friend just bought a flat for £280,000 in a building where I bought a flat for £1 or actually, I secured the price at £135,000 a few years ago and now it is worth the same price as he paid: £280,000. He bought it through an estate agent and I got this deal through what I learnt on a course that cost me £500. My friend thought that the £500 for a seminar was expensive. He told me he couldn't afford the money or time, so he just waits for the price to go up.

Goals

I would write down 10 Daily Goals every day and to do this I have created a list for you to help.

1. **Believe**
   You must absolutely believe that you can transform your life. Everything started as a thought so make your thoughts turn into a reality.
2. **Visualise**
   Know what you want for your life and focus on making it happen.
3. **Write it down**
   This is the key to your success.
4. **Purpose**

Knowing your 'Why' you want to achieve your goals.

5. **Commit**
Commit to making it happen.

6. **Stay Focused**
Stay focused to Manifest your goals and do this daily.

7. **Action Plan**
Know what you want by writing down a list of tasks to achieve your goals.

8. **Do It Now**
Think of something that you can do now to show commitment towards your goals, even if you do a little thing every day towards your goals that will help you and get you closer to your dreams.

9. **Be Accountable**
Tell friends and family about your goals and seek outside help (like trying to find a mentor).

10. **Review**
Each day to make sure you are on track because sometimes life gets in the way, so it's important to follow this list to see if you are on track.

Do these steps daily and you are on your way to achieving your goals.

Daily Goal Setting

Every morning, write down your ten top goals with a pen and a piece of paper. Don't look at the ones you wrote yesterday, think about what you want most and write them down. It's important to always write goals in the present tense and set a deadline for each one. Do this for each of your ten goals.

An Action Exercise

Use a notebook and a pen to write down your goals. Every morning, write down ten goals, don't look at the day before. And make them happen.

Going to bed at night listen to inspirational quotes and affirmations. The subconscious mind absorbs this positivity if you project it – you can become more positive and achieve your dreams while becoming more focused.

Okay, so we have: improving your credit score, getting a buddy, going on property courses, reading books, your power team, goal setting, and making your mindset positive. Do you have any more advice

as to practical things one can do to make success in property more attainable?

I would read every morning for about half an hour or 45 minutes, maybe an hour. Sometimes, I'd end up reading a book every single day on property. If you don't like reading, then listen to the audiobook.

Continue to learn, go to more events and network with like-minded people. Focus, have a plan and get started TODAY. Because there is no time like the present and if you do something every day that gets you one step closer to you achieving your goals then the journey will be worth it.

Create your own Mastermind Team of Go-Getters.

Surround yourself with people who do things better than you can.

The way to success is to continue learning.

Influence your own subconscious mind with affirmations and positive thoughts.

How do you suggest choosing which course to take in property? When you're first starting, you hear all

these words coming at you – Rent To Rent, Deal Sourcing, Lease Options, Serviced Accommodation, HMOs – there's just so much to take in. You end up thinking, "Well which is the best one for me? Is it this one, or should I be going to Auctions? Which subject do I learn?"

I would say to go to monthly networking events and ask people if they have been on any course and what course do they recommend. Go online, search for reviews, and see if anyone has written a book linked to the course you want to go on and maybe read the book first so you will start to get a feel of whether what this person is teaching would be useful to you with what you are trying to achieve.

How do you suggest cutting through all the analysis-paralysis to narrow your focus?

Good point. There is so much, and I think when I first went on the courses they would talk about just trying to find an absolutely crappy, terrible property that's so rundown that you can turn it into a goldmine and add value to it. That's what I first did. I went to all the estate agents.

I then re-mortgaged my own property, pulling some money out to use as a deposit for the new property. I did that before even finding the property, so I had the deposit money ready because it takes time to re-mortgage your property, so you want to be in the right position straightaway. From there I just contacted the estate agents went with that as my strategy. Just focus on just one strategy at a time.

When I ran out of money and couldn't buy any more property, I thought about how to do the lease options. I totally focused on that and turned all of them into holiday-lets; I then focused on holiday-lets. You're right that you can end up focusing on too many things, so my advice would be just try to focus on one thing and do that well, and then repeat it.

The thing that people become hung up on is how to choose the right property. How do you choose the right area? Is there a good area in the country to choose? A lot of people say don't buy anything in London, because there are cheaper properties up north but I have always thought that doesn't make sense to me because I live in London and I only want to buy property in London because the value of

properties in London goes up a lot more than anywhere else in this country.

Well, I live in London and I've been there many, many years. All the people that I was learning from and paid to go on their courses never invested in London. I wanted to try to find someone that was actually teaching or buying property in London, because they were teaching about properties all outside of London in all different parts of the country. To me, those areas didn't interest me at all. I wanted to buy in London, and then, even when I spoke to the people teaching the course to say, "Look, I'm not really interested anywhere apart from buying in London." They'd say, "Oh, London is very expensive," and "You know, it's very competitive."

They'd tell me all the reasons why it wouldn't be possible, but they were the ones teaching a course, so it was just that they probably had tried and failed. I just thought, "You know, I'm sure there's a way to do it," but I never met anyone that could teach me. *That's what I'm trying to do now for other people by writing this book to explain how I did it.*

You cannot really go wrong with London. Obviously, property prices do go up and down in value, but, traditionally, they double in value every 10 years. When I went on these courses, the person teaching would say something like: they bought a property for £50,000 and 10 years later it's worth £100,000. I thought that if I could buy a property in London for £250,000 or £300,000, then in 10 years' time the same property would to be worth £500,000 or £600,000.

Even if I buy fewer properties, I think it would be much better for me to buy properties in London because I would have to buy so many properties up north to get to that level. You need to find an area. I just thought, *"Okay, well, there are certain parts of London that I like and feel comfortable with."* It is important to note some areas in London increase far more than others.

Another tip: look into areas where people are getting repossessed the most. I think there are websites out there that can show you statistics on which areas of London where properties get repossessed. Maybe you could flyer and leaflet those areas. With a website, I would get calls from all over London from all sorts of different people. Just try to make sure the deal works for you. I look for capital growth and if the deal works for me. Some people are different – maybe you want cash flow now. If that's the case, maybe buy council properties. They are a lot cheaper to buy, but they give you a much better rental income, but they will not appreciate in value as much.

What about the more formal aspects of business – analysing the deal, or making sure that the figures stack up – do you have any sort of system for doing that or do you work on a deal-by-deal basis?

I just do it on a deal-by-deal basis. Whatever deals come my way, I research the area. I would then go on Rightmove.co.uk, for example, and look at comparable properties in that area, with that postcode, that have sold. I'd also call, maybe, three to five local estate agents in that area, and say: "Hello. I've got property that I'm looking to sell." Now, they normally would always not give a figure over the phone. They'd always want to view the property, and of course, you can't give them the address (the street address is ok but not the number) because they may take the deal from you and because you haven't bought it yet and you're talking hypotheticals.

I always say, "I'm looking to sell. I know, normally, you'd have to come around to view the property, but could you give me a ballpark figure? It's a one-bedroom flat or two-bedroom flat." Whatever it is, describe it to them, and say, "On average, what would a property like this, sell for, if I was to put it on the market?

I'm just trying to get an idea of what to do at the moment to sell or maybe even to rent it out."

You know, some of them will give the information: "Oh, well, I sold one recently, let's say, just down the road from there for X amount." I ask them, "Could you send me some details of that, just so I can have a look?" and get them to email it to you. Speak to their lettings team as well: "How much could you rent it for?" You need to try to do your own due diligence.

Do you have a checklist for things doing due diligence?

What I do is look online at properties that have sold. I check RightMove.co.uk for comparable properties that are for sale in the area and that have sold. I also speak to local estate agents and get an estimate of what the property is worth. I visit the property and I know my area well where I am investing so I can tell if it's a good deal or not. This takes time to learn but once you know your area and constantly check online you will know how much the properties are selling for. I visit estate agents and letting agents to go and view other compatible properties for sale to see how they compare to the one you are buying. You will get to know if it is a good deal or not.

Do you have any tips for building up relationships with estate agents, or do you think it's better to deal directly with the owner?

Both, really. It depends what works for you. I've tried both and both have worked for me. Personally, I like to build up relationships with people that I'm talking to over the phone or in person. I have done more deals talking to the owners directly, but I've done deals with estate agents as well.

I would recommend that once you've done a deal with an estate agent, for example, then you should go back to them and say, "Great! Thank you." Buy them a gift, as well – a bottle of champagne or whatever they like, a bunch of flowers, nice chocolates, a box of donuts or a football ticket – and say, "Great. Thanks a lot for all your help with the property. Where's the next deal?" Now they know you're serious, and now they should put you at the top of the list to bring you more and more deals.

The Power of Belief is to Believe

Laurence Lameche

Chapter 6
The Power of Belief

I have gone to many sold-out events over the years and I always get a ticket at face value or sometimes for *free*.

It's just brilliant, and you should try it, too, because it always works for me. Whenever I am on my way to the event, I always visualize getting a ticket from a fan who has a spare ticket and I never pay more than the face value of the ticket.

All I do is I go to these events about one hour before they start, and I choose the place where the most people enter the event (because some events have many different entrances). I go to these sold-out events all over the world, and I just have a little sign on an A4 piece of paper that I take it with me and it simply reads: *One Ticket Wanted, Cash Paid, Thank You*. I always get in; I have never failed. Sometimes people offer me tickets for free or give me their tickets for less than the face value.

As I am about to leave my home to go to these events I already see, feel, and believe myself already in possession of the ticket and visualize someone coming up to me to give me their spare ticket. It works every time I have done this.

Because I believe 100% with certainty and with absolute faith that I will get into the event, there is never any doubt in my mind. I already know the outcome that I will always get a ticket and this gives me the result I desire.

Here are some of the many sold-out events I have gone to over the years:

- The Olympics in London 2012 (I got 15 tickets to all the sold-out events and even someone gave me a £725 ticket for FREE to see Usain Bolt and Mo Farah win their second gold medals) .
- Live Aid at Hyde Park, London in 2005 (I got into the VIP section).
- Wimbledon Men's Tennis Final in 2014.
- FA Cup Final in 2015 Arsenal v Aston Villa at Wembley Stadium.
- Champions League Finals in 2006 in Paris, Arsenal v Barcelona.

- Champions League Finals in 2013 at Wembley in London.
- England games at Wembley.
- Arsenal's last game of the season in 1998 against Everton where Arsenal won the League.
- Old Trafford to see Manchester United v Arsenal on 8th May 2002 where Arsenal won the League (I had to sit with the Manchester United fans, but it was worth it).
- White Hart Lane to see Tottenham v Arsenal on 25th April 2004 where Arsenal won the League (I had to sit with the Tottenham fans and again it was worth it).
- Royal Albert Hall 'Music For Montserrat' Concert on 15th September 1997.
- Royal Albert Hall in 1999 'Concert for Linda' on 10th April 1999 a memorial concert for Linda McCartney.
- Royal Albert Hall in 2002 'The Concert for George' on 29th November 2002; this was a memorial concert for George Harrison to mark the first anniversary of his death.
- US Open 2001.
- Barcelona v Arsenal on 6th April 2010.
- Many different concerts in London.
- Many different Theatres / Musicals in London.
- Seminars and Events.

Warning: beware of ticket touts

Never buy a ticket from a ticket tout because they will always want a lot more money than the face value of a ticket. It's easy to spot these people: they are usually older or middle-aged men who just walk around the venue or stand there saying "Tickets? Anyone need tickets?" If you approach them, they may want you to walk off with them—don't do it because sometimes the tickets they sell are not even real and won't get you into the venue.

How to buy a ticket at face value for all sold-out events

If you would like to print my sign and use it for yourself to get tickets at sold out events, use the example of it on the next page (or you can just take this book along with you, hold it outside the venue, and wait for people to come up to you and offer their tickets to you). Trust me, it works!

ONE
TICKET
WANTED
£ CASH PAID £

THANK YOU

Chapter 7
How To Network Without Talking To People

Every event I go to I take with me my business cards. Even if – like me – you're scared to network with people and are a bit shy at these events, you must see it as a great opportunity to meet new people and to push out of your comfort zone.

I have come up with a quick way to speak to lots of people and to collect as many business cards as possible.

When I was at these events, I was normally stuck with the dullest person in the room, and they wouldn't ever shut up or go away. I just couldn't ever think of a polite way to excuse myself from that situation to get away from them. I knew I'd be stuck with that person and I wouldn't be able to network or try to meet anyone else. That's why I invented this sign to say, "Can We Swap Business Cards" or "$1,000,000 for your Business Card?"

I've produced all these different signs to grab people's attention, and they'd always give me their business card. I do it as soon as the event finishes. Because people would be rushing off to go home, so they wouldn't talk to me for that long, which was brilliant. I could capture so many business cards, and if people did try to talk to me by saying, "Well, what do you do?" I reply, "I Buy Property in London For £1 or A Football Ticket?" "Wow, how did you do that?" My response: "Well, if you give me your business card, I'd be happy to tell you. Let's catch up after the event." If people say to me *"Well, I'm not interested in property*, then I ask them, "What do you do," and I listen to them for about ten seconds. After I learn a bit about them, I suggest that maybe we can help each other in our businesses and offer to swap business cards.

If they are being difficult, they may say something like, *"What's the catch? What are you trying to sell me*?" I will reply, "I have nothing to sell. All I am looking to do is to network with like-minded people and to make new friends, and who knows, maybe we could help each other in the future." Then I would start to walk a few steps to my left or right, so I could catch the eye of someone else. Remember, if you argue with a fool, you become one!

Then I just excuse myself by saying I have to meet more people. I'm always looking for the next person, the next business card. You've got to network quickly with people and so try to talk to each person for thirty seconds to one minute—if they are interested in you, say, *"Let's catch up after the event, it was nice to meet you"* and move on to the next person.

Important to remember: Sometimes I have gone to events, seminars, and courses and held up my sign because I am shy and this is how I prefer to network with people, but the organizers don't always like me doing this and request I do not put my sign up. When I ask them why, they simply say I can't do this otherwise I have to leave. So I just walk outside onto the pavement on the street and then I make sure that I talk to everyone who comes out of the entrance to ask them for their business card. They can't stop me there and they can't stop my abundant mindset and attitude.

Here are some of the examples below of the signs that I use at these different seminars, courses, or networking events. Feel free to use them. Don't worry about feeling scared because I always do! What I have learned is to feel the fear and do it anyway!

$1,000,000
For Your

Business

Card
Thank You

Are You Interested In *Property?*

Can We Swap Business Cards?

Thank You

Let's Swap Business Cards?

Thank You

How to have an abundant attitude

Here is my list of what to do to have an abundant attitude so that you can create your own daily living routine in order to increase and attract good things into your life and so that your goals and dreams come true at a quicker rate.

A: Abundance in thoughts, feelings, and actions

B: Believe in yourself and in your dreams

C: Create a magical life

D: Determination to succeed

E: Excitement to live your dream life

F: Focus on your goals

G: Grow and learn

H: Hope there is always hope

I: Imagine what is possible

J: Just do it now

K: Kindness to kittens and to yourself

L: Laugh because life is meant to be fun

M: Motivation to make it happen.

N: Never give up.

O: Optimistic for the future

P: Positive mind

Q: Quitters never win

R: Risk challenge yourself every day

S: Success be the superhero you were born to be

T: Thank you for having the time to enjoy life

U: Unique and special are words to describe you

V: Visualize in your dreams and goals in life

W: Wealth and Wisdom

X: X-factor—you have it, so use your talent.

Y: Yes, you can do it

Z: Zest for life

How to get closer to reaching your goals

Now it's time to get motivated and to start to take action so you can accomplish your dreams and goals in life.

If you want to accomplish one thing at a time, within the next week write down what you want to see happen, and just do it, it's that simple. Get something else done in week two, week three and so on. There's fifty-two weeks in a year; you can accomplish a lot if you break a year down into doing one thing every week, or even one thing every month which is a start and your momentum will build up like a snowball on top of a hill.

All you need to do is start by doing something each day that will move you towards your goal.

Like in that Chinese proverb that states 'a journey of a thousand miles begins with a single step,' it may take a long time to get it finished, so we must take the first step. You have to take the first step. You just have to do something. Take action today. Many people don't take action or do anything at all.

My goal in writing this book is to inspire you to Take Action, to buy a property for £1 or with a football ticket. Maybe you want to increase your salary or start that business, so dare to dream big, because you can have anything you want in life. Be anything you want, do anything you want. Remember that opportunities are all around us. Be brave and stand out from the crowd and make your dreams become a reality.

Begin Your Dream Right Now, Whether You Are Ready or Not. Your Willingness to be Bold has Genius, Magic and Power in It

Laurence Lameche

Buying my dream home In London

Now, what I am doing is looking to buy my dream home in London. Although I must say I wasn't looking to buy anywhere for perhaps the next three to five years, but recently a few months ago I walked along The Bishop's Avenue, which for decades was known as "Billionaire's Row," one of the most expensive roads in London where you can find many mansions.

My mother used to drive me down there when I was younger to inspire me before I moved to London. I used to love going to London when I was a child, seeing these mansions thinking, just like the TV character Del Boy would say from 'Only Fools and Horses': "This time next year, we'll be millionaires!" I'd always think to myself, "I will also figure out a way to one day become a millionaire."

In the summertime this year, I was walking around a food festival in Wimbledon, and it was such a beautiful sunny day that I walked around the park. I hadn't been to that area before. Then I stumbled across The All England Tennis Club (where the Wimbledon tennis matches take place each year).

I remember walking there and thinking, "Oh wow, these properties are amazing." Then I walked all the way around the park and there were other bigger mansions, and I wondered how much it would be to live there. I was just thinking it was such an unbelievable dream to imagine living there. I rushed back home, got on the Internet, and started to look.

One of the properties I liked was for sale at £5,000,000, and I thought, "Wow, one day if I work hard enough I will buy it." Another one was around £10,000,000, another one was £15,000,000; they were all just amazing dream homes.

Recently, I rented a flat in Paddington from a landlord as a Rent2Rent, which means I am renting it out as a serviced apartment / holiday let in London. It was completely unfurnished; it didn't have anything – no bed, no furniture, none of that. I had to try to find ideas how to decorate it nicely. It's in a beautiful building and I could rent it out to holidaymakers for between £250 to £300+ per night and the rent I pay for the flat is £2,000 a month. Even at £250 pounds a night, that's £1,750 a week or £7,500 per month.

I thought I should have a look at these multi-million pound properties to just inspire me for ideas on how to decorate this new flat, so I was just looking and searching online. I went page after page after page looking at how they decorate the living room and what furniture they chose. In a lot of the photos there are two sofas and a nice rug, a coffee table sometimes wooden or glass, and a beautiful mirror above the nice fireplace.

I appreciated the attention to detail – you know, the dining table and chairs, the bed, the matching bedside tables and lamps, how they decorated it with many pillows, wardrobe, chest of drawers and desk. Most of the homes looked like show homes and they were all just so beautifully decorated.

I just wanted to search online so I'd get an idea, "Oh, that looked good, wow look at how they have decorated that room," and then I came across this unbelievable property and as soon as I saw it, I thought: "Wow, I'd love to live there, this is my dream home." At the time I thought it was way out of my league; I thought I couldn't even possibly imagine buying something like that, right now. Then I thought, "No, that's a limiting belief. Why can't I live there?" Then I thought, "This property is perfect – it's the most beautiful home I've ever seen in my life. It's in a really nice part of London." I thought I just had to go and view the property.

Next year I'm coming to a significant birthday. A good friend of mine always wears this expensive Rolex watch, and I, for years, always wore a watch that was hardly worth anything. Even though it was a special watch to me because I bought it for myself when I took my mum to New York one Christmas; I had the watch for over fifteen years.

I always wondered how my friend felt wearing such an expensive watch. He's like, "Ah, I feel like a million dollars when I wear it, it makes me believe I can achieve anything in this world. I feel powerful; it makes me feel amazing. Every day when I wear the watch it makes me want to work harder."

I said to him, "How can you afford to pay for something like that? It's so expensive." He said, "Oh, it's quite simple. It's like buying a car." He was paying it off a little bit every month and you can get financing over the course of maybe two or three years. I never knew about this form of financing. I'd thought that to purchase it I would have to have the money in my bank account, to pay it off or to use a credit card. How on earth does someone pay something like that off if they don't have the money?

I thought it was a great watch, and that I had to get one in order to feel that I've made it. Then I would be able to walk through the door of my dream property and it would make me feel like a million dollars. I bought myself two nice watches from Bond Street and then I contacted the estate agent, and he said, "Unfortunately, the property has just been removed from the market. It's not for sale anymore." I said, "Oh, no. You don't understand. This is my home. I am meant to buy it. I've waited a few months to call you. I've been busy, writing 'this book'. Is there any way I can view the property?" He said, "No, sorry. It's been taken off the market by the owners." I said, "Why?" He didn't know and gave no reason at all. I said, "Look, you don't understand. With the property I have now, I knew that I would buy it before I even saw it. I have the same feeling with this property. I love the property so much. You don't understand – it's not just a home. This is my forever home. I absolutely love it – I have to see it." He said, "Just write me an email and I'll talk with the owners and get back to you."

I did that, and a few days later, he came back and said, "It's your lucky day, the owner is going to let you see it one time, and one time only. You have to view it on this day at this time." I said, "Yes, no problem, fine." I hired a Mercedes Benz taxi to take me there in style and the agent took me around. Then the owner came back home, and I said, "You have the most beautiful home I've ever seen in my life. I just absolutely love it – and thank you so much for allowing me to view it. I bought you these flowers to say thank you." The owners, husband and wife, were very touched by the flowers, but it meant a lot to me to see their property.

A week later, there were about four or five other properties in that same area that were also for sale. I wanted to see them, but I didn't have the same feelings for any of them. I posted the owner a letter because I always like the personal touch of trying to speak to the owner to try to figure out the reason why they are selling their property. If I can understand that, then hopefully I can figure out a win-win deal for both of us.

Two hours later, I was by chance in the area, and the owner drove past, recognizing me from behind, and said, "Oh, hello Laurence." I said, "Oh hi there, how are you? It's nice to see you again." I said, "Look, I do love your home. Is there any way I can take your number and talk to you about it some time?" He gave me his number and then from there I was talking to him.

I said, "The trouble is I don't have any money to buy it because all my assets are all tied up in the property I own. I'm going to have to sell quite a lot in order to buy it. Where I live right now, I've loved living there, and I would never before consider selling it. I'm a bit scared to sell it. In case the deal with you falls through, can we meet up and talk about it?"

Anyway, we talked a bit about it, and we talked again about it and he kindly said, "Look, we like you, me and my wife. We want someone that loves our property to buy it." When I met them, I told them, "Your home is the most beautiful home I've ever seen. I probably shouldn't tell you this because it's not good for negotiation, but I absolutely love your home and I would love to live here. It's an actual dream come true.

Ever since I saw it advertised online, every single night, every single day I can't stop thinking about it. I'm thinking about it all the time. When the agent showed it to me, he gave me a brochure of the property and I have it on my desk; so every single day I look at it and I visualize living there.

The owner said he would take it off the market for a year if that would give me enough time to try to buy it. For that, they wanted a small deposit payment from me into their solicitor's account, just to hold it for that time. If I didn't complete, they keep the money; if I do complete, it would be taken off the asking price.

Because I told them that I don't have any way of raising money without selling something, which I don't want to do. They have since said, "Look, if you want we'll just keep it off the market," and they told me another idea would be to not ask me for a deposit, but maybe they could allow me to have eight months to try to find a way to buy the property. They also said that they don't want any deposit from me, if that helps me to try to figure out a way to buy it.

I've spoken to a few mortgage brokers and they said on the property portfolio that I have (with the properties that I have bought for a football ticket and the other £1 properties I've acquired in London and my other properties I own) that they reckon I can do it and buy my dream home. I don't have to sell any property. I had thought I'd have to sell quite a lot and will have to pay capital gains tax. I always wanted to keep the properties that I have, thinking that the ones that I pay off would provide me with a path to retirement.

However, the mortgage brokers and the people I've been speaking to have said that I could get my dream home through taking out a bridging loan with the money I have built up in equity in the properties. Then, within twelve months, I would need to get a mortgage to purchase it. As I write this book, I'm thinking about standing outside The Bank of England, Liverpool Street Station, City of London, and Canary Wharf with a sandwich board saying: *"Help Me Buy My Dream Home, I Will Pay You A High Interest and A Charge Against The Property"* to see if any investors would be interested in helping me.

I'm looking for investors, so if you know anyone who has money sitting in the bank not earning anything – most banks pay less than 1% interest – I'm willing to pay a very high interest rate to borrow the money from an investor or investors to buy my dream home.

It would all be secured; you'd have first charge on the property and I'd pay you a high interest rate. If you know anyone who can help, please contact me: laurence@thelondonpropertybuyers.co.uk

I also have other assets and property that I'd be prepared to put towards getting my dream home, so there is less risk for an investor. In the next edition of this book, I'll talk more about it, and I will have a photo of me outside my dream home, because I'm going to go ahead and buy it. I'm just trying to work hard to figure out the best way to do this deal and to raise the money I need.

It doesn't matter whether you're rich or poor because we all have one thing in common and that is time. However, every day that goes by, you get one day older, which means you have one day less to achieve the wealth and success you desire.

Dream Big and Believe that Anything In Life Is Possible. I Wish You Every Success In The Future.

About the Author

Laurence Lameche moved to London and, as he didn't have a penny to his name, he slept in his car. He was hungry for food (and success!) and was determined to succeed but he lacked any business experience.

Laurence graduated from the school of hard knocks, life. He is now a multi-millionaire property investor, entrepreneur and motivational speaker.

He specialises in Rent2Rent, Serviced Accommodation / Holiday Lets in London, Lease Options / Purchase Lease Options and Instalment Contracts, with these strategies allowing him to control property with little or no money, or maybe the cost a Football Ticket.

Every single strategy shared in this book, has been experienced by Laurence on his journey to success. There have been many ups and downs but he has just given things a go and doesn't let the rules stop him, as he finds legal ways around the rules and you can too!

This book shares many simple principles which can be followed by anyone wanting to achieve success in the property market, in or out of London! By following these simple ideas, you too can have a million-dollar business card, network like a pro, set big goals, step out of your comfort zone, learn from failure and achieve great success!

You too can learn how to buy property in London or anywhere in the World with No Mortgage and No Deposit. Or for the price of a football ticket or for as little as £1.

Many years of experience buying property in London with no money, then renting them as serviced accommodation to generate maximum rental income, is just one of Laurence's specialisms. Laurence's properties are owned by him, controlled by him and also rented from other landlords and letting agents. He also offers a full management service, which is hassle free for landlords and can earn them up to double their normal rental income, or he can guarantee a fixed rental income every month for landlords in London to give them piece of mind in knowing what rent they will receive month in, month out. Contact Laurence directly if him managing your property is something which you would like to discuss:

Email:
info@citybooker.co.uk

Website:
www.citybooker.co.uk

If you need to sell your property in London then please also feel free to contact Laurence.

Website:
www.TheLondonPropertyBuyers.com

Laurence now teaches the strategies he has refined and explained in this book in more detail in live training events. He also offers a one-to one-consultancy service for anyone wanting more information, advice and guidance on their property issues and supports first-time investors to get started in helping them achieve their property goals.

He can be contacted by email:
laurence@thelondonpropertybuyers.co.uk

Recommended Reading

The Magic of Thinking Big by David J. Schwartz

How to Think Like a Millionaire by Charles-Albert Poissant

Think and Grow Rich by Napoleon Hill

The Power of Positive Thinking by Norman Vincent Peale

The Secret by Rhonda Byrne

The Slight Edge by Jeff Olson

One Minute Millionaire by Robert Allen

Eat That Frog by Brian Tracy

The Richest Man in Babylon by George S. Clason

Twisted Knickers and Stolen Scones by Watt Nicoll

Screw It Let's Do It by Richard Branson

How to Win Friends and Influence People by Dale Carnegie

Millionaire Property Author by Stephanie J. Hale

Property Magic by Simon Zutshi

Awaken The Giant Within by Anthony Robbins

How To Be A Money Magnet by Mary-Clare Carlyle

The 4-Hour Workweek by Timothy Ferriss

The 7 Habits of Highly Effective People by Steven R. Covey

How To Persuade People Who Don't Want To Be Persuaded by Joel Bauer

The Journey by Brandon Bays

Marilyn Monroe: The Final Years by Keith Badman

Printed in Great Britain
by Amazon

Identifying Man-made Gems

Identifying
Man-made Gems

Michael O'Donoghue
M.A., F.G.S., F.G.A.

Colour photography by Dr Edward Gübelin C.G., F.G.A.

N.A.G. Press Ltd
London EC1V 7QA

Published in 1983

© N.A.G. Press Ltd and Michael O'Donoghue, 1983

ISBN 7198 0111 7

Printed and bound in Great Britain by
Clark Constable (1982) Ltd, Tanfield, Edinburgh
EH3 5JT, Scotland

Contents

List of Colour Plates

The author and publishers wish to acknowledge their immense debt to Dr Edward Gübelin of Switzerland and to thank him for permitting them to reproduce the colour plates which come from his collection of gem-inclusion photographs.

1. Verneuil Ruby
2. Verneuil Ruby
3. Verneuil Ruby
4. Verneuil Ruby

5. Fremy Ruby
6. Early Hydrothermal Ruby
7. Early hydrothermal ruby
8. Early hydrothermal ruby

9. Chatham ruby
10. Chatham ruby
11. Chatham ruby
12. Chatham ruby

13. Chatham ruby
14. Chatham ruby
15. Kashan ruby
16. Kashan ruby

17. Kashan ruby
18. Kashan ruby

19. Verneuil sapphire
20. Verneuil sapphire
21. Verneuil sapphire
22. Verneuil sapphire

23. Chatham sapphire
24. Chatham sapphire
25. Chatham sapphire

An Introduction to
Man-Made Gem Materials

Any study of materials must ensure that its readers understand exactly what is meant by the terms used by the writer. Much labour has been wasted in attempts to clarify terms after a study has been published and, in order to avoid this, I shall try to clarify my terms from the outset.

By 'gemstone', I mean any substance – inorganic or organic – which is reasonably durable and attractive and which has been, or may be, used for ornamental purposes.

By 'man-made', I mean any substance which is artificial, whether or not it has a natural counterpart. Thus, for clarity, emerald and strontium titanate are both referred to (when appropriate) as man-made for the purpose of this study; even though one has a natural counterpart and the other has not. The adjective 'synthetic' should be used only for man-made items with a natural counterpart.

Although I have included the term 'organic' above, readers will understand that almost all materials used for ornament are inorganic. This study covers organic materials comprehensively where they have been manufactured (coral) and in passing where they have been altered in some way by the action of man.

Man has also been instrumental in altering the colour of inorganic substances. Examples of this activity are included in this book; purchasers of stones whose natural colour has been 'improved', should know about it, because in certain circumstances the practice may be viewed as undesirable. In any case, it is always better to know the full facts about items which you intend to buy, even when such facts may be unpalatable. Furthermore some countries have legislation which specifically states that items offered for sale should be correctly and fully described; penalties for concealment or omission can be severe.

Readers should also bear in mind that many artificially-made substances were originally made for industrial purposes and that their ornamental application was (and perhaps still is) secondary or even accidental. In the course of the book, some details of industrial application will be mentioned where appropriate, since there are cases in which a particular property of a substance has made it desirable for both types of application. It is interesting to note that many substances have appeared in faceted form in one or two examples only. The task of identification and description is made more exciting because, at the time of first encounter, no one knows whether or not the material will appear on the market in a commercially successful form.

Nassau (1976) lists some criteria for the correct use of the term 'synthetic'. They include:

1. Same chemical composition with some allowance made for substitutional variation as in much natural material;
2. No filler or binder of a foreign substance should be present;
3. Crystal structure, as seen by X-ray diffraction, should be the same as that of the natural equivalent;
4. Sub-microscopic structures must be essentially identical (e.g. the diffraction grating effect in opal); and
5. The man-made product should appear the same to the eye as the natural one.

Methods of crystal growth have been documented in a wide variety of texts but, for the purposes of this book, I have considered it best to outline the chief methods which have produced gem-quality materials without including such details as phase diagrams and tables. However, those who want to know why one method is preferred for the manufacture of a substance rather than another will find explanations of the reasons. I shall also show why particular characteristics (inclusions, variations in constants) arise during growth. The literature on crystal growth is now very large and I have only chosen those texts which are both fairly easy of access and of understanding for inclusion in the Bibliography. Many substances which come within the scope of this book are described in patents and I have included the appropriate numbers in some important cases.

During the discussions of particular materials, references to features of the natural material will also be given for the purpose of comparison. Details of man-made stones will, in many cases be given more than once; firstly in the chapters dealing with manufacturing methods, and secondly in the chapters covering the particular species of gemstone.

It is an unhappy fact that a proliferation of undesirable trade-names has accumulated over the years. These are given in a list which makes no pretensions to completeness. My opinion of these names is that they will die if no one repeats them but, where trade-names are in common use, the reader will be cheated if they are not explained.

I hope that this book will be used; I should like to see it on the bench, on or near the counter (depending on the type of business!) and, most important of all, in the classroom, though, since this is not intended as an elementary gemmology textbook, I have omitted explanations of and references to phenomena whose details are easily found elsewhere. With an eye to the future, I have included some substances which are not (at the time of writing) in general ornamental use. Perhaps some of them may never be used as gems but, equally, there may come a time when crystals are collected for their own beauty, whether or not they are man-made. Then many of these substances will come into their own.

MICHAEL O'DONOGHUE   LONDON
                                                     JUNE 1982

Note: To convert nanometers (nm) to Ångstroms, multiply by 10.

PART I

METHODS OF GROWTH

1. The Structure and Development of Crystals

A crystal may be defined as a solid three-dimensional body with long-range order of its component atoms; atoms in liquids and gases do not display this kind of order (since they are in rapid movement). In fact almost every solid substance known is crystalline; the one exception of real importance is glass, in which the atoms only display order over a very short range. Crystals may be bounded with plane (flat) faces which make the whole body recognizable; but most crystalline substances occur as apparently shapeless lumps, due to the various conditions of growth. It is worth noting here that synthetic crystals, grown in a controlled environment, frequently display a very beautiful and recognizable set of faces.

The special outward shape taken by a crystal is called its 'form'. This word has a special significance to crystallographers because it means the particular shape taken by a crystal and forced upon it by the operation of elements of symmetry, which themselves depend upon the chemical composition of the crystal. Many forms are not often seen in actual examples, because conditions of growth hinder development of faces which the symmetry of a perfect crystal would demand. Compare a snowflake to an ice cube in a refrigerator. However, it is vital to realize that, whatever the crystal looks like from outside, inside the symmetry is still that regular type which the particular substance requires; only X-ray studies can prove this.

Symmetry in crystals extends geometrical symmetry, as it applies to three-dimensional rather than to two-dimensional bodies. Axes of references (or crystallographic axes) determine how crystals can be grouped into six recognizable and independent crystal systems. These systems can be further divided into classes and space groups. (There are 230 of these, some of which are not represented by actual material, either natural or synthetic). However such details are not necessary for the purposes of this book.

The crystallographic axes are imaginary axes which intersect at various angles and are themselves of varying lengths. For example three axes, mutually perpendicular and of equal length, would be the obvious framework or scaffolding around which a cube could be constructed. If one of these axes is a different length from the other two, a cube cannot be constructed because it will be longer or shorter in one of the dimensions. For similar reasons, axes meeting at angles other than 90° will produce shapes which are more obviously unsymmetrical. Further details of the systems can be found in mineralogical or gemmological textbooks.

Three important symmetry elements are:

1. Axes of symmetry;
2. Planes of symmetry and
3. Centres of symmetry.

Axes of symmetry can be imagined by passing a line through a crystal and rotating the crystal so that it appears the same to the observer two, three, four or six times during a complete revolution. For example, an axis passing through the centre of a cube face would be an axis of four-fold symmetry, because the observer would apparently see the same face four times during the revolution. An axis passing through the larger faces of a matchbox or a brick would be one of two-fold symmetry. Planes of symmetry divide a crystal in such a way that each part is the mirror image of the other.

A centre of symmetry will have like faces and edges on opposite sides of it. We shall see how this can sometimes affect the behaviour of crystals; especially when the centre is not present. The combined operations of axes, planes and centres of symmetry give the crystal its form.

We have seen how the six crystal systems can be distinguished from each other and how each of the systems has particular degrees of crystallographic symmetry. Each of the systems has certain forms associated with it which, in some cases, can only occur within that system. One form cannot always be distinguished from another by eye, but many crystals will show, however distorted they may be, some of the forms which will give a clue to their identity.

Since the special terms used to describe forms are so important in the description of crystals at all stages, they can be conveniently listed and explained:

1. Prism: A form containing faces meeting in parallel edges: e.g. the sides of a matchbox, the top of a table. Strictly speaking, cubes are prisms, but since this is a unique form, it is normally referred to simply as a cube.

2. Pyramid: A form containing groups of faces which will intersect all the crystallographic axes, produced if necessary.

3. Pinacoid: A form which intersects the vertical crystal axis, but which is parallel to the horizontal axes.

4. Dome: A form which intersects the vertical crystal axis and one of the horizontal axes but which is parallel to the third axis.

Many of these forms will not make a complete body on their own; they need to combine, as when the prism and pinacoid forms together make a brick shape. There are some forms, however, which can complete a solid on their own. Examples are the cube, octahedron, tetrahedron, rhombic dodecahedron and icositetrahedron. Such forms are known as 'closed'; those which need another form to complete the body are described as 'open'.

While the final form depends on the symmetry operators, the exterior conditions of growth also modify the growing crystals: i.e. they change their habit. It is obvious that, in nature, crystals growing in a pocket enclosed by hard rock, can only take on the shapes which the environment will allow. Some will be shortened when compared to the ideal crystals of the species which the symmetry operators should be making. Local conditions are not the only modifiers of shape; the addition of chemical impurities to the growing crystal can also affect it. Such impurities can also affect the growth of man-made crystals, even though such environmental considerations as space may be more freely available. Common adjectives to describe various types of habit include:

Tabular: flattened (as in some crystals of ruby).

Botryoidal: like a bunch of grapes (as in some malachite).

Prismatic: where the prism is the predominant form.

Acicular: like needles (as in rutile).

Reniform: kidney-shaped (as in some hematite).

The final appearance of a crystal depends on its form and habit. Both these interact to some extent, but it is the chemical composition of the crystal which dictates how the component atoms will fit together. This fitting together decides the crystal system of the particular substance. The shape of a crystal is called its 'morphology' and the study of crystal morphology is an important branch of crystallography. Crystal growers need to know in advance what is the particular morphology of the crystal they are attempting to grow; it may be important to have a particular set of forms for some industrial purpose or, for gemstone use, a thick crystal would be more useful than a thin one.

Summary
Crystals are solid bodies with regular and predictable internal atomic structure. They can be classified into six systems on the basis of the symmetry operators which also give characteristic shapes (forms) to the crystals. While form is imposed on a crystal 'from inside', habit is imposed from outside, although owing something to internal symmetry as well. The study of the way crystals are shaped is called crystal morphology.

Crystal Growth
We have seen that crystals possess internal symmetry which is sometimes suggested by their outward shape. We have also seen that, by the action of the symmetry operators, crystals can be placed in systems and classes. How do they come to take up the forms that we see by eye or by X-rays?

Bearing in mind the internal arrangement of atoms in a crystal is orderly, we must now examine how crystals grow. As it is obvious that they cannot grow 'from the inside', they must take their 'food' from substances available to their surfaces. It is also obvious that, in growth conditions (either in nature or in the laboratory), some parts of the crystal will be touching the rock, other crystals or the bottom of the container in which growth is taking place. This partly explains why it is quite rare to find a large crystal with all the faces possible in the particular symmetry system to which it belongs; the feed material cannot normally reach all parts of the crystals equally.

Atoms of the feed substance, on joining the surface of the growing crystal, immediately arrange themselves in accordance with the underlying symmetry. Under natural conditions, when chemical and temperature requirements permit, many crystals of the same substance may begin their growth in the same place and at the same time. These may then interfere with each other and the result may be a polycrystalline mass rather than several single crystals. The minute crystals composing this mass all obey the symmetry laws for the material, although each one takes a different direction.

Crystals of different substances grow at different rates but, even in a substance with quite a slow rate of growth, up to 100 molecules per second can accrete on the growing face. Since they need to obey the symmetry laws appropriate to the material, there is a certain amount of twisting and settling to be done in a very short time. It is during this settling time that imperfections may arise. We shall be seeing some of these in due course; all we need to know now is that they occur at this stage.

The material from which crystals grow is a solution. We can see for ourselves that when some solids are added to a solution (e.g. salt in water) they will dissolve. After a certain amount of the solid has dissolved, the solution will take no more so that the undissolved material remains unaltered; heating the solution may enable it to dissolve more of the solid. When a solid is dissolved in a hot solution up to the point where no more can be dissolved, crystals will usually form when the solution is cooled. They can also form when a solution evaporates to the point where there is not enough liquid left to keep the solid in solution.

When a solution is unable to dissolve more solid it is called 'saturated'. Sometimes a solution will dissolve a solid at a given temperature until it can dissolve no more, but on heating it will be able to dissolve more solid. If, at this point, the solution is poured into another container, leaving out any undissolved solid, and allowed to cool back to room temperature, it may or may not reject the extra solid that was added on heating. Where there is no such rejection, the solid is called 'supersaturated'. Let us review what can happen:

1. Solid added to a liquid will dissolve.
2. Solid added to saturated solution will remain unaltered.
3. Solid added to supersaturated solution will increase in amount.

A solid added to a supersaturated solution will grow until the solution has returned to its saturated state. Speed of solubility is much reduced the nearer a solution approaches saturation from both the unsaturated and supersaturated directions.

It is possible to think of an unsaturated solution as being in a stable state; it may evaporate but can easily be prevented from so doing and, in such a case, will undergo no change in composition for an unspecified time. A supersaturated solution is not so stable; it can be made saturated by adding solid, which will attract more of the solid from the solution until it is saturated once more and the supersaturation is exhausted. The area in which such a solution can be induced to reject excess solid is quite critical; as stated earlier there are occasions in which the supersaturated solution will not immediately reject the excess solid; it needs an impetus before deposition of the excess can begin.

This impetus can be given by introducing a piece of the solid upon which the excess can be deposited. This is how some types of crystal growth begin. These solutions give up the solid most efficiently when a piece of the same solid is introduced. It is also possible for a super-saturated solution to begin to deposit solid not merely on cooling but when stimulated by tiny particles of airborne dust. Again deposition may start when the solution is stirred or shaken. For example, a saturated solution of sodium chloride (common salt) will, on cooling, begin to deposit crystals, although it is difficult to make a supersaturated solution. On the other hand, a solution of sodium sulphate may be kept unaltered for years, but will crystallize on the introduction of a particle of very small size. Such particles do not always have to be of the same substance as the solution, although for the artificial growth of single crystals they usually are.

When it is desired to grow a layer of one substance upon another (like butter on bread), it will be found that the overlying material will take up the same orientation as that of the underlying material, so far as angular differences allow. This is called 'epitaxy' and is very important for the growth of materials needed for solid-state devices, such as transistors.

Crystalline Defects

It has been said that crystal-growing is as much of an art as a science and experience seems to bear this out. Apart from the great difficulty of obtaining crystals of some substances of any useful size, it is also quite difficult to obtain smaller crystals of 'easier' materials sufficiently free from defects to be useful for the purpose for which they were grown. One of the defects, quite tolerable and even desirable in some mineral specimens, is 'twinning'. This refers to a condition where two crystals either grow together or are intergrown. This can rule out most natural quartz crystals from use in electronic devices. But apart from twinning, other qualities which are unacceptable to the grower and the user can also arise in crystals.

One way in which alterations might be expected to occur is when atoms of different substances occupy sites which, in a 'pure' crystal, would be occupied by atoms of the 'rightful' substance. For this to happen, atoms of the two substances need to be roughly the same size; crystals of this kind are called 'mixed crystals'. Ruby, in which chromium atoms fit certain sites, is a good example. In other cases, atoms of one substance will fill certain sites even if the sites are in different positions with respect to one another; in this case, only a small amount of the foreign substance will be accepted by the crystal.

Atoms of an alien substance which are of sufficiently small size may also be accepted by the growing crystal. These may fit into spaces left by the atomic arrangement of the host. Because they fit into interstices, they are known as 'interstitial impurities'. Although these atoms are usually small compared to those of the host, they can in some instances, providing there is enough room, be as large as those of the host. An example is hydrogen in germanium.

One of the results of crystallographic symmetry is that, if a crystal is 'ideal', then all the individual unit cells – the smallest pieces still possessing all the qualities of the crystal – are identical. In this case each unit cell represents the crystal as a whole and, by examination of one unit cell, those of the whole crystal can be predicted. Symmetry operations require that, if a particular site is occupied by an atom of a particular kind, then all equivalent sites should be occupied in the same way. This is not the case when we consider defects, since there is no longer a typical unit cell.

The most 'perfect' crystal is not really so since there are always defects where the structure is incomplete or otherwise irregular. 'Point defects' is the term used to describe a number of conditions where some atoms are either missing from their rightful place or are occupying some site where they have no right to be. When an atom is missing from its right position there is said to be a 'vacancy'. Temperature fluctuations may cause these vacancies in the crystal lattice (the 'scaffolding' arrange-

Fig. 1.1. The two-phase inclusions in a Gilson emerald which form the veil-like 'feathers'.

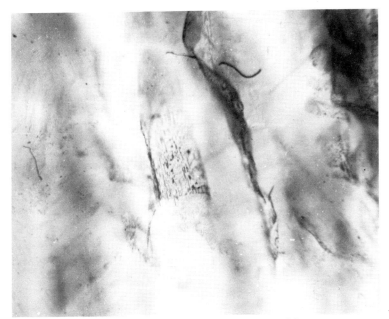

Fig. 1.2. A fingerprint inclusion in a synthetic emerald.

ment of the constituent atoms). Where an atom is found occupying a normally vacant site there is said to be a 'Frenkel defect'. If a pair of electrically balanced ions (charged atoms) is missing, then this is called a 'Schottky defect'. Crystals grown from the melt have fewer concentrations of such defects than those grown from high-temperature solutions.

So far, we have seen how crystals may depart from perfection in their internal atomic arrangements. While growing, crystals may also acquire other types of defect. Some of these for example, the presence of myriads of veil-like structures, each composed of liquid-filled cavities, can be attributed to a growth rate, too fast for the substance. A slower rate of growth should reduce the size of these cavities. At some point, the size of the cavities may well be such that they could contain no liquid but merely be vacancies. The speed of growth might be such as to stop the filling of these vacancies before a fresh deposition of atoms starts a new layer.

Some types of defect can give rise to colour centres. These occur when certain events happen in the life of a normally colourless crystal. One of these events may be an imbalance of the normal chemical constituents: e.g. an excess of sodium in a crystal of sodium chloride. Another may be the proximity of ionizing radiations and yet another the presence of certain impurities. Whichever set of conditions is fulfilled for a particular crystal, the result is that absorption of light takes place and the crystal appears coloured.

The gemmologist recognizes by the general name of 'inclusions', several of the peculiar internal phenomena of the crystal. These inclusions may be solid (i.e. portions of other minerals or minute pieces of the vessel in which the crystal was grown); they may be liquid (water, carbonic acid) or gaseous (carbon dioxide). Liquid and gaseous inclusions are, in fact, quite rare in crystals grown from solutions, although the gemmologist will learn to recognize some especially familiar ones.

Probably the most typical inclusions seen in man-made gemstones are the veils seen in many of the emeralds grown by the flux-melt process. They occur when supersaturation is low at the centre of a crystal face. This causes layers to spread from the corners and edges of the face and to grow over the central part, thus trapping any 'undigested' growth liquor in that area. They may also arise from cracks which develop during growth and which enclose films of solvent when the crack heals by later growth. At this stage, the veils tend to break up into tiny droplets. The various types of inclusions characteristic of man-made gemstones are shown in the chapters on the stones themselves.

2. The Flame-fusion Method of Crystal Growth

A practical method of growing crystals by flame fusion, based on a process devised a good deal earlier, was announced by Auguste Verneuil in 1902. The commercial aim was to make ruby of gem quality. By far the greatest number of synthetic stones on the market are manufactured by this process. The cost is much less than, for example, the Czochralski method of growth. The ready availability of hydrogen is one of the most important factors in the assessment of cost-effectiveness of the Verneuil process. For high-melting oxides, this is a specially useful method of manufacture (corundum and spinel have melting points between 2050°C and 2150°C). Size is not particularly difficult to attain and sapphires with a diameter of up to 75mm (2.95 in) are regularly grown.

The Verneuil Process

The method is quite a simple one. Feed material, in the form of a fine-grained powder of calcined ammonium alum, is scattered from a container through an oxy-hydrogen flame and reaches the surface of a seed crystal. The surface of this crystal is covered by a thin melt film and an amount of matter, corresponding to the powder flow, is crystallized on the film; the crystal is pulled downwards at the same rate as it is growing towards the flame. Powder flow and crystal motion are stopped when the crystal has reached the desired length. The grown crystal takes on a characteristic form (boule) with a broadening phase which leads on to a main part with a constant diameter.

The main features of the apparatus are shown in **Fig. 2.1**. Powder is induced to leave the chamber by a vibrating mechanism (a hammer is sometimes used); it falls through the oxygen stream and, by way of a two-stage burner, proceeds with the hydrogen to the flame. This, along

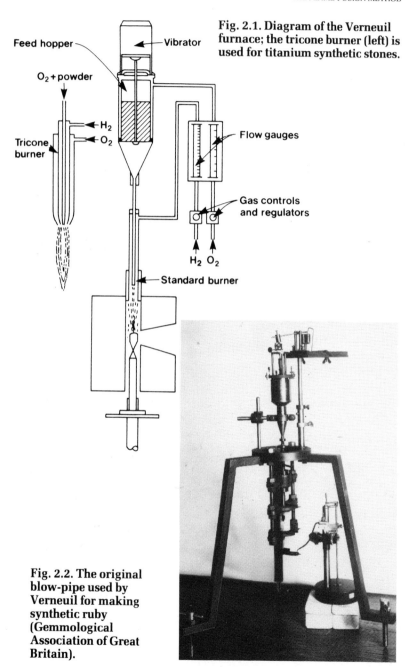

Feed hopper

O_2 + powder

Tricone burner

H₂
O₂

Vibrator

Fig. 2.1. Diagram of the Verneuil furnace; the tricone burner (left) is used for titanium synthetic stones.

Flow gauges

Gas controls and regulators

H_2 O_2

Standard burner

Fig. 2.2. The original blow-pipe used by Verneuil for making synthetic ruby (Gemmological Association of Great Britain).

with the growing crystal, is enclosed in a vertically-positioned growth chamber of tubular section.

Crystal perfection depends on both the properties of the flame and on the supply of powder. To produce a satisfactory transition from powder grain to liquid droplet, small grain size, low density and a constant flow are needed. Chemical purity is also essential. When the powder quality, plus a satisfactory feed, burner and growth chamber are established, it is necessary to determine constant growth rate. At too high a rate, the mechanical strength of the crystal decreases. When it is needed to grow crystals of large diameter (say above 40mm), it will be found desirable to rotate the growing crystal. Fast rotation drives the melt outwards by centrifugal force so that the speed can influence the nature of the growth front. Since the flow of gas determines the broadening of the crystal, sapphire and Mg-Al spinel, when grown in an excess hydrogen atmosphere, can be altered in shape simply by altering the oxygen flow.

If the powder reaching the melt film is not entirely molten, the small thickness of the film is critical for crystal perfection. Cooling is also critical, because it is hard to control the temperature gradients. If the cooling is not uniform, stresses may develop leading to plastic deformation of the crystal (i.e. twinning, fracture). It is well known that corundum boules have a direction of weakness in the vertical plane. Some residual stresses may be removed by reheating to just below the melting point (annealing).

In the growth of Al-rich spinel, striations can be seen which represent the changing shape of the melt film as the crystal cross-section increases during growth. The stages are convex, flat, concave. These striations are due to heat loss through the body of the crystal. Crystals of corundum frequently show bands corresponding to growth additions; because the flow of feed powder into the apparatus has been 'smoothed out', these lines (resembling the grooving on a gramophone record) seem less prominent. They are usually seen best on the 'alexandrite' type of corundum; they are less visible on the reds and greens, and can hardly be seen at all on yellows. Against these lines, tadpole-like structures can be seen; these arise from undigested grains of feed powder. Although we shall see in Part 2 exactly how the synthetic products differ from the natural, it is interesting, while considering some of the mechanical stresses to which Verneuil crystals can be subjected, to note that crystals of spinel (isotropic), which have non-stoichiometric composition, show circumferential and axial stresses (giving rise to the anomalous double refraction seen between crossed polars).

Materials made by the Verneuil Process

Many materials have been grown by the Verneuil process; apart from corundum, spinel, rutile and strontium titanate (the best-known products of this method for the gemmologist), emeralds have been attempted. (The experiments were abandoned because beryl melts incongruently and for commercial reasons.) Forsterite (Mg_2SiO_4) and ZrO_2 (zirconia) have also been attempted; the latter product was unsuccessful because the high gas pressure gave rise to fused material. Stoichiometric* crystals of spinel crack very easily as compared with those rich in alumina (red spinel boules made by this method are stoichiometric) so that most spinel crystals needed for industrial use are grown from the melt (see Chapter 4). Burners with afterheaters, or with other special modifications, went some way towards rectifying the difficulties encountered with the flame-fusion growth of spinel.

Some of the crucible sections, preserved in the Museum of Natural History in Paris, show crystals lining them. They are quite small, which was one of the problems facing Verneuil; the use of larger crucibles did not help much. It is now thought that one reason for the smallness of the crystals was multiple nucleation arising from the local cavities found throughout the porous mass of the crucible. The multiphase medium provided by the apparatus made this nucleation occur more easily.

Probably the first true synthetic gemstone with a possible jewellery application was the so-called 'Geneva ruby'. This was long thought to be 'reconstructed', although this is now known not to be the case. Verneuil's announcement of the synthesis of ruby by the flame-fusion method came in 1902 and was seen to be an improvement on all existing

* With exact proportions of elements.

Fig. 2.3. Surface structure of a 'twin' boule of synthetic spinel. 15x

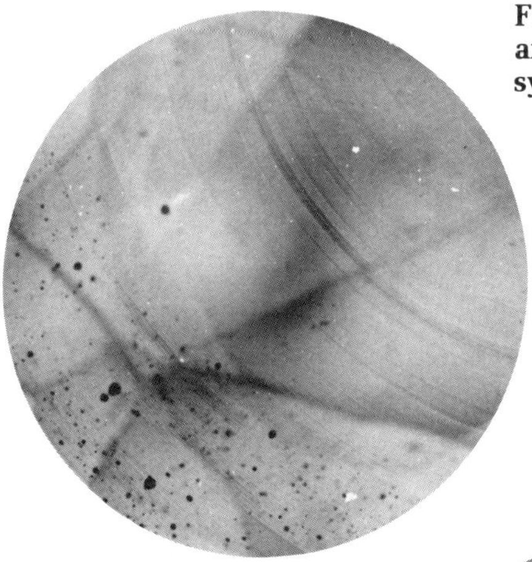

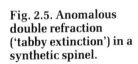

Fig. 2.4. Curved growth lines and gas bubbles in a synthetic ruby. 25x

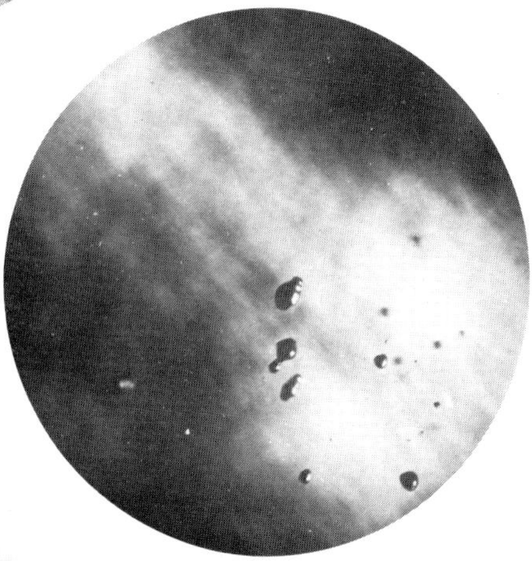

Fig. 2.5. Anomalous double refraction ('tabby extinction') in a synthetic spinel.

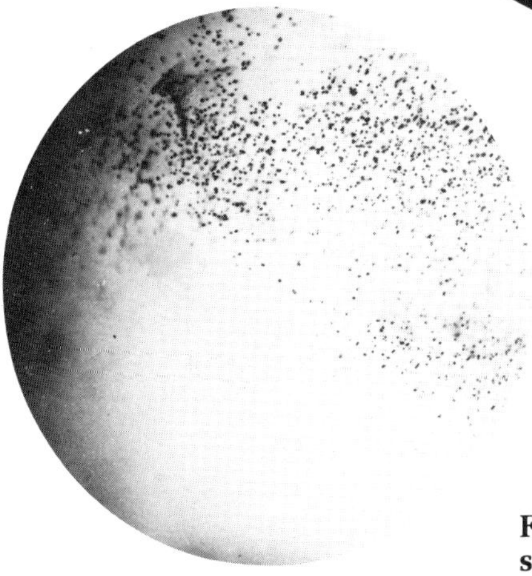

Fig. 2.6. Bubble cloud in a synthetic violet sapphire. 25x

stones. In fact, Geneva stones were made by a three-step flame-fusion process; the boule was rotated while growing and at least two torches were used in the last stage of growth. Feed powder was delivered down a platinum tube between the torches. Cracking the boule was a problem with this method (it comes into contact with the support after it reaches a certain size). Verneuil succeeded in overcoming this to some extent by reducing the contact area to as small a size as possible.

A report issued by Verneuil in 1904 (the only report to give full details of the construction of the apparatus and methods of growth) shows that the growth period lasted for about two hours, after which the gas and oxygen were shut off abruptly. After 10 minutes the boule, which was still fixed to the aluminium support rod, could be removed. Stones weighed about 2.5 to 3g (0.09 to 0.11 oz) with a diameter of about 5 to 6mm (0.22 in). This would give a weight of about 12 to 15ct. Verneuil decided that a flame rich in hydrogen and carbon was needed to avoid bubbling in the melt and the consequent addition of gas bubbles to the product. He also decided that a gradual solidification of the thin layers from the bottom upwards was needed to maintain transparency; and that the minimum of contact area between the boule and the support was needed to minimize cracking. Curved growth lines could not, however, be eradicated.

Looking at the method as a whole, although it has not been found possible to grow crystals with a high degree of optical and mechanical perfection, this is to some extent due to a diminishing reliance on the process. With the advent of the Czochralski method, crystals (of ruby for example) were easily available with the right degree of perfection so the impetus for the further development of the Verneuil method declined. It must be admitted that some aspects of the method, such as the stability of the melt film with the use of high temperatures and the over-rapid cooling, need more investigation. However the use of powdered corundum with a grain size of 80 mesh should prevent the build-up of undigested powder referred to earlier, which at present makes identification possible for the gemmologist.

Corundum

To make ruby by the Verneuil method, about 3 per cent Cr_2O_3 is added to the feed powder and the melting point reached is about 2050°C. The boules have a very roughly hexagonal or rounded cross-section. Care must be taken that no iron is present as this would give a brownish tinge. Orange can arise from the incorporation of magnesium, through the coupled substitution Mg^{2+}-Cr^{4+} replacing two Al^{3+}. Spinel boules tend

Fig. 2.7. Synthetic star sapphire.

towards a cubic cross-section and have a characteristic rough feel to them, resulting from tiny overlapping platelets of the material.

Although in some parts of the trade, the term 'reconstructed' or 'reco' can still be met, there are no truly reconstructed rubies (i.e. whole crystals made up from fused fragments of corundum). Despite the story being current for years that they had been made near Geneva, work by Nassau has proved that these stones were early Verneuil-type synthetics. The same writer, in his latest book *Gems Made by Man* (1980), makes the commercially important point that a wide variety of colours needs to be manufactured, at least where corundum is concerned. This is because, with a wide range, both small and large gems can be made to match.

The manufacture of star corundum by the flame-fusion process involves the preparation of a feed powder with 0.1 to 0.3 per cent titanium oxide in addition to the alumina and the desired colouring agent. The finished boule is heated usually for about 24 hours at 1300°C. At this temperature, the TiO_2, previously undetected in the clear boule, precipitates out in fine needles. This produces a six-rayed star when a cabochon is cut with the optic axis perpendicular to its base. As titanium tends to move to the outside of the growing boule, some stars may be incomplete and show transparent regions. In a modification of the original process, the temperature of the system was varied by altering the oxygen flow intermittently so that the growing boule solidified in successive layers. This kept the titanium in place and ensured a complete star. Some natural corundum may produce hitherto unsuspected stars on annealing.

Bubbles in synthetic corundum are usually of gas and take characteristic shapes. Small isolated bubbles are often spherical but, when groups are examined, some will be found to be distorted and there is a

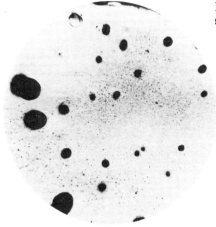

Fig. 2.8. Profuse bubbles in a synthetic ruby.

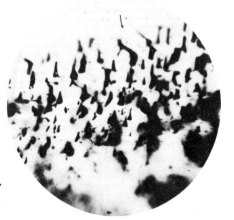

Fig. 2.9. Unusual triangular bubbles in a synthetic sapphire.

tendency to form clots. Frequently bubbles are found enclosed in triangular cavities. It should be noted that the outline of gas bubbles is always bold; this indicates a considerable difference between the refractive index of the bubble and that of the host.

One advantage of the Verneuil technique is that, since growth takes place not in a closed container but in open space, there is much less likelihood of contaminating the crystal. This contamination often occurs in other methods where crucibles are employed, because unwanted elements enter the crystal from the container or other parts of the apparatus.

Plasma torch heating (plasmas are gases from which electrons have been removed by very high temperatures) have been used as heaters for flame-fusion crystal growth; they give an intensely hot flame. Another method employs two large parabolic mirrors between which the growing crystal is placed. A carbon arc is focussed on the crystal and the incident energy from it is enhanced by the mirrors, focussed upon a small area giving great heat in that spot. This is a good method of crystal growth, since light alone is used as the source of heat. This eliminates undesirable elements met with in other growth methods.

Identification

Identification of stones grown by the Verneuil process is not difficult in most cases. Although full details will be given in the chapters dealing with the stones themselves, a summary will be useful at this point, since these are the most common synthetics.

RUBY

Synthetic rubies are always a noticeably bright red and suspiciously clean. Although their specific gravity and refractive index do not differ from those of the natural material, the 10× lens will show several features which will make their origin apparent. Most typical are the curved growth lines, resembling the grooves on a gramophone record; these are best seen when the stone is immersed in a liquid with a refractive index close to that of the stone. As methylene iodide has a refractive index of 1.74, this serves admirably. The lines may be seen even better if the stone is photographed while immersed, using a narrow beam of light and with the lens at its narrowest aperture. Generally speaking curved lines can best be seen at right angles to the table, because the stone is cut with the table parallel to the sides of the boule. In addition, structures resembling tadpoles can often be seen. Other bubbles without tails but showing, under magnification, bright centres and a dark outline, are also characteristic.

The colour distribution in synthetic ruby grown by this method will also be curved, rather than angular as in natural stones. However colour banding is more characteristic of sapphire than of ruby. An absence of natural inclusions (i.e. crystals of other minerals) is worth noting.

The spectroscope will show a more decided absorption spectrum than most natural stones will give; the three bands in the blue, in particular, are prominent and there is a strong emission doublet in the red. Dichroism through the table facet of a ruby will strongly suggest a synthetic stone as they are normally cut either with the table parallel to the optic axis or randomly. More elaborate tests will show that the synthetic stones are more transparent to short-wave ultra-violet light than are the natural stones and that they will phosphoresce after irradiation by X-rays.

Early Verneuil rubies were very clear and rhombohedral in shape. The feed powder included a small amount of potassium dichromate with some barium fluoride as well as alumina. The reaction was carried out in a ceramic crucible at the temperature of 1500°C; diffusion of humid air through the crucible wall was found to be vital to the process. The crystals produced were up to 3.2mm (0.13 in) in diameter and up to ⅓ct in weight. The colour varied from colourless to red, blue, violet: some crystals had red on one side and blue on the other.

BLUE SAPPHIRE

Around 1909, Verneuil began to work on the synthesis of blue sapphire. It is interesting to note that he realized that it was necessary to oxidize the ferrous iron which was produced in the reducing part of the flame to ferric iron. This was done by the titanium, added to the feed powder in a proportion of about 1.5 per cent iron oxide to 0.5 per cent titanium oxide. The titanium lowered the valence state of the iron and thus, by a process of intervalence charge transfer, produced the blue colour:

$$Fe^{2+} - O - Ti^{4+} \rightarrow Fe^{3+} - O - Ti^{3+}$$

Blue sapphires show a more pronounced curved colour banding than ruby and a stone will show them well when immersed. Details of the banding are coarser than those of the growth lines which can also be seen in the correct orientation.

Blue sapphires will not show the 450nm complex of absorption bands, although some faint banding in this region has sometimes been noticed. However the band in natural blue stones, when faint, is quite narrow and measurable, whereas the banding in synthetic sapphires is vague and only roughly related to the 450nm position. It should be noted that any absorption banding in a synthetic blue sapphire is exceptional. The reason for its absence in the majority of stones is that the iron, which causes the absorption, migrates to the edge of the boule. It is therefore either lost in cutting the stone, or it has already evaporated during the melt process.

Under short-wave ultra-violet light, blue synthetic sapphires show an unmistakable greenish glow which seems to be on the surface only. Some stones also show a bluish-white glow. Natural sapphires never show this. If the stones are viewed on their edge rather than through the table facet, the effect is seen to greater advantage and is accompanied by

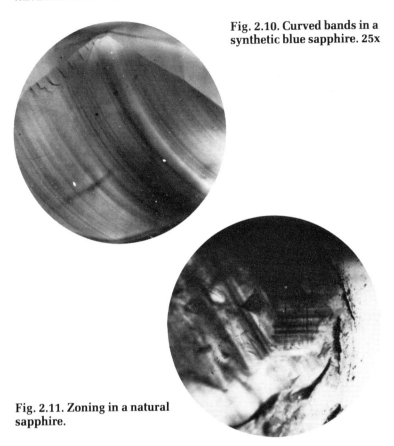

Fig. 2.10. Curved bands in a synthetic blue sapphire. 25x

Fig. 2.11. Zoning in a natural sapphire.

an enhancement of the curved structure bands. It should be said that some blue synthetic stones have been found to give a red fluorescence, but these are exceptional.

YELLOW SAPPHIRE

Some yellow synthetic stones, with a trace of chromium in their composition, may show a red glow under X-rays with some phosphorescence. The curved growth lines are less easy to see and some workers maintain that they are never encountered. Fortunately most natural yellow sapphires will either show a characteristic absorption spectrum or will fluoresce. Yellow synthetic stones will do neither of these things.

GREEN SAPPHIRE

Apart from the presence of curved growth lines, the best test for synthetic green sapphire is the absence of the three absorption bands in the 450nm area, always shown by the natural stones.

OTHER SAPPHIRES

Colourless corundum may show curved growth lines but they can only normally be seen when the stone is immersed and then photographed. They cannot be seen with a 10× lens. In this case, we need to rely on the other inclusions typical of the flame-fusion process and the absence of natural inclusions. Since the stone is colourless – and few natural sapphires without colour will be cut (most apparently colourless natural stones will in fact betray a trace of blue) – specific gravity and refractive index tests should be sufficient to distinguish the stone from whatever natural stone it may be intended to imitate.

A corundum with an amethystine colour has been seen on occasion. It shows a reddish fluoresence under long-wave, and bluish-white fluorescence under short-wave, ultra-violet light.

'ALEXANDRITE' CORUNDUM

'Alexandrite'-like corundum, to which vanadium has been added and sometimes some chromium, shows very prominent growth lines and has a strange and very characteristic purple-mauve colour according to the light in which it is viewed. It shows a band at 475nm in the absorption spectrum which is quite distinctive.

STAR CORUNDUM

Star corundum (see above) is formed by the addition of TiO_2 to the feed powder and by the annealing of the boule after formation. This causes the rutile to precipitate out at right angles to the vertical crystal axis and form a six-rayed star. Stones can be identified by the perfection of the star and the brightness of the body colour. Most natural star corundum either has a poor colour or an off-centred vague star. Bubbles are almost invariably present and curved colour banding is noticeable. Flat backs are usually found; most natural star stones are distinctly heavy or lumpy.

Spinel

The story of the manufacture of gem-quality synthetic spinel by the Verneuil flame-fusion process involves an interesting mistake. The workers were trying to grow blue sapphire by adding cobalt to the powder used to make corundum, as it was believed that cobalt was the colouring agent in blue sapphire. Attempts to grow such crystals had proved fruitless, so magnesium was added to the feed mixture to act as a flux; but the resulting crystal was spinel rather than corundum. Deviation from stoichiometry by the addition of 1½ to 3½ Al_2O_3 produced a better crystal and improved growth.

Spinel is now commonly grown by this method to give colours which imitate other gemstones rather than natural spinel itself. Common colours include a blue, which could be mistaken for zircon or aquamarine; a colourless form used to imitate diamond, especially in small sizes; and a colour somewhat like a dark green tourmaline, but with red flashes. This last has been offered as an imitation of alexandrite, but can be distinguished by its S.G., R.I. and lack of birefringence.

RED SPINEL

Red spinel has not been grown successfully, though a few stones and boule sections are sometimes offered. This is because the boules have a distinct tendency to fragment; their composition is equimolecular rather than having the excess alumina needed to grow spinel of other colours. Any synthetic red spinel encountered should be checked for the inclusions typical of the flux-melt process (see Chapter 4). The

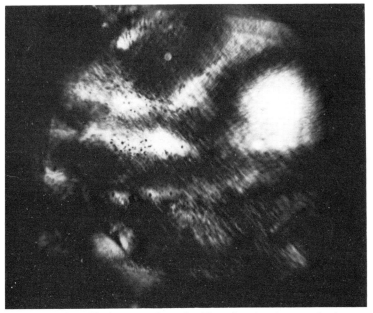

Fig. 2.12. The telltale anomalous double refraction in a synthetic spinel.

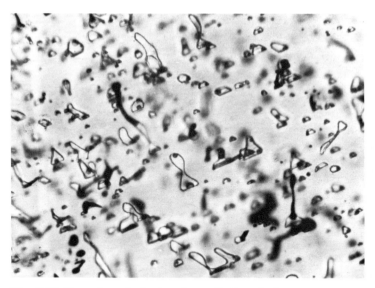

Fig. 2.13. Two-phase inclusions in synthetic spinel.

occasional Verneuil red will not show curved growth lines, but will show swathes of colour and tiny gas bubbles.

Since extra alumina needs to be added to most spinels, the constants reflect this when they are compared to those of the natural material. The specific gravity of natural spinel is around 3.60, while that of the synthetic material is around 3.64; the refractive index for natural spinel is 1.718, while that of the synthetic is 1.728. Additionally spinels grown by this method will show an anomalous double refraction, again as a result of the excess alumina. This can be seen between crossed polars as a striped effect, like the stripes on a tabby cat; it has been given the name 'tabby extinction'.

BLUE SPINEL

Blue synthetic spinels are coloured by cobalt to resemble dark blue sapphires. They show red through the colour filter since cobalt transmits a certain amount of red light. They also show an absorption spectrum typical of cobalt: three broad bands between the orange and the green portions of the spectrum. These are very strong in deep blue spinels and may coalesce to givethe impression of total absorption in this region. Sometimes these stones have chromium added with the result that some red may be seen between crossed filters* or under ultra-violet light.

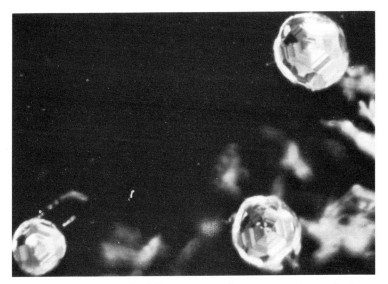

Fig. 2.14. Inclusions which have a natural appearance in synthetic spinel.

OTHER SPINELS

A pink variety of spinel which might be mistaken for pink beryl (morganite) contains some iron. A very odd-looking lime-green-yellow type, with a strong fluorescence and two absorption bands in the violet, is coloured by manganese.

Another interesting result of the non-stoichiometry of most spinels grown by the Verneuil method is the moonstone imitation obtainable by adding as much 5.5 Al_2O_3 for each MgO. This gives a schiller when the boule is annealed, as a fine precipitate of the excess alumina forms at that stage. The variation in stoichiometry does give a considerable colour range since at a ratio of 1:1 chromium gives red; at 1½:1 it gives brown; at 2:1 it gives greenish-brown; and green at 3:1.

INCLUSIONS

Inclusions in synthetic spinel include characteristic bubbles; these are isolated and may take on shapes such as hose-like tubes, furled umbrellas, or long flasks. These are, in fact, negative crystals with a hexagonal shape when seen in cross-section; they may also be grouped into hexagonal patterns.

---

*The stone is illuminated through a copper sulphate solution and observed through a Chelsea filter.

Some workers have noted that two-phase inclusions can be found in synthetic spinel; they consist of cavities containing gas or liquid and a bubble, sometimes joined by a tube to a similar cavity.

Rutile

As well as forming an important part of star stones this has also been made by the Verneuil method in its own right, as a possible simulant of diamond. It first came on the market in 1949 and was manufactured by a modification of the Verneuil process in which an outer jet of oxygen is added to the apparatus in addition to the oxygen already provided. The material forms boules which, when removed from the flame, are black, owing to the tendency of TiO_2 to lose oxygen when heated to high temperatures. To lighten the black, the boules are heated again to about 1000°C in a stream of oxygen, whereupon they become much lighter in colour, though never attaining complete whiteness.

The absorption spectrum invariably shows a cut-off in the extreme violet and the stones have a yellow tinge on this account. From time to time attempts have been made to alleviate this unfortunate situation by adding such agents as strontium oxide. Stones have also been coated with a film of synthetic corundum which seems both to lighten them and to preserve their somewhat fragile surfaces. However, since the advent of other more successful diamond imitiations, not much more work in this direction is likely to take place. Other colours of rutile have been made, but these are rare, although they look quite attractive. Browns, blues, reds and an orange-brown are all known.

The constants of synthetic rutile are sufficient to distinguish it from gemstones which might be confused with it; the specific gravity is 4.25, the hardness is 6, and the refractive index is 2.62 (ordinary ray) and 2.90 (extraordinary ray). The double refraction is very high at 0.287, which immediately rules it out as a serious imitator of diamond. It also displays a very high dispersion at about 0.300 (compared to 0.044 for diamond). The first examination of a synthetic rutile will show an unmistakably fuzzy appearance due to the huge birefringence; the dispersion causes the stone to show an almost opal-like play of colour.

A star rutile was made at one time by adding about 0.5 per cent magnesium oxide and annealing the boule in oxygen at around 1300°C. 'Star-Tania' was the name given to this product.

Strontium titanate

Strontium titanate is another material grown to imitate diamond. Since it is cubic, it shows no birefringence. It is soft (about 5½) and has a

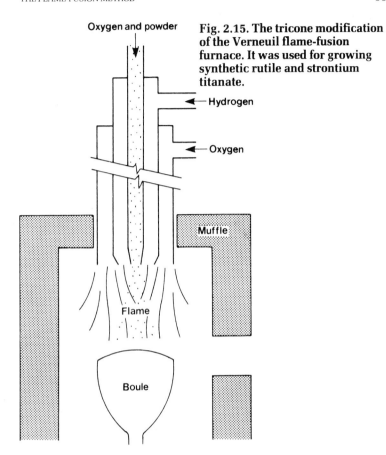

Oxygen and powder

**Fig. 2.15. The tricone modification
of the Verneuil flame-fusion
furnace. It was used for growing
synthetic rutile and strontium
titanate.**

Hydrogen

Oxygen

Muffle

Flame

Boule

notably high specific gravity (5.13). The refractive index is 2.41, very
close to that of diamond; however the high specific gravity, softness,
and high dispersion (about 0.200) all serve to separate the stone from
diamond.

The surface can be marked with a needle and tiny inclusions,
resembling a ladder with rungs but without uprights, have been noted.
X-rays which will pass through diamond are impeded by strontium
titanate and there is no fluorescence. This material has no natural
counterpart. As with rutile, colours have been made by adding various
dopants.

3. Crystal Growth by the Hydrothermal Method

The hydrothermal method of crystal growth, as its name suggests, involves the use of water and heat. It also involves high pressures, which in turn make the process expensive (since special equipment is needed) and dangerous, so that the products can be more expensive than those grown by the simpler and less dangerous flame-fusion method (see Chapter 3). If we remember that almost all crystals grown by the hydrothermal method are quartz, we shall have its use in the correct perspective.

Hydrothermal growth methods are used for materials with a low solubility, which can be increased by operating at high temperatures and pressures. In addition to quartz, calcite and corundum are regularly made by this technique. Temperatures for the method as a whole are usually in the region of 700°C and pressures are around 3000 atmospheres. Such conditions are very similar to those obtaining in the Earth's crust, where many minerals were formed.

The equipment needed for hydrothermal growth comprises an autoclave (or pressure vessel), furnaces, thermocouples, temperature controllers and a temperature recorder. The autoclave must be able to withstand the high temperatures and pressures encountered in operation and is usually made of a strong steel with extremely thick walls. A liner made from platinum (sometimes with gold or silver) ensures freedom from contaminants such as iron. As might be expected, the seal on the autoclave is a critical part of the apparatus and various models are in use.

The Method

The simplest method of hydrothermal growth requires the nutrient material to be dissolved in one part of the autoclave and subsequently transported to another part by convection. This continuous transporting of materials makes it possible to grow larger crystals than does the cooling of a saturated solution. Generally speaking, the temperatures used for hydrothermal growth are between those used for flux-melt growth and for growth from aqueous solutions at atmospheric pressure.

Possible advantages of the hydrothermal methods over other types of crystal growth include the ability to create crystalline phases which are not stable at the melting point. This is because of phase transitions or glass formation (as in some silicates, where high viscosity prevents fast growth). Materials which have a high vapour pressure near their melting points (such as zincite), can also be grown successfully by the hydrothermal method. (Zincite (ZnO) can, with suitable doping, be

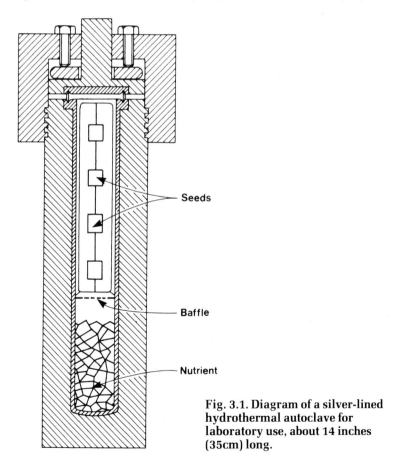

Seeds

Baffle

Nutrient

Fig. 3.1. Diagram of a silver-lined hydrothermal autoclave for laboratory use, about 14 inches (35cm) long.

used as a gem material.) The method is also particularly suited for the growth of large good-quality crystals while maintaining good control over their composition. Disadvantages of the method include the need for special apparatus, the need for good quality seeds of a fair size and the impossibility of observing the crystal as it grows.

Since the growth of quartz is typical of the method as a whole, it might be interesting to describe it more fully. By quartz, the crystal-grower will understand SiO_2 in its α or stable form. Early in the present century, attempts to grow quartz were made using a sodium metasilicate solution with a container of quartz chips. This was held at a temperature of 330°C at the top of an autoclave with a truncated quartz crystal suspended further down at a temperature of 170°C. This attempt gave too slow a growth rate to be further applied. Later, silica glass was used to produce growth on quartz seeds but, although the glass was more soluble than quartz, a heavy deposition of quartz took place on the autoclave sides; this was due to the high degree of supersaturation. Additionally, devitrification of the silica glass took place after some hours, forcing the workers to grow crystals in layers about 1mm (0.04 in) in thickness.

The temperature gradient method is now most commonly used; this involves a vertical autoclave with a seed in the upper and cooler part plus quartz chips as nutrient in the lower and hotter part. Although water was used in early work, later studies have shown that solubility increases by an order of magnitude if an alkaline solution is used – this is usually sodium carbonate or sodium hydroxide. A typical set of constants for the growth of quartz using one of these solutions includes a nutrient temperature of 400°C, a seed temperature of 360°C, 80 per cent degree of filling and 1500 atmospheres pressure.

Temperature gradients are more extreme for sodium hydroxide than for sodium carbonate. To avoid twinning (which must be shunned at all costs for the industrial use of quartz), growth must be carried out below the temperature of 573°C, at which α becomes β quartz.

Seeds are cut in the basal plane (0001) which is perpendicular to the optic axis. They may also be cut parallel to the mirror rhombohedral face (1$\overline{1}$0$\overline{1}$). Growth on the basal plane takes place at a lower degree of supersaturation which, in turn, leads to a lower likelihood of crystallization occurring by spontaneous nucleation on the walls of the autoclave. Good-quality growth on the basal plane will be obtained provided that the rate of growth is about 1mm (0·04 in) per day.

Growing Corundum

More important to the gemmologist is the hydrothermal growth of emerald and corundum, although there is no significant commercial production of the latter. In the largely experimental growth of ruby and sapphire, the mineralizer NaOH was found to be the best agent for the promotion of satisfactory crystallization. The red needed to give the colour for ruby is provided by the addition of sodium bichromate. A major problem is the corrosion of the container by the solvent.

Ruby with a well-documented history was produced in 1958 by Laudise and Ballman of Bell Laboratories. In this case, the nutrient is either corundum or gibbsite $[Al(OH)_3]$ which is placed in a silver container. This container is then filled with sodium carbonate. Seed crystals, which may be either synthetic or natural ruby, are suspended from a silver frame at the top of the container. Heat up to 400°C is applied to the base of the container and this causes currents to form in the melt. So the warmer part of the mixture in the region of the nutrient passes to the cooler area at the top while the cooler solution sinks to the bottom where it comes into contact with the heat and reascends. Corundum is precipitated upon the seed crystals; growth is at the rate of 0.05 to 0.25mm (0.002 to 0.01 in) per day, according to conditions. The basal plane face shows the fastest growth rate; the final crystals will show prominent flattening and little of the prismatic form. One per cent of chromium (sodium chromate) will give a satisfactory ruby red. If the vessel walls are of iron, a green colour will result.

Examination of rubies produced by this method is prone to error, since the constants are virtually identical with the natural material. More alarming is the presence of natural inclusions in the seed (unless, of course, this is made from synthetic ruby). Again, at certain orientations, the seed can often be seen. In experimental ruby, one may from time to time come across a seed made from colourless material.

The most typical inclusions of hydrothermally-grown ruby are partially-healed fractures with undigested drops of liquid. At the junction of seed and overgrowth, look for tiny bubbles which appear to coat the seed. In the outer layer, look for swirled wispy structures made up of minute liquid-filled tubes.

Emerald

Hydrothermal emeralds are grown in a similar way but can be identified with some success by examination of their characteristic inclusions. The seed can be seen and tubes, which taper in the direction of growth, lead away from the seed. The seed is often cut obliquely to the main crystallographic direction of its original crystal, so that the tiny tubes appear to be at an angle to the growth direction of the host. Some productions have inclusions resembling strokes of a brush.

Lechleitner emeralds (shallow overgrowth on a seed already cut to the shape of the finished stone) show a long series of cracks; two-phase growth tubes can also be seen. Phenakite crystals from which growth tubes lead are also common; I have found these especially noticeable in a new hydrothermal product, the 'Regency' emerald.

Yttrium Aluminium Garnet (YAG)

This has also been made hydrothermally, although this is not the main way of making the material (see Chapter 4, on crystal pulling). Stoichiometric quantities of Al_2O_3 and Y_2O_3 were placed in platinum capsules with solvents of NaOH, KOH or K_2CO_3. A 48-hour growth period showed that YAG formed in all cases, regardless of the type of solvent used.

One advantage claimed for the hydrothermal method over other growth methods is that, since the temperature is relatively low, crystals can be grown with lower strain content. Other methods impose large thermal gradients.

4. Growth from the Melt

When a crystal is grown from a state of liquid-solid equilibrium (which can be thought of as 'controlled freezing'), much less difficulty in the areas of equipment and control is experienced than with some other methods. The method is probably more used than any other, and almost all synthetic emeralds and rubies are made in this way, together with numerous other stones. There are some disadvantages, including the possibility that the material will decompose before it melts, or that it may melt incongruently (unevenly). Also the material may sublime before it melts or have too high a vapour pressure at its melting point.

Sometimes the modification of a particular polymorph* is wanted and the equilibrium within the melt will create an alternative polymorph so that good crystals of the wanted polymorph are not obtained. Some substances have melting points so high that growth is impractical; some dopants will not be compatible with crystals grown this way.

The Czochralski Method
The technique is often referred to simply as 'pulling', because it involves the pulling of a long rod-like crystal from a melt. Czochralski first used the method in 1917. To obtain successful results, the crystal should melt evenly (together with its dopant where required); it must not be reactive with the crucible nor with the atmosphere present during growth. Oxidizing or reducing atmospheres can be provided. The melting temperature should be below that of the crucible.

Control of growth with the pulling method is very efficient as the seed and crystal can be seen at all times. Where a seed can be correctly

---

*Material that will crystallize in different forms with the same chemical compositions.

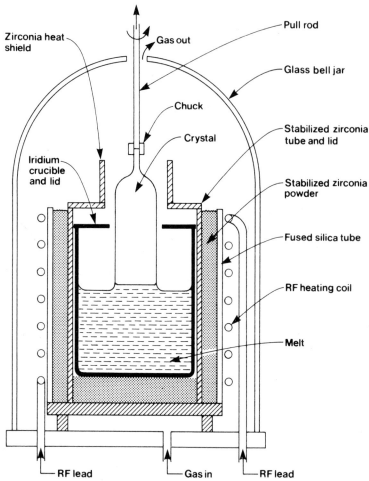

Fig. 4.1. Growing from the melt — this apparatus is used in the Czochralski method. The crucible can measure 6 inches (15cm) across.

oriented, any direction of growth is theoretically practicable. When a seed is not available, it is possible to originate spontaneous nucleation on a wire. From the polycrystalline mass thus obtained, and with the temperature and pulling rate suitably adjusted, one of the crystallites will dominate the others so that, with further adjustment, the crystal will become the desired single crystal. When the method was first used (1917), crystals of low-melting point metals such as tin and lead were grown; but today the process is most used for the growth of semiconductors and of single crystals of ruby, YAG, scheelite, etc.

To grow crystals by the Czochralski method, the amount of necessary equipment is small; it includes a crucible of suitable material, a means of heating the melt which includes some form of temperature control, a means of rotating the seed and of withdrawing it (i.e. the actual pulling), and some method of atmosphere control where desired. Heating is carried out by radio-frequency (R.F.) or resistance heating. With radio-frequency heating, the frequency needs the melt or the crucible to be sufficiently conductive to couple to the radio-frequency field. Alternatively a susceptor can be used as an intermediary. A power of up to 20kW is needed to heat an iridium crucible so that YAG can be brought to its melting point of about 1900°C.

The Method
Dislocations and polycrystallinity, which may be propagated through the crystal, need to be avoided while growth continues, once it has been initiated. It is therefore necessary to balance the pulling rate and the thermal conditions. The thermal gradient across the crucible and in the vicinity of the seed and the thermal gradient normal to the growth interface, are very critical. The arrangement of the heaters can be influential in this, as well as the depth of melt in the crucible. If the crucible is less than full, the walls untouched by the melt may act as after-heaters.

As the melt begins, the temperature is raised slightly above that of the melt and the seed is introduced. This ensures that a small part of the seed is melted so that growth can begin on a clean surface. On decreasing the power, the temperature of the melt is lowered and growth begins. At the 'right time' – the grower will almost sense when this occurs – the pulling is started. The diameter of the growing crystal is controlled by careful adjustment of the heater controls. At the end of the run, the melt temperature is raised so that the crystal can be withdrawn without causing thermal shock and consequent imperfections. When these are known to be a possibility with a particular substance, the crystal is allowed to cool while still keeping contact with the melt.

Specific Crystals
Many crystals suitable for laser applications have been grown by the Czochralski method. One of the first was calcium tungstate (scheelite), reported as grown by this technique in 1960. The melting point of scheelite ($CaWO_4$) is 1570°C and it is best grown in an iridium crucible. Since no special atmosphere is required, it can be grown in air and growth rates between 6.4 and 19mm (0.25 and 0.75 in) per hour are usual. Nd, as a dopant, has been satisfactorily incorporated in the

crystals. Since Nd^{3+} is at a site normally occupied by Ca^{2+}, charge compensation is necessary and this is achieved by adding Na^+.

Lithium niobate ($LiNbO_3$) has also been grown by the Czochralski method, starting materials being mixtures of Li_2CO_3 and Nb_2O_5. Any contact between the melt and the iridium walls of the crucible instantly turns the crystals brown. The melting point is about 1265°C so that control of growth is not difficult and allows several types of heater to be considered for use. Platinum is favoured as a crucible material because of the problems of discolouration. For crystals of 5 to 20mm (0.6 to 0.8 in) diameter pulling rates of about 6 to 8mm (0.25 to 0.3 in) per hour would be typical. Heat shields are essential, because the material tends to crack during cooling.

Recent developments in Czochralski growth include the automatic control of diameter so that a smooth parallel-sided crystal is obtained. This has been achieved with lithium niobate, gadolinium gallium garnet, lithium tantalate, and also with some semiconductors.

Ruby has been grown by the Czochralski method principally for use in lasers. The melt is contained in a precious metal crucible which is heated by radio frequency induction; the seed is a small diameter corundum rod for which any crystal orientation can be chosen. The seed is rotated at speeds between 10 and 60 revolutions per minute and it is withdrawn from the melt at speeds between 6mm (0.25 in) and 25.4mm (1 in) per hour. Sizes up to 25.4mm (1 in.) in diameter and 63.5cm (25 in) in length are regularly grown. It is possible, by growing ruby by this method, to minimize misorientations, particularly that of the optic axis which is very common with crystals grown by the flame-fusion method.

Crystals grown at 60 degrees to the c-axis show very little misorientation. Scattering sites (voids or inclusions larger than about ½ micron causing light scatter) are of very low density in Czochralski ruby (about 1 per cubic cm [0.035 cubic in]). Some have been identified as platelets of crucible material, others are small gas bubbles. Other factors which need to be eliminated are central chrome-rich cores in some crystals.

YAG (yttrium aluminium garnet) grown by pulling usually shows distorted drops of undigested melt. In some places these congregate together to form gas- or liquid-filled structures resembling bunches of grapes. Triangular black crystallites can sometimes be seen; they may also be square or shapeless.

The Bridgman-Stockbarger Process
Some large single crystals can be grown by the Bridgman-Stockbarger process. This involves cooling the starting material in a shaped

container, normally a cylinder with one end tapered. The material is allowed to cool slowly until it is close to freezing point, at which the temperature is lowered at the tapered end to allow the formation of a single seed crystal at the extreme tip. The reason for having a shaped vessel is that single crystals are more likely to form this way. On cooling, the crystal grows into the container until the single crystal occupies the whole of it. A number of halides and oxides are grown by this method as well as sulphides and a number of metals. Cadmium sulphide (in nature the mineral greenockite) is one example with possible gem application. Large fluorite crystals have occasionally been cut. They include rubidium manganese fluoride, coloured a light pink; and calcium fluoride (fluorite) which is coloured red by uranium or green by samarium.

The Kyropoulos Method

The Kyropoulos technique of crystal growth is a variation of the Czochralski pulling method. Here the crystal itself is not moved; instead the temperature of the melt is lowered from the seed downward. In many cases, this is accomplished by allowing the crucible to pass down a temperature gradient so that, as the material freezes, the crystal grows from the seed. Good crystals, with a diameter large in proportion to the length (Czochralski crystals are the reverse), are obtained in this way.

Flux-melt Growth

A method of crystal growth known either as flux-growth or fluxed-melt growth is of considerable gemmological importance. Components of the desired substance are dissolved in a solvent (flux) and growth takes place at relatively low temperatures; the method is especially suitable for crystals needing to be free from thermal strain. It also avoids the need for very refractory crucibles, since the addition of the flux may lower the melting point sufficiently for a platinum or similar container to be used. Materials which enter a different phase at temperatures above their melting temperatures, can be flux-grown (with a lower temperature) although they cannot be grown simply from a melt. Phase changes such as that undergone by ZrO_2 (it transforms from cubic to monoclinic at 1150°C) are avoided.

Many crystals grown by this method display natural facets so that they can be used for optical experiments without the need for further polishing. A disadvantage is that the crystals are relatively small and that ions of the solvent phase enter the crystal lattice. This can usually be avoided or minimized by the use of the appropriate flux.

Growth by the method may be by spontaneous nucleation (i.e. no seed is used) or growth may take place on a prepared seed. Gemstones commonly grown this way may or may not have a seed, according to what is wanted by the grower.

The crucible used is almost always platinum. Emerald in particular may show included platinum crystals when grown this way. Pure platinum seems to be more resistant to attack: on attack by the melt, other alloys will enter it and the finished crystal may contain a high proportion of the metal. Nucleation takes place either at the surface of the melt or on the platinum wall, a site that may be preferred if the crucible is old, because the surface will be rougher and so encourage nucleation.

The Method

The actual method of growth is simple. A saturated solution is prepared by keeping the constituents of the desired crystal and the flux at a temperature slightly above the saturation temperature long enough for a complete solution to form. The crucible is then cooled through a temperature range in which the crystal desired is known to precipitate. Nucleation usually takes place first in the cooler part of the crucible; there is usually a cooler part although efforts can be made to keep the

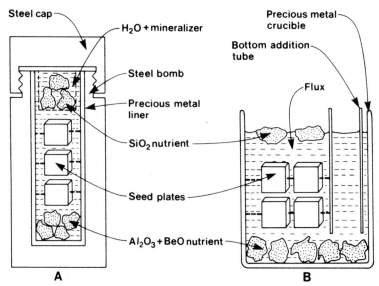

Fig. 4.2. Making synthetic emerald — this compares hydrothermal growth (A) and flux-melt growth (B).

crucible isothermal. Once nucleation has taken place, no more will occur so that crystals from the initial sites will be maximum size. When cooling is completed, crystals are removed from the crucible by hand or by chemically dissolving the flux.

Growth on a seed gives a greater degree of control of perfection, doping and orientation than spontaneous nucleation. Two methods are commonly used:

1. Growth by slow cooling with a seed, and

2. Growth on a seed which is placed in a cooler part of the system while the rest of the solute is in contact with the solvent in a hotter part of the system (growth in a thermal gradient).

The latter is similar to hydrothermal growth. The advantages are that the crystal quality and clarity are good because the inclusions of flux are much less and a faster rate of growth can be achieved. The amount of supersaturation can be kept lower than that which is needed to achieve nucleation on the platinum, so that all growth will therefore take place on the seed. On the other hand, growth with a seed needs more elaborate equipment and more careful control of the growth process. The choice of flux is also more critical. Seeds may have to be specially grown and need to be orientated before growth takes place on them.

The choice of a suitable flux depends upon a number of criteria. It needs to have a low melting point; it should be a good solvent, dissolving from 5-30 weight per cent of solute* at the maximum temperature intended; it must not form a compound with the solute and it should be compatible with platinum over the intended temperature range. It should have low volatility, if growth is to be by slow cooling; otherwise a lower temperature range and a faster rate of cooling will be needed. This will often cause nucleation at the melt surface. The flux should have low viscosity and be non-toxic if possible. It should also be relatively easy to separate from the crystals at the end of the run.

The advantages of growth by flux evaporation, as compared with growth by slow cooling, are that the growth occurs at a higher temperature so that the desired substance does not form compounds with the flux. This is more likely at lower temperatures. If the run is completed, almost 100 per cent of the possible yield is achieved and crystals free from a coating of flux are obtained. Large well-formed crystals should be obtained from the crucible base, although this will not always happen. On the other hand, there is less control over the process and slow cooling will produce better quality crystals.

*A substance dissolved in another.

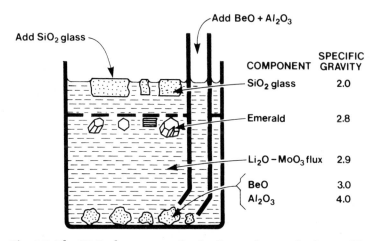

Fig. 4.3. The IG-Farben process for the flux-melt growth of emerald.

YAG has traditionally been grown by the flux-melt method; one form of growth employed a flux of lead oxide and boron oxide. A mixture of PbO,B_2O_3, Y_2O_3 and Al_2O_3 was heated in a platinum crucible for four hours at 1250°C and cooled at 1°C an hour to 950°C. The crucible was then removed from the furnace and cooled, the solvent being leached out with hot nitric acid. Crystals as large as $10\times7\times7$mm $(0.4\times0.28\times0.28$ in) were obtained. Another method used a flux of $PbO-PbF_2$ and B_2O_3. Crystals up to 100 g (3.5 oz) and with good optical quality were obtained.

Growing Emeralds by Flux-growth
In the 1930s, emerald was produced by the German IG Farbenindustrie with a flux reaction technique in which pieces of silica were floated on a solution of beryllia and alumina in the correct proportions. Emerald was then precipitated by dissolution and diffusion. Later apparatus separated the reactants from the growth regions by diaphragms. For a flux, alkali vanadates, molybdates and tungstates are suitable; emerald was grown as far back as 1888 using a flux of lithium molybdate and lithium vanadate. A patent granted in the United States in 1967 uses the same flux and, in this case, the emerald is grown on a seed. It is preferable to use materials having a high degree of crystalline perfection and a minimum amount of water as seeds. These are usually high-quality natural beryl, aquamarine, or emerald which has been heat-treated before using it as a seed. Seeds where the faces of the plates are orientated perpendicular to the c-axis are preferred.

The method of growth is as follows: a flux of, say, Li_2O 2.25-3.25 MoO_3 is placed in a platinum crucible which is positioned in the lower section of a vertical tube furnace. The central portion of this furnace is heated to about 1000°C, subjecting the crucible to a reverse thermal gradient as the hottest part of the melt is at its surface. Chips of beryl or powdered oxide are first added to the melt to adjust the solute-flux composition to an equilibrium state. Then one or more seed plates of natural or synthetic beryl are positioned in the lower, cooler part of the furnace.

A test seed of known weight can be used to help assess achievement of equilibrium growth conditions. By frequently removing and weighing a test seed, a point can be found where solution stops and crystallization begins. At this point the seed plates of emerald can be lowered into the melt. It is also possible to keep a test seed plate immersed in the melt and to remove it periodically to assess the growth rate on the other seeds. When emerald crystals of the size required are achieved, the crucible is removed from the furnace and the crystals recovered by pouring off most of the flux and dissolving the rest by boiling in an alkali solution. This method of growth confines crystal growth with beryl structure to the seed and much of the production is optically transparent and substantially flawless. Spontaneous nucleation and twinning on the seed is minimized. Favourable growth rates over a long period can be achieved.

The earliest synthetic emeralds could be identified with some confidence by their typical bright red through the Chelsea colour filter and by their notably low specific gravity and refractive index (for which typical figures might be a specific gravity of 2.65 and a refractive index of 1.56-1.57). Even today the constants for synthetic emeralds are lower than for most natural stones and the red through the filter is still marked.

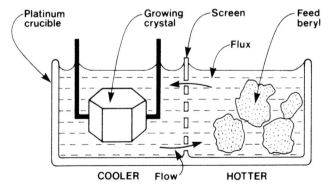

Fig. 4.4. The Gilson process for the flux-melt growth of emerald.

For a while, Gilson added iron to his emeralds and this had the effect of raising the constants to higher figures and at the same time diminishing the fluorescence. More details are given later in the section on emerald. For the moment, it may be said that any emerald showing red under ultra-violet light or between crossed filters should be regarded with suspicion.

The best way to detect synthetic emerald is with the microscope or the 10× lens providing the stone is sufficiently large. The most characteristic inclusion is the profusion of twisted veil-like structures which I call 'frozen cigarette smoke' from its resemblance to cigarette smoke drifting in a room where the air is still. Admittedly in the finest Chatham and Gilson stones, these veils are kept to a minimum; but I have never seen a stone from which they were totally absent. When closely examined, the veils are seen to be made up of cavities connected by channels which may contain two- or three-phase inclusions.

In addition we may sometimes see squashed liquid drops and, under magnification and polarized light, it can be seen that the flat sections of the channels contain crystals. Probably while the crystal was being grown, some of the melt passed into cracks in which it crystallized on

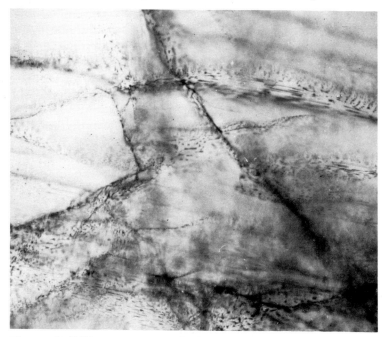

Fig. 4.5. Veil-like structures in Chatham emerald.

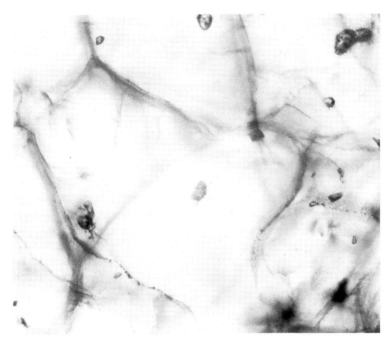

Fig. 4.6. Phenakite crystals in a Zerfass emerald.

cooling. Crystals of phenakite are quite common (phenakite is beryllium silicate, Be_2SiO_4) and they may be seen to be faceted (i.e. showing natural crystal faces). They may come about through modification of the growth process at some stage. It is also possible to find in some stones crystals of platinum (from the crucible) or hexagonal tables of ilmenite (iron titanate).

An important test for synthetic emeralds is that almost all known *natural* specimens are opaque to ultra-violet rays shorter than about 300nm. Synthetic Chatham emeralds at least transmit ultra-violet rays quite freely down to about 230nm. Those with the appropriate equipment will also find that, in some (hydrothermal) emeralds, infra-red spectroscopy will reveal the presence of water; this is also seen in natural stones, but not in the flux-melt product.

Other Gemstones

Although emeralds are the most important gemstones grown by the flux-melt technique, they are not the only ones. Ruby for industrial purposes is more commonly grown by the Czochralski pulling method, but quite a lot of rubies made by the flux-melt method have appeared on the market. They are characterized by drops of flux which sometimes resemble the marks made when a full paint-brush is slapped on a wall. Drops of melt forming feather-like structures can also be found. It is interesting to note that the occasional mesh formation of undigested flux can have a roughly hexagonal shape. All elongated cavities found in flux-grown rubies are grouped and parallel and look whitish to the naked eye. Other constants are not so revealing since specific gravity, refractive index and absorption spectrum do not differ from those shown by the natural material.

Crystals of YAG (yttrium aluminium garnet) are, like ruby, more commonly grown by pulling methods; but those grown by the flux-melt process usually show liquid-filled channels with two-phase inclusions; the channels are often jagged in outline and may lead into a network of intermingled feathers and resemble the twisted veils so characteristic of synthetic emerald.

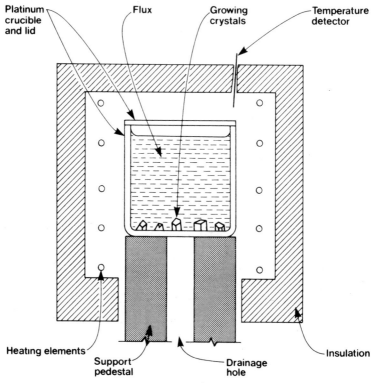

Fig. 4.7. Cutaway diagram showing the platinum crucible inside the flux-growth furnace.

Alexandrite has been grown by the flux-melt method and shows characteristic inclusions – the twisted veils, tiny crystallites and particles of undigested flux.

Spinels of various colours have been grown by the flux-melt method; it may be that some red spinels on the market and clearly not natural, may be these productions. I have seen reds, greens, yellows and blues; and in all cases the colours are quite unlike those shown by the Verneuil-grown stones. Typical inclusions are botryoidal or other irregular shapes with residues of the melt and other gaseous or liquid fillings.

Skull-melting

Cubic zirconia so far has been manufactured by a process unlike the hydrothermal, flux-melt or flame-fusion techniques. Efforts to grow the material by the flux-melt method have resulted in the monoclinic or tetragonal phases of zirconia so that a new method was required to give the cubic, stable phase. Because zirconia has a very high melting point (2750°C) no known crucible material can be used. Therefore a technique known as 'skull-melting' has been developed which overcomes most of the difficulties. It is interesting to assume that the material must have been regarded as important, as so much work has gone into its manufacture.

The 'skull' consists of a cup with sides made up of copper tubes

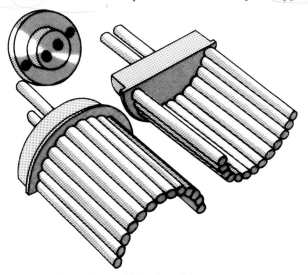

Fig. 4.8. Split halves of a small skull-melting apparatus.

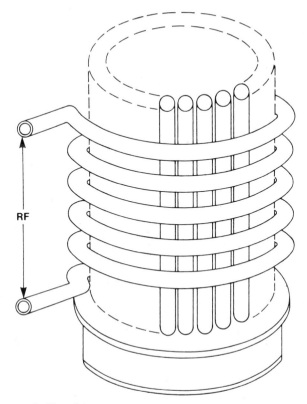

Fig. 4.9 A skull-melting apparatus set up for use. (RF = Radio Frequency)

resembling the fingers of a hand, concave and parallel. These are cooled by water. The skull is placed inside a copper coil connected to a radio-frequency source (4MHz and 100kW). The energy imparted by the radio-frequency enters the skull between the fingers. The skull is filled with zirconia powder mixed with stabilizer (calcium or yttrium); this will not become hot until some zirconium metal is added. When the metal is hot, it heats up the powder near to it which then conducts the electricity and melts. The metal reacts with oxygen in the air to provide more zirconia. The zirconia melts leaving only a thin layer next to the copper fingers so that the melt is confined in a container made of itself, also preventing contamination from the copper.

Fig. 4.10. (Opposite) the process of solidification during skull-melting crystal growth: (A) formation of a porous crust; (B) growth of parallel columns; (C) the whole melt has solidified.

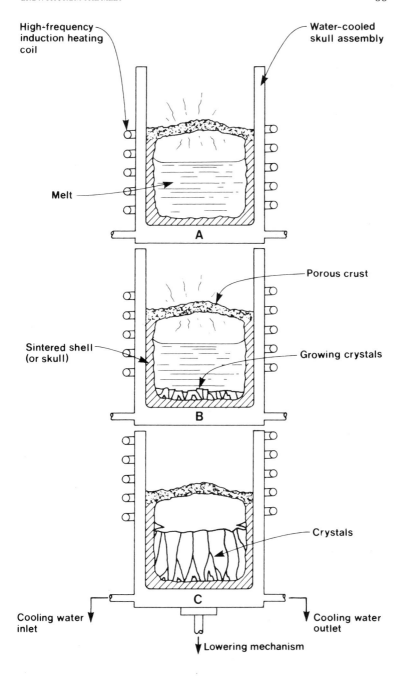

High-frequency induction heating coil

Water-cooled skull assembly

Melt

Porous crust

Sintered shell (or skull)

Growing crystals

A

B

Crystals

C

Cooling water inlet

Cooling water outlet

Lowering mechanism

As the heat is reduced, a skin forms over the contents of the skull while crystal growth begins at the bottom. Columns of crystals parallel to each other nucleate near the bottom and grow upwards, stopping when the melt is used up. On separating the columns, the crystals can be removed.

With a charge of 1kg (2 lb 3 oz), a maximum of 500g (1 lb 2 oz) of facetable material has been obtained. Cerium added to the powder gives orange to red; a number of different additives give yellow; and nickel gives brown. Blue and green have presented some difficulty.

5. Irradiation, Staining & Coating

The practice of subjecting gemstones to various forms of irradiation, in order to improve their colour, has been carried out for many years and appears to be on the increase. In many cases (though the stones involved are so far among the less expensive categories), the practice cannot be detected; although the experienced eye will know that the colour seems unusual. The only safe course to adopt when a stone with an unusual colour is encountered, is to send it for laboratory examination. As always, diamond is a case apart and examples of treated diamonds are dealt with in Chapter 8 on diamonds.

Reports on Individual Cases from the Literature
Stones which had been subjected to beta-ray irradiation were reported by Schlossmacher some years ago. They included rock crystal which turned smoky, though not uniformly; colourless, white and pale pink tourmaline crystals which turned to rubellite (red); and some crystals, green at one end and white at the other, which turned to rubellite at the white ends. All the crystals cracked. Kunzite and colourless spodumene crystals turned green, but quickly faded after exposure to sunlight for a few minutes. Pale green and yellow spodumenes were not affected. Colourless and blue topaz turned a rich brown in zones, but the colour faded quickly in sunlight. Pink topaz obtained from heated brown material turned brown and kept its colour. Colourless stones from the Thomas Mountain range in Utah turned a rich reddish-brown and kept this colour for months despite exposure to daylight.

Yellow to amber colours were taken by corundum (original colour not specified), but the change was not permanent. Pale emeralds became greyish-green; an emerald from Brazil turned more strongly dichroic, with bluish-violet and grey-green colours. Colour induced in emerald did not survive exposure to sunlight. Pale aquamarines and some colourless beryls turned pale yellow and this colour remained for some time after exposure to sunlight; heating drove it off much more quickly.

Heat-treated Indo-Chinese zircon crystals were the only zircons affected. All the white and blue stones turned reddish-brown, but this may have been the original colour of the stone. Weakly irradiated stones reverted to blue or colourless, but those irradiated for longer retained the colour even after long exposure to sunlight. Some clear pale scapolites turned an amethystine colour but the colour was not stable; a similar instability was noticed in a yellow which was induced in phenakite.

No response was noted in the various types of chrysoberyl, strontium titanate, synthetic rutile, some apatite (colours not specified), brazilianite, benitoite and euclase.

Sinkankas (1963), reported that some pink tourmaline crystals from the Himalaya mine, California, and some blue crystals from the Tourmaline Queen mine, Pala, California were irradiated by some process, the exact nature of which is unknown. The Himalaya pink stones and some pink stones from the Tourmaline Queen turned a deep purplish-pink with the exterior zones showing the most intense colour. Pale portions of some of the blue crystals also changed to this colour, but portions which were originally a decided blue showed no change. The induced colours had persisted for at least seven years (at the time of writing of the report).

Topaz coloured by radium was reported by the Gemological Institute of America in 1949. The colour was originally pale blue and, after exposure, it changed to deep rich brown. The stone was exposed to 3g (0.1 oz) of radium contained in 30 glass tubes; these tubes were stacked to a depth of 5cm (2 in) in a lead container and the stone placed on top of them in a paper envelope. After one week the stone had turned to a light amber and after two weeks to a deeper amber. After three weeks and four weeks, there was no further change.

A yellowish-white sapphire crystal turned dark amber in two weeks with no further change after four weeks; a purplish-white sapphire turned olive in one week with no further change after four weeks. In one week, a blue-grey star sapphire turned to a more pronounced grey; after two weeks it had changed to grey with a tint of olive; and after four weeks there had been no further change. No change was reported in a blue sapphire and a brown star sapphire after four weeks.

A zircon from Thailand was heavily irradiated with radium and turned violet, the original colour being brown. The violet, almost that of amethyst, faded to some extent when the stone was exposed to diffused daylight for four weeks.

Irradiation of smoky quartz gives a range of colours from pale tan through to pitch black. Since the process is identical with that taking place in nature, it is not possible to distinguish between treated and untreated stones. A greenish-yellow quartz can be obtained by heating smoky varieties. Heating must be carried out in stages, because a sudden application of excess heat will drive off all colour. Again there is no possibility of separating natural from treated stones.

Topaz of a fine dark blue is now on the market; no means exist of distinguishing this undoubtedly irradiated material from naturally-coloured topaz, though very little natural material shows so dark a blue. Irradiation of brown topaz shows that almost all material turns yellow from 'Imperial' colour to a cinnamon brown. These colours, due to the action of colour centres, are unstable and revert after exposure to sunlight for a few hours. Blue topaz turns an olive-brown colour (the combination of the colour centre mentioned above and another one giving blue). After the brown is lost by exposure to light, only the blue colour remains; it appears to be stable to light and heat (Nassau, 1977). Since the colour may be produced the same way in natural blue topaz, it may not be possible to identify a treated stone with certainty (though they are a much darker blue than almost all natural stones).

Tests on gamma-irradiated topaz and quartz were reported from the GIA's New York Laboratory in 1973. A cleavage section of topaz, which was originally colourless, became dark reddish-brown after an exposure to gamma rays for a short time. This colour was only seen in half of the section; the other half did not change in colour so presumably something in the structure of the stone prevented the irradiation from accomplishing its effect. Half the stone was then covered with black tape and exposed to sunlight for two weeks. The exposed part of the coloured section faded to about half of its original colour and became smoky rather than brown. Some 'Imperial' topaz became a fine orange after exposure to sunlight (only a few days). Rock crystal exposed to gamma rays became smoky; some coloured unevenly and showed colour zoning reminiscent of that sometimes shown by amethyst. Again exposure to sunlight faded the stones appreciably.

A report in Gems and Gemology (Winter 1981) states that a number of blue irradiated topazes have been found to be radioactive and that the colour of stones showing this effect is not restricted to very deep blue. Generally the irradiation used to colour the stones leaves no radio-activity behind, because this contamination cannot occur with gamma irradiation. However, if the stones are subjected to neutron irradiation in an atomic pile, they may then keep dangerously high levels of radioactivity. In one case, at least four radioactive elements were found in a blue topaz. One stone, which showed a level of 0.2 milliroentgens per hour, was unsafe for wear, let alone for long-term handling such as might occur with a gemstone dealer.

Radioactivity has also been reported from Maxixe-type blue beryl and from some tourmaline which has been irradiated to give a dark red colour. Fading of colour or subsequent heat treatment does not dispel the radioactivity.

Stones irradiated by neutron bombardment are reported by Burbage and Jones (1957). For the purpose of the experiment, a range of pairs of stones was assembled; one of each pair was then subjected to neutron bombardment for a period of three to six days. A colourless corundum boule became brown, showed strongly through crossed filters and developed strong dichroism. A boule of synthetic ruby darkened, with some increase in dichroism, but fluoresced less between crossed filters. A pink synthetic sapphire, originally strongly dichroic with the colours yellow and pink, became brown with little change in dichroism. Two blue synthetic sapphires, which were exposed for six days, varied in their response; one became dark brown and the other greenish-blue with strong directional dichroism. One of the so-called 'alexandrite' corundums became a garnet-red with dichroic colours of yellow and red.

A blue synthetic spinel became pale greenish-brown and a pale blue spinel became a more steel-like colour. A pink topaz reverted to a sherry-brown; a pale yellow topaz became darker and greenish with pink and very pale green dichroism, which was stronger than in the original. Zircons, both blue and golden, were exposed for three days and became a very deep reddish-brown, which was almost black.

Gamma-irradiated topaz showed strong dichroism (yellow-green and reddish-brown); it also showed a very low refractive index for topaz. A stone placed in an atomic pile and originally a pale brown (Mexican stone) became a very dark reddish-brown and the colour appeared to be permanent. The refractive index of this stone was 1.612-1.620 and there was strong dichroism.

Kunzite turned deep green on gamma irradiation; this colour bleached on subsequent exposure to light or heat. The green colour resembled that of natural hiddenite. Another kunzite became sherry-brown after irradiation, with pink and brown as the dichroic colours.

An orthoclase feldspar on subjection to irradiation (type unstated)

turned sherry-brown with dichroism in two shades of brown.
Irradiated morganite turned to a deep greyish-blue. The bands in the spectrum were at 675, 659nm with fainter bands in the orange.
Some colourless sapphire was irradiated by X-rays. Natural stones turned canary yellow very quickly, but synthetic stones were unaffected after five minutes' exposure. It was noticed that there was a distorted interference figure in the synthetic stones; the strain giving rise to this may also have prevented the alteration of colour.

Staining

For staining or coating techniques to be successful, the material needs to be porous although some porous stones should not need any improvement of this kind (e.g. opal). Detection is quite easily carried out in most cases with a 10× lens, because the dyestuff, which concentrates into cracks (often at the base of the stone), will be seen as a darker area of colour. Many agates are stained as a matter of course, the colours being rather gaudy. Again detection is easy and, in fact, the practice is acceptable; few customers will stipulate that their agate must be unstained!

The staining of jadeite can be a more serious matter, particularly when the stone is mounted in a setting in such a way that only a portion of the top of the stone can be closely examined. The spectroscope is the most useful tool in this case, as bands from the dyestuff never resemble the chromium bands seen in the best green jadeite. For commercial reasons, only the finest colours are worth reproducing.

Lavender jadeite known to have been dyed, gives a distinctive absorption spectrum with bands in the red and in the yellow-green; the 437nm band is also visible. There is a pink fluorescence.

Dyed aventurine has been seen offered as purple jade. The colour is not specially attractive.

'Pink jade' which is, in fact, dyed quartz has been seen on the market. As is usual, the dye can be seen concentrated in cracks. Another dyed quartz was violet in colour and showed a broad absorption band from 590 to 550nm. Again the dye concentration in cracks could be seen.

A green-coloured chalcedony reported by the G.I.A. in 1966 had a colour between that of 'green onyx' (dyed chalcedony) and chrysocolla. Lines in the red in the absorption spectrum were similar to those found in natural jadeite, but a chalcedonic structure could be seen by transmitted light. Under magnification, the flat back of the cabochon showed a brownish zoning parallel with it. It is thought that this brown was caused by heat generated by rapid polishing of the back.

A fine-grained calcite dyed to resemble green jadeite was seen forming part of a bracelet. The dyeing was selective to give the impression of the white mottling so characteristic of jadeite, but the easy cleavage of calcite soon caused the bracelet to break. Selective dyeing has also been reported on true jadeite, the green colour appearing on top.

A report by Jobbins (1975) showed that walrus ivory can be stained. A necklace submitted for examination was a spinach-green in colour and had been at one time offered as jade. The general structure could be seen as nodular with many small cavities; the colouring was very uneven and it appeared that the beads had been dyed. Scrapings were immersed in oil and showed anomalous double refraction, low birefringence and a mean refractive index just above 1.55. Beads had a hardness between 2 and 3 on Mohs' scale and were sectile. The specific gravity was 1.99; on heating the minute scrapings gave off the smell of burning protein and became blackened. Microchemical analysis showed that the phosphate radical and a major amount of calcium, with lesser amounts of magnesium and copper, were present. This suggested that the material consisted of bones or teeth which had been stained by copper salt. Identification with known organic material showed that the beads were walrus ivory (i.e. the enlarged canines from the upper jaw of the animal). Whereas elephant ivory shows the lines of Retzius, resembling eleborate arcs drawn with a pair of compasses, the structure of the walrus ivory could be seen to be fine-textured on the outside of the tooth with a much coarser inner core with nodules or whorls. The necklace was fashioned from the inner part of the tooth.

Dyed wollastonite has been offered as a jade simulant and is reported by Liddicoat (1977). The material had a green colour with a dye spectrum, a specific gravity of about 2.94 and a refractive index about 1.62; the hardness was 4½ to 5. There was a bluish fluorescence under long-wave ultra-violet light and under short-wave; under X-rays, the fluorescence was yellowish. Wollastonite is a calcium silicate.

Some poor quality sapphire can be dyed to give a ruby colour; likewise a better blue can be given to a sapphire by the introduction of dye to any cracks.

Some pearls are dyed blue or rosy.

Some rings, especially those with closed ('gypsy') settings, contain apparently good quality emerald. These are, in fact, poor grade stones (pale green or blue) backed with a bright green substance. Dichroism and an emerald absorption spectrum will be shown. If the colouring matter separates from the stone, a white spot in a green background may be seen.

Coating

Coating gemstones will give increased internal brilliance (in the case of colourless stones); stones with tinges of yellow will appear whiter and most other stones will have their colour enhanced. The film commonly applied (which is similar to that applied to camera lenses) has a hardness of about 6 so that it serves to protect the surface from some kinds of damage. The coating is soluble in boiling water and 30 per cent hot acetic acid and in some other strong acids. However, at the time of writing (Gübelin, 1950), the stones so treated were said to be too gaudy to pass as untreated gems. Various chemical tests to detect the film are quoted, but the practice seems now to be little followed.

Recent Developments with Corundum

Over the past few years, it has become apparent that certain corundum varieties, especially ruby and sapphire, have undergone some form of treatment with a view to the enhancement of their colour, clarity or asterism. A detailed review of the treatment is given by Kurt Nassau in *Gems and Gemology* (Fall 1981) and his findings are summarized here.

The significant parameters are the temperature-time relationship, the oxidation-reduction conditions and the presence of chemicals which can interact with the stone. Nine different processes have been identified, but it is not yet apparent whether or not their use should be disclosed as a normal part of a selling operation.

The first process is the development of asterism in a stone containing a sufficiency of titanium oxide. The oxide is converted after heating to titanium dioxide (rutile), which then takes up the characteristic star pattern. Heating (perhaps 1300°C for 24 hours) is the only method necessary to produce the asterism.

The second process removes unwanted rutile from a stone; it might either be producing asterism or the profuse network of crystals often known as 'silk'. The stone is heated at a temperature between 1500°C and 1700°C and this enables the rutile to dissolve in the corundum. The process has been used on rutile-rich Australian sapphire and on milky white stones from Sri Lanka ('geuda stones'). This material is also turned blue by the third process. It is possible to get a good star stone by using process two to dissolve rutile followed by process one to get it to precipitate out correctly. The use of a heat treatment to remove silk and/or asterism may be detected by the presence of a dull chalky green fluorescence and by the absence of the iron band at 450 nm. It is reported that Burma rubies have had silk removed with consequent enhancement of colour.

The third process, in which a fine colour is developed in a stone with a potential for blue, depends on the charge transfer between titanium and iron atoms. A sapphire with some iron and titanium oxides but with too little ferrous iron will be pale blue, green, yellow or colourless in its first state. If it is then heated in a reducing atmosphere, some Fe^{3+} will convert to Fe^{2+} – this can be done either by heating the stone for some time in a hydrogen atmosphere or by packing the stone in a carbon-producing material (such as charcoal or graphite) so that combustion with a small amount of air will produce carbon monoxide. If the temperature is high enough and if enough time is taken, the new colour will penetrate right through the stone, although bands from impurities will still be present if they were before. A chalky green fluorescence and no band at 450nm are again clues to the treatment. Internal stress fractures, pockmarked facets and doubling of the girdle (through some of the original girdle being missed on repolishing) are clues as well. The original colour is replaced by a fine deep blue.

In the fourth process, on the other hand, the colour in the original material is too dark (as in the inky sapphires often found in Australia). Heating the stone for an extended period in an oxidizing atmosphere may lighten the colour, because much of the iron may alter to Fe^{3+}. A colourless stone may be the result of a long period of heating. Where a yellow colour is possible, heating may produce green or yellow; and where purple sapphire with a chromium content is heated, ruby may be the final product (oxidation does not affect chromium colouration). One result of this process may be a distinct green dichroic direction in blue sapphire. It is thought that many brownish 'Siam' rubies are also treated in this way, as far fewer rubies of this type are seen on the market nowadays.

Process five involves the diminution of banding such as that seen in stones made by the Verneuil process. Heating at temperatures up to 1600°C and over for several days allows a diffusion of the impurities causing the banding into the remainder of the stone; however the process is very slow. This process is reported to be in use in Bangkok on Verneuil blue sapphire. With the simultaneous application of process six (introduction of natural-seeming inclusions), the result can be a very difficult stone for the tester to identify. The removal of banding also makes application of the Plato test difficult. Gas bubbles cannot be removed however, and, as they are so characteristic of Verneuil stones, they should be looked for carefully.

The sixth process introduces inclusions reminiscent of the 'finger-prints' characteristic of natural corundum and may be produced by using a flux-type chemical agent (perhaps sodium bicarbonate or borax). The inclusions are close to the surface of the stone; so far no actual evidence of this kind of treatment is available.

The seventh process is used when a corundum contains insufficient rutile to form a satisfactory star. It may be possible to diffuse some rutile into the stone as a thin layer just below the surface. In one process, a slurry of aluminium titanate in water was painted on to the stone which was then fired at 1750°C for several days, then cooled. After cooling, further heating caused the star to develop as happens with the familiar Verneuil star stones. The depth of penetration is very shallow. Stars produced in this way are much sharper than would be seen in natural stones. Uneven colouration, an increased depth of colour around fractures and pits, together with pockmarked surfaces and stress fractures are indications of this treatment.

The eighth process involves adding a blue colour by diffusion. This requires a reducing atmosphere and gives a blue colour when insufficient iron oxide or titanium oxide is present in the stone. The original colours are pale blue, yellow, green or colourless. The penetration is very shallow. Colours other than blue can also be added by diffusion; chromium gives a red 'skin'; nickel gives yellow; while nickel and chromium together give orange. All colours produced by this method are stable.

To summarise, the characteristics which can identify heat-treated blue sapphires are:

1. Areas where there were finger-print inclusions, appear glassy;
2. Silk which is very fine and dot-like;
3. Pock-marked facets;
4. Pock-marked girdles; and
5. A chalky blue-green fluorescence with or without a 450nm spectrum band.

6. Testing Man-Made Gems

For the most part, gemmologists will be familiar with the testing methods needed to identify almost all the synthetic stones likely to be encountered. As a brief guide, I have mentioned the colour filter, cathodoluminescence and the reflectivity meters separately since they will test more than one variety of stone. Most materials and their means of identification are listed in the Chapters dealing with the materials themselves. There is still no real substitute for the 10× lens; most synthetic emeralds can be identified with it and, with some practice, synthetic opal (the Gilson product at least) can also be spotted. Where a birefringent stone is offered as a natural isotropic material, the lens will make all clear (e.g. lithium niobate for diamond, rutile for diamond). Specific gravity tests, the refractometer and the spectroscope are mentioned in the appropriate contexts.

Reflectivity Meters
These do not measure refractive index, as has been erroneously supposed, but rather the relative reflectivity of the surface of the stone. This surface needs to have a high polish and to be clean. The best results (and the most useful) are those given when testing stones with refractive index values over 1.80 – this of course includes diamond and most of its simulants. Since heat and incident light affect the accuracy of the instruments (which also need to be calibrated), care should be taken with them and control stones used in all cases.

Colour Filters
The colour filter is still useful in gem testing. Where synthetics are concerned, it will still arouse suspicions when an emerald glows a bright red; when blue synthetic spinel or cobalt glass glows red; or when

stained green chalcedony glows a faint pink. Most green glass and doublets will remain green, although some soudé (doublet) stones will show red.

Cathodoluminescence

Cathodoluminescence can be used to some extent in gem-testing and is reported by Gaal (1977). Briefly, when gem materials contain activator ions or structural defects, they may fluoresce in an electron beam and show features not visible in normal light. The Gemological Institute of America has used the Nuclide Luminoscope ELM-2A, which can be operated in conjunction with a microscope. This enables the phenomena to be observed under different magnifications.

The operation of the apparatus allows electrons to be drawn from a cold cathode by an anode; these are then passed along a metal tube with magnetic conductor objective lenses. The lenses focus the beam on to a small area of the specimen, exciting cathodoluminescence with some thermoluminescence and some X-rays. The specimen must be placed in a vacuum chamber to avoid attenuation of the electron beam and to permit its free passage. The electrons strike the specimen and their momentum is stopped; some of the kinetic energy is dissipated as heat and some is radiated back as light (cathodoluminescence). How much depends upon the state of the lattice, whether or not it is distorted, and upon the presence or absence of impurity ions and imperfections. Such imperfections as structural defect centres or the presence of elements as impurities, will cause cathodoluminescence because they create a change in the electronic state of the material. It seems from work carried out that the cathodoluminescence arises from a very thin layer either on or near the surface.

When examining stones, there is no requirement to prepare them in any particular way. There is no need to make them conductive by coating them with a conductive solution, because charge neutralization takes place very quickly. Stones should be cleaned with distilled water and placed in the vacuum chamber which is raised to a pressure of 15-30mtorr in less than three minutes. The cold cathode discharge source is turned on and the beam voltage is adjusted to produce luminescence. The response of the stone is then recorded, giving details of colour, intensity, patterns and phosphorescence.

Zirconia was found to give a broad band with a peak at about 475nm with a small secondary peak at 612nm. Dyed jadeite gave discontinuous areas of luminescence. Carbonates seemed usually to give a red luminescence; those with an iron content did not show this colour.

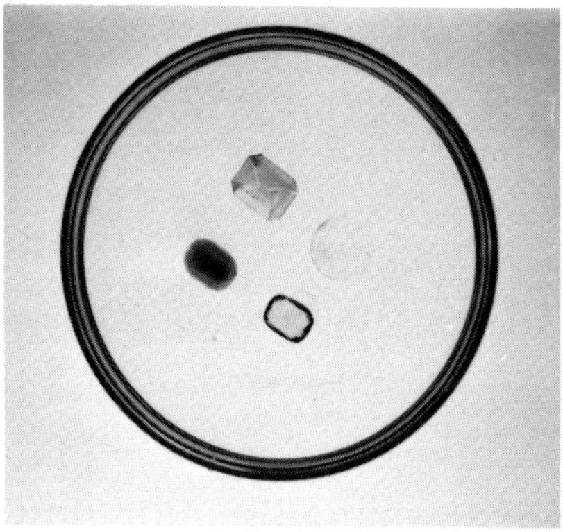

Fig. 6.1. Comparative relief of gems in colourless iodine (Refractive Index 1.49) (clockwise from top): Lechleitner partly synthetic emerald (R.I. 1.57-1.58); colourless natural sapphire (1.76-1.77); natural zircon (1.93-1.99); and blue sapphire. The petri cell holding the liquid was lit from below.

Strong zoning was observed in synthetic alexandrite. Diamonds gave a wide variety of patterns and colours. Synthetic diamonds gave intense yellow, blue and green luminescence. Linde synthetic emerald gave an intense red, as did Chatham stones; some natural stones appeared to give no reaction. Kashan synthetic ruby gave a weak red; other synthetics and the natural stones were an intense red.

7. Photographing Gem Inclusions

A file or album of photographs of inclusions to supplement pictures in books or articles is a valuable asset to a gemmologist's reference library, not only for guidance in identification but also in the, hopefully rare, instances when identification is necessary in the case of loss or theft of a customer's property. Colour photographs are often so beautiful that they have become an art form in their own right, as the reader has no doubt realized by looking at the pictures in this book by Dr. Edward Gübelin, who has specialized in the field for many years and whose book *The Internal World of Gemstones* (ABC Verlag, Switzerland, 1979) is a magnificent pictorial expression of the unexpected beauty of what were once contemptuously dismissed as flaws.

Micro-photography – photographs of small subjects generated by using a camera with extension tubes or bellows – produces images which, for technical reasons, cannot be enlarged more than about ten times. In gemmology, magnifications are normally more than this, 30x being the most common, and a microscope adapted for photography is needed. The use of this is known as photo-micrography. Again, for technical reasons, the eyepiece (the removable lens at the top of the microscope) should not have a magnification of more than 10x. Greater magnifications are obtained by varying the lens at the bottom of the microscope tube – the objective – usually by having a turret with several objectives that can be moved into place. An alternative which has useful applications in gemmology is a microscope with a built-in zoom lens.

Photo-micrography requires knowledge, suitable equipment, skill and above all patience. The inclusion has to be located through a microscope, the most suitable view selected, illuminated adequately, and photographed without too much or too little contrast. Adequate depth of field is important for it to be recognized and the final picture can be a print or a transparency.

There are basically two methods of photographing through a microscope. The first is by using a camera with its own lens, set at infinity, on top of the eyepiece of the microscope. Attachments are made to hold the camera firmly, generally by straps. This system was devised for cameras with fixed lenses and is now outdated. As most cameras used for photo-micrography today take 35mm film and have lenses that can be removed, the second system is preferred. In this, the eyepiece of the microscope and the camera lens are removed. A special tubular adaptor is employed to attach the camera body to the top of the microscope tube which acts like an extension tube, with the objective at the bottom being employed as the camera lens.

Using the camera body implies that it has the shutter mechanism incorporated in it, i.e. that it has a focal plane shutter, which is almost universal with interchangeable lenses. A camera with a fixed lens usually has a 'Compur' shutter in the lens system. The shutter must be released by means of a cable because pressing a button on a mounted camera is liable to produce vibration and blurr the picture during slower exposure times.

Vibration is not an important factor in ordinary microscope work, but becomes so as soon as a camera is introduced. The equipment must be placed on a steady bench free from shake caused by movement of the floor through traffic, human or otherwise, if serious work is to be undertaken. Unnoticed shake can cause serious lack of definition in the photograph. Fixed monocular microscope tubes are sometimes upright and sometimes sloping. The vertical version is much more suitable for gemmology because the stage is horizontal and refractive liquids in glass cells will stand on it. It is the most reliable for photography also, because it is steadier when the camera is attached. Some microscopes with horizontal stages have binocular eyepieces which are at an angle to the vertical body tube. If a camera is attached to one of these, it is wise to provide extra support for the camera because shake is likely to occur unless the exposure is very brief.

Some horizontal microscopes are used in gemmological work because they have the advantages of making the stone being examined more manoevrable in air and particularly in a refractive liquid. Special horizontal tube attachments for cameras are available but again, especially if the camera is heavy, there is a risk of camera shake during exposure because of the long overhang of the tube, which should be supported to avoid vibration.

Fig. 7.1. Horizontal microscope by System Eickhorst suitable for inclusion photography.

Choice of magnification depends on the gemmological needs of the subject and, as mentioned, is usually relatively low, around 30x. It presents no more problem than in any gemmological work. Low magnifications have a photographic advantage because the higher the magnification, the greater the risk of camera shake, as anyone who has used a telephoto lens will know. Depth of field is also reduced as magnification is increased.

A 35 mm camera with a through-lens viewfinder is almost essential because the operator sees exactly what he is photographing and is able to compose the picture to his needs. Another advantage is provided if the camera has a sensitive built-in exposure meter. Calculating exposures otherwise is not easy because of the difficulty of using a separate meter in the small space available and of calculating for reciprocity (longer exposures needing extra exposure over the meter reading). In any case, it is wise to bracket exposures to make extra exposures that are larger and shorter than those indicated and not just to rely upon meter reading or automatic exposure. The meter averages the light to calculate the exposure. The automatic exposure system of the camera should have aperture priority: in other words, it should change the exposure time to suit the subject being photographed.

In some cameras, the shutter speed has priority and the meter alters the aperture. This type will not give automatic exposure with a microscope because the aperture is fixed by the microscope and cannot be altered.

The adaptor attaching a camera to a microscope must have the correct fitting – screw or bayonet – for the make and model of camera. If it is part of the equipment made for the microscope, it will probably have a special fitting for that too. If not, it will probably have a clamp to hold it round the top of the microscope tube with a small matt black inner sleeve to prevent extraneous light from entering. Some vertical microscopes have an extra tube extension above the sloping monocular eyepiece or binocular eyepiece so that a camera can be fitted on top without having to remove the eyepiece. This applies also to the horizontal microscopes referred to earlier which have a horizontal tube fitting for the camera below the binocular eyepiece. When there is true binocular vision, i.e. with two objectives, the camera only photographs through one objective, so there is some parallax error, that is, the photograph is off-set slightly to one side or the other.

Monocular microscopes sometimes have alternative binocular fittings, which give a better view of the subject but not a stereoscopic one because there is still a single objective. If the two eyepieces are lined up so that their focii are identical, a camera can be attached to one and the other used to focus the inclusion. Unfortunately, however, this is sometimes impossible because there is insufficient room for seeing through the free eyepiece.

Advantage is taken of this arrangement in an ingenious system known as the Photoscope, devised by the Gemological Institute of America for use with their Gemolite binocular microscope. A Polaroid camera is mounted on one eyepiece and on the other, a special fibre optic cable which is linked to the lightmeter (to control exposure) in the camera. Thus if an inclusion can be located and focused through the eyepiece before the light cable is slipped on to it, exposure time is selected automatically when the exposure is made. The system is practical and easy to operate and produces pictures of acceptable quality for record purposes.

Some of the best and most consistent pictures and transparencies can be obtained with a microscope made for photography. One type is a vertical tube monocular model with a special film or plate holder or a Polaroid film holder on top as part of the microscope fittings. This may be larger than 35mm; others are a normal 35mm. A separate eyepiece projecting at an angle from the body of the tube is lined up exactly with the focal plane of the film or plate so that when the subject is focused by eye, it is in focus for taking the picture. One version by Nikon also has a binocular eyepiece that can be swung to one side when taking the photographs. The only problem is the length of exposure, but some models take care of this, too, by provision of a computerized meter which is linked into the optical system.

Focusing through a microscope eyepiece is easy, but when the camera cannot be aligned with the eyepiece, focusing has to be done on the camera viewfinder, if the camera is a through-lens reflex. This is not always easy, especially if the stone is dark and lighting level low. The subject itself can also cause difficulties. A well-defined inclusion such as a gas bubble or crystal can be focused upon, but a milky or wispy cloud often gives no hard outline. It will then be found that the ground surface of the screen in the camera is coarser than the feature on which one is trying to focus, which makes focusing impossible. Some cameras have interchangeable screens, of which one may be found better than another, but no screen is a satisfactory substitute for focusing through the microscope eyepiece.

Insufficient depth of focus can cause problems if an inclusion is large. With a camera, depth of focus can be increased by using a shorter focus lens, a more distant subject, or a smaller aperture. The same options are not open in photo-micrography. However, there is a way round the difficulty of photographing, say, a thick inclusion satisfactorily. This is to photograph it at a lower magnification, with all of it in focus, and then to enlarge the resulting photograph. This can also be done with a transparency, although with those for projection it is usually more convenient to find a compromise magnification to save copying in colour. It should be noted that although the enlargement is greater, the resolution (fineness of detail) remains the same. No kind of enlargement of the photograph will increase the detail in it, it will only make the detail larger.

Changing the aperture to achieve a similar result is a different matter. In the old system of using a complete camera, the iris could be closed down, which might work, but the only way with the camera body only is to use a separate iris below the objective. Such irises or diaphragms are available commercially. Experiments with a small hole in black matt card in front of the objective may be worth while.

Choice of film depends upon several factors, the most important of which is usually the film speed, expressed in ASA or DIN number. Because the lighting level is often low, a relatively fast film consistent with good quality is usually chosen, say of 200 or 400 ASA. Lighting conditions can vary widely, even when photographing the same inclusion from different angles. In addition, gems themselves vary considerably in translucency and colour and, while a medium or fast film will cope with many of them, it might produce better results to use, say, fine grain 64 ASA film for transparent stones; but even these in dark field illumination can have a very low light level. A particularly suitable black and white 35mm film is Ilford XPI because of its extremely wide exposure latitude and fine grain characteristics. Although normally rated at 400 ASA, it can be exposed over a range of 50 to 1600 ASA (18 to 33 DIN) and still produce fine grain negatives that give excellent prints. For best results, however, it must be processed soon after exposure.

When taking colour transparencies, the speed of the reversal film is even more important because of the narrow exposure latitude of colour stock. Fortunately, correct colour rendering is not always important for inclusions, and film speed can take priority because different makes of film have different colour biases.

Kodachrome, usually preferred for reproduction, is rated at 64 ASA, but Ectachrome is available in 200 and 400 ASA, which may persuade the photo-micrographer to overlook the bluish bias. The greens of stones such as emerald are difficult to render accurately although Fujichrome (100 ASA) is said by some photographers to be good in this range. Colour stock is made for daylight use or artificial light use. The daylight films are faster, generally, than those for artificial light, but can be corrected by use of an appropriate blue filter over the lens objective or the light source, with some reduction in speed but not as much as by using artificial light films. A photoflood bulb should give the correct colour temperature for the film but it is often difficult to obtain correct colour rendering in photo-micrography of gems although plenty of colour is often produced.

Every film has a brightness latitude – the range of contrast it is able to render – which varies with the type and speed of film. The range is much less than the eye's, so that what may seem acceptable to the eye might not be reproduced satisfactorily on film or slide. When illuminating an inclusion under magnification there are often extremes of contrast which may be useful for focusing, especially through the camera body, but are better reduced by lowering the light intensity before photography. On the other hand, some banding feature, for example, might present too low a contrast, which has to be increased by different lighting. In general, illuminating a highly reflective surface can be useful during examination, but will present difficulties in photography.

As lighting is as important to the microscopist as it is to the

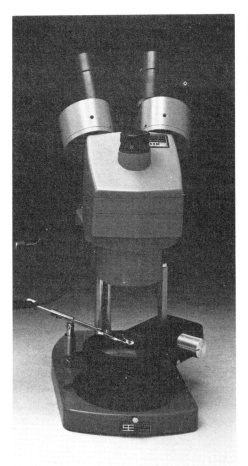

Fig. 7.2. The System Eickhorst microscope with dark field illumination, which aids inclusion photography.

photographer, he should already have a good idea of what is needed. Translucent or transparent gems can be lit by transmitted light from a lamp directed at a substage mirror and reflected up through a substage condenser and through a hole in the stage to the gem, which is fastened in a holder or is in a cell containing refractive liquid. If a specimen is opaque and a surface feature is being photographed, a beam of light should be shone on the surface from some point above it. A mineralogical microscope usually provides a beam of light through the body of the microscope; this avoids awkward reflections.

For substage illumination, it is useful to have a high intensity lamp in which the brightness and cone of light can be varied; however, its flexibility is limited considerably by the mirror and substage condenser. This is avoided by an intensity lamp with fibre glass optics. The flexible arm carrying the light beam can be adjusted to the most useful position for illumination without need for the mirror and condenser. Even more valuable is a version with several fibre glass channels of different diameters, so that a stone may be illuminated by 'spot' or 'floodlights' from two or more angles. A drilled pearl or bead can be illuminated from inside the hole.

Gemmologists commonly use dark field (also called dark ground) illumination by which the specimen is lit from all round the sides against a black background. The effect is to produce a bright inclusion against a dark ground. With dark field illumination there is only limited adjustment of the lighting.

The effect is produced by a bowl-shaped reflector, around or just below the specimen, illuminated by a small bulb in the base of the bowl. A black disk over the bulb prevents direct light from reaching the specimen and provides the dark background. The disk can usually be swung to one side to allow inspection by direct light. Some models have an iris near the top to alter the diameter of the rim of the ring of light. Lighting is varied by moving the stone, which is held in universally jointed tongs with small projecting handles, within the area of the dark field.

Another version of dark field illumination, by System Eickhorst, employs a small circular fluorescent light shielded at the top and mounted on a rack so that it can be raised or lowered to obtain the effect needed. The stone is held by universal tongs, described later, so that it can be moved to the most suitable position. An advantage of dark field illumination is that the interior features of even a highly refractive stone, like diamond and most of its simulants, are highlighted so that it is not necessary to place it in a refractive liquid.

The Diamond High Council in Antwerp has introduced a special diamond grading microscope, known as the DHC-microscope, which has a third version of dark ground illumination. Instead of a fluorescent tube, a light-emitting ring is used, fed by an optical glass fibre cable from a separate high intensity lamp. The light intensity from the ring can be varied by an electronic control. To hold the diamond being examined, the microscope incorporates a device called the Potterat-master, which employs three small wheels to provide completely universal movement of the stone.

When using understage lighting with an ordinary lamp or a high intensity lamp, the lighting has to be adjusted very carefully because it is responsible for many photographic failures. Good results can be obtained with simple equipment such as a diffused light from a frosted bulb or a photoflood bulb. The image of the bulb should be focused in the plane of the substage diaphragm with the iris partially closed. If the eyepiece is removed, the rear lens of the objective should be seen on looking down the body tube. In photography, the image of the bulb then becomes out of focus. It is important to exclude any light that spills from the lamp, whether an ordinary bulb or a high intensity lamp. The objective of the microscope will accept a cone of light up to an angle that is controlled by the substage condenser. Any light over this angle can result in loss of contrast and in glare. The light spill should be eliminated by using an iris or diaphragm on the lamp, or by making an internally blackened tube if there is no iris.

Heat is not normally a problem in photographing gem inclusions, but if it is necessary to reduce heat, a cell containing water can be placed between the bulb and microscope substage. Heat problems do not arise with a fibre optic high intensity lamp, nor with a fluorescent ring light and light spill problems do not arise with dark field illumination.

The standard universal holder for stones was developed by the Gemological Institute of American and a version is now fitted to most special microscopes for gemmological use. It comprises a specially shaped pair of spring loaded tweezers on a short arm with a grip on the other end. In the centre is a universal joint attached to the microscope stage. It has become an invaluable aid for handling polished stones unless very small, and also stones mounted in small items of jewellery.

It is easier to see a specimen with a high refractive index, particularly by transmitted light, if it is immersed in a refractive liquid. The liquid should be placed in a shallow dish, such as a Petri dish, over the hole in the microscope stage. The liquid can be of quite low refractive index

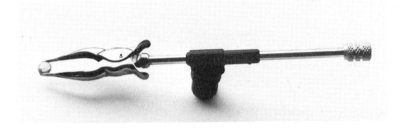

Fig. 7.3. Gem holder for inclusion photography.

compared with the stone because it acts as a refractive stage in the viewing. Monobromonaphthalene (RI 1.66) is often used, but a cheaper and better alternative is toluene, which has an RI of 1.49 and evaporates fairly quickly off jewellery or stones removed from it, whereas monobromonaphthalene has a rather persistent smell and has to be cleaned off. Although having an RI of only 1.36, surgical alcohol (ethyl alcohol), obtainable from a chemist, also has uses as an immersion liquid.

Universal tongs are not usually satisfactory for holding a stone in refractive liquid on a horizontal stage because of the angle, so some other means has to be adopted. One is to use a piece of plasticine or Blu-tac, small enough not to obscure the light, attached to the bottom or side of the cell. The stone can be stuck to this by part of the table or pavilion, or by the girdle. It is a tedious method if the position of a stone has to be changed a number of times.

The difficulty is overcome by a System Eickhorst horizontal microscope which includes a deep cubic transparent cell to hold the refractive liquid. The stone is held by a universal clamp pointing downwards into this and viewed through the side of the cell by the microscope. The cell can be raised or lowered and the position of the stone changed by the univeral holder. Illumination is provided by a high intensity lamp, with a dimmer and iris control to narrow the beam, mounted on an arm that can be swung around the cell.

A feature of some gemmological microscopes, including the horizontal one just mentioned and the Gemolite, is a zoom lens which will provide magnification from about 10x to 30x. It is a useful feature for photography because the right degree of enlargement or depth of focus can be obtained without an (or with only a small) adjustment in focusing, otherwise necessary when a lens turret is employed. Also, any enlargement is possible between the two extremes. A further benefit, when taking 35mm transparencies for slide projection, is the possibility of making the best composition within the frame. For most gemmological purposes, photo-micrography through a zoom lens is excellent, but for certain very high quality work or work where dimensions are important, the less complicated light path of a fixed focus objective will give better results.

Gemmological equipment is available from Gem Instruments Ltd, Saint Dunstan's House, Carey Lane, London, EC2V 8AB in the UK; the GIA Gem Instrument Division, 1660 Stewart Street, Santa Monica CA 90404 in the U.S.A. and from Eickhorst & Co., Hans-Henny-Jahnn Weg 21, D-2000, Hamburg 76, West Germany.

PART II

IDENTIFICATION

8. Diamond

Although diamond in sizes small enough for industrial use have long been synthesized this book will not deal with them; nor will it cover the many attempts to manufacture diamond (in all types of quality) which have already been adequately described elsewhere. For some years now, diamonds of gem quality have been grown, although their total number is still very small. The process, at the time of writing, is too expensive to allow for regular gem production. Production of gem quality synthetic diamonds was announced by the General Electric Company of America in 1970. Stones so far reported (I have seen a number of them) do not much exceed 1 ct in weight.

The apparatus uses a 'belt' (a tungsten carbide ring) of which the centre forms a cylinder with flared ends. Hydraulically-powered pistons drive into opposite ends of the cylinder. A pyrophyllite container is placed in the hole and filled with graphite or some other form of carbon, together with nickel or tantalum. Pyrophyllite has the special property of having a melting point which rises in relation to the rise in pressure; its melting point can be as high as 2720°C. Pressure is applied to the container by the pistons and heat is applied electrically. The pyrophyllite flows and allows the pistons to compress the metal. The pressures involved are in excess of 10,342,500kPa (1,500,000lbf/in² or 100,000 atmospheres) and temperatures over 2000°C with transient peaks in the region of 3000°C occur.

To manufacture diamonds of gem quality, a small mass of synthetic diamond crystals is placed in the centre of the cylinder and, on each side of the mass, is placed a bath of the catalyst (iron or nickel). This melts when the apparatus is working so that free carbon atoms traverse the bath. In the hotter central part of the cylinder, more carbon is dissolved so that free atoms tend to crystallize at the ends. Although graphite

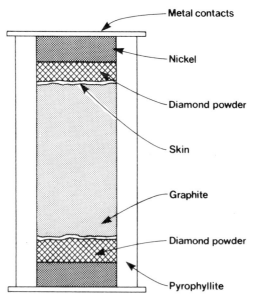

**Fig. 8.1. The pyrophyllite container used in the belt system for growing
synthetic diamond grit.**

would be expected, rather than diamond, the presence of diamond seed
crystals at each end enables the atoms to locate themselves until the
whole carbon supply is exhausted. The rate of growth is said to be about
2-3mg an hour. This rate is increased with an increase in the distance
between the centre and ends of the pressure chamber; a typical
difference would be 28°C to 33°C.

Temperatures are held for several days at a pressure of about
6,205,500kPa (900,000lbf/in^2 or 60,000 atmospheres). The best quality
crystals grow at the bottom of the molten bath; because any dirt and
smaller poorer crystals move upwards and out of the way. A variety of
impurities can be deliberately added to achieve special effects of colour,
electrical properties, hardness and so on.

The first crystals were white, canary yellow and pale blue: faceted
stones were cut from them. Apparently the polishers detected no
difference between them and natural crystals so far as the polishing
process went. Later on it was discovered that, with the absence of
nitrogen, crystals of a good white colour could be made; added boron
turned the crystals blue. The first synthetic gem diamond crystals were
truncated octahedra with modified cube faces (the white and blue
crystals); yellow crystals showed well-shaped octahedra with one point

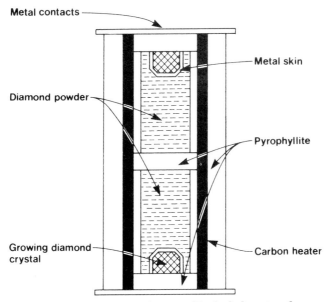

Fig. 8.2. The pyrophyllite container used in the belt system for growing synthetic diamond crystals.

diminished. Internal conditions ranged from clear (flawless grade) to imperfect. The latter showed round or plate-like nickel inclusions. All of them showed very fine dust-like white particles under high magnification. Blue stones also showed a whitish cross under high magnification; this may have been groups of the dust-like particles.

All the diamonds were semiconductors except the yellow stones; in nature only blue stones have this property. None of the stones show any absorption spectrum; again few natural diamonds are free from at least one absorption band. Later production by General Electric showed interesting properties with a cross-like extinction between crossed polars. Details of luminescence are given on page 88.

It was reported that diamonds were made in the USSR in 1967 (at the Kiev Synthetic Diamond Research Institute); these were cut in Belgium and found to be very hard. The colour of the rough was said to be straw and the clarity very good. After cutting the stones were said to be colourless. No further production has been seen and it may very well be that the costs were too great for further work to be done.

The General Electric Synthetic Diamond

There can be no doubt that, before very long, such stones will begin to appear on the market, even though costs at the time of writing are said to be too great to make the proposition economic.

The luminescence of natural diamond varies a great deal. Not all stones luminesce, nor does the luminescence confine itself to one colour. The General Electric stones do not fluoresce under long-wave ultra-violet light (about 10 per cent of natural diamonds do); however the General Electric stones do fluoresce under short-wave ultra-violet light, showing either a yellow or a green colour. Only natural blue diamonds show phosphorescence under short-wave ultra-violet. More important still, the General Electric stones phosphoresced after the radiation was switched off. The phosphorescence continued for some time, except in some dark blue stones. All General Electric stones apart from the yellows were semiconductors, whereas only natural blue diamonds have this property.

The absorption spectrum of natural stones, and of those that have been subjected to some kind of bombardment, varies; none of the G.E.C. stones, however, show any absorption bands. Only the finest white natural stones show no absorption bands.

The later General Electric production (an 0.28ct round brilliant examined by the Diamond Grading Laboratories in London) was characterized by numerous tiny inclusions under the table, which could be seen clearly under 10× magnification. A Maltese cross pattern could be seen through crossed polars and there was a slight yellowish-green fluorescence under short-wave ultra-violet light. This persisted for several minutes as a blue-green phosphorescence. A similar fluorescence colour was seen under long-wave, but no phosphorescence was seen after this type of irradiation. Under X-rays, there was a strong light blue fluorescence (similar to that shown by some natural diamonds) and this was followed by a light blue phosphorescence lasting several minutes. No absorption bands could be seen with the hand-held spectroscope.

Improving Natural Colour
Although man-made gem-quality diamonds are still a rarity, it is an unfortunate though interesting fact of gemmological life that many ways have been found to improve the colour of diamonds whose natural appearance left something to be desired. Anyone buying diamonds will know that it is common practice to sell yellowish stones in packets with a bluish lining. The reason for this is that yellow and blue are complementary colours and that a yellow object surrounded by blue will appear less yellow.

When indelible pencils were commoner than they seem to be now, they could be used to mark the back of the stone (it could be the culet, pavilion facets or the girdle). This had the effect of improving the overall colour and, in a closed setting, the stones could deceive the unwary. However the marking looked uneven and could be removed by water, general wear and tear, or by chemical action.

Coating

A later development of this process was to coat the stone or part of it with a bloom, similar to that used on camera lenses to reduce unwanted reflections. This bloom is not so easy to remove and acid is necessary to effect this. Later still, by the time of the Second World War, thinner coatings could be applied to diamonds. From about 1962, it was found possible to apply very thin coatings, the development of which had been given an impetus during work on the transistor. These coatings (applied by firms which advertised their services) were much harder to spot and it is said that the prices of coated stones could be increased by up to 25 per cent more than uncoated ones. Grading too is made virtually impossible. When the coating can be detected, it can be seen as a spotty or granular area near the girdle with pitting like that seen in some natural glasses.

Coatings are only a fraction of a wavelength in thickness. On one occasion, a stone known to be coated was submitted to the Gemological Institute of America. Boiling the whole piece (the stone was set in a ring) in sulphuric acid removed the coating and revealed that the stone had a yellowish body colour.

Although most coatings are applied to cut stones, it has been known for certain diamond crystals to be burnt so that they take on a whitish appearance through oxidation of the surface. A yellowish crystal may then appear to be a white one with a frosted surface. One cutter is reported to have purchased a whole parcel of these crystals which became yellow on cutting.

Irradiation

However coating diamonds is not largely practised since a number of better ways to improve colour are known; some kind of irradiation is the commonest method. Such treatment is relatively inexpensive and large numbers of stones can be treated at one time. So long as stones so treated are sold as such, there is no legal prohibition on their sale.

In 1904, Sir William Crookes experimented with radium as a medium for the colouration of diamond. The stones took on a green colour – one of them may still be seen on display at the British Museum (Natural History) in the Mineral Gallery – and can be distinguished by leaving the stone overnight on a photographic plate when an image of the stone will develop. This is called an autoradiograph. The colour is usually reminiscent of a tourmaline green; although some stones, perhaps overexposed to the radium, look darker than this. Stones so treated still show some radioactivity, although it would not be dangerous.

Diamonds placed in the patch of accelerated subatomic particles in a cyclotron may undergo a change of body colour. The particles may be alpha, neutrons or deuterons and the colours produced are green, bluish-green, yellowish, or brownish-green to black. After heat treatment (not at very high temperatures), yellow-orange-brown or brownish-pink stones may be obtained. Stones treated in a cyclotron may be distinguished by the presence of an umbrella-like mark encircling the culet. Zoning of colour may also be seen. The colour imparted by the bombardment is usually not very deep and can be polished away. This colour is believed to arise from colour centres, which are caused by the removal of electrons from their regular places in the crystal structure and their subsequent settling into vacant positions outside their normal sites. This movement causes an absorption of energy in the visible region and therefore the stone appears coloured.

Stones which have been subjected to neutron bombardment in an atomic pile, have a colour which penetrates throughout the stone and which is not removable by polishing. There is no sign of colour zoning or of the umbrella-like markings which characterize cyclotron-treated stones. When the stones emerge from the atomic pile, they are green and are usually then altered to yellowish-brown by heating. When this has been done, the stones usually show a sharp absorption band at 592nm. Other lines, at 498nm and 504nm, can also be seen. Those expecting (if not hoping) to see the band at 592nm should remember that it is much easier to see if the stone is placed near ice, because the band tends to disappear when the stone rises a little above room temperature. It should also be noted that British writers tend to quote the band at 592nm as 594nm. Anyone trying to see absorption bands in diamond ought also to remember that reflected light techniques with the spectroscope work much better than those which use transmitted light.

In natural diamonds of the 'Cape' series, there is a prominent line at 415.5nm, the forerunner of a set of bands extending into the near ultra-violet. There is also a band in the blue at 478nm, with others at 465, 451, 435, and 423nm. In practice the band at 478nm is easier to see than that at 415.5, because the further down the spectrum the harder it is to

Fig. 8.3. The 'umbrella' around the culet of a bombarded diamond.

make observations (this is because of the decreased efficiency of the eye in these regions). These bands are unchanged even after bombardment, so they obviously represent some quite stable condition in the crystal lattice. When the observer sees them in addition to bands at 594, 504, and 497nm therefore, it must be clear that the stone has been treated. It also shows that the original stone, however fine the colour (usually a bright yellow) now seen, was a common or garden 'Cape' stone with much lower value. It should be noted that some treated stones tend to give a greenish fluorescence under long-wave ultra-violet light. Another interesting point is that natural brown stones, which show the bands at 540nm and 497nm, show the former more prominently; in treated stones the reverse is the case.

Almost all green diamonds known to be of natural origin show characteristic trigon markings or 'naturals' on the girdle. No deep green

Fig. 8.4. Girdle 'natural' on a diamond.

diamonds can be looked at without suspicion, since all green stones seem to show these markings. Although green treated stones would normally show the bands at 498nm and 504nm, some treated stones have been reported in which the bands do not appear (nor do any others). More recently some yellow diamonds and some brown stones have been showing the band at 594nm; but with green stones, the band is either absent or very strong at 540nm. Therefore, if no green naturals are seen, the stone must have been treated.

Recently it has been reported that a yellow diamond has been seen without the line at 594nm, although the stone was known to have been irradiated. When the annealing temperature is raised to 1000°C (from the usual range of 700°-800°C), the line disappears. A further report (Read, 1979) shows that the absence of the line at 594nm does not prove that a yellow diamond is natural.

From time to time, irradiated diamonds of red, blue or purple shades may be encountered. Stones of Type Ia and Ib (with nitrogen in platelet and randomly dispersed form respectively) can be treated but not other types. Diamonds are transparent to X-rays while their imitators are opaque. Photography will help in this conclusive test.

The Classification of Natural Diamonds

To enquire further into the behaviour of treated diamonds, it may be found helpful if the accepted classification of natural diamond into 'types' is given. The original study in 1934 placed diamonds into two classes, one of which (Type I) absorbed ultra-violet light strongly after 330nm and showed absorption bands in the infra-red. Type II stones did not absorb ultra-violet rays until about 220nm and showed no infra-red spectrum. Later studies showed that almost all diamonds have some characteristics of both types, although in each stone the characteristics of one of the types will predominate. When a diamond shares the characteristics of both types, it will show anomalous birefringence (seen as a striped effect between crossed polars). The cause is believed to be distortion of the crystal lattice.

Treatment	Ia	Ib	IIa	IIb
neutron irradiation	green	green	green	green
neutron irradiation with heating	yellow-amber		brown	red-purple
electron irradiation	green	blue or greenish-blue	blue or greenish-blue	
electron irradiation with heating	yellow-amber	red-purple	brown	

Of the two original types, Type II is the rarer. It includes most, if not all, of the larger stones and is often found in shapeless lumps. Type I stones are less pure, but often occur as octahedra or other more obviously symmetrical forms. In 1959 nitrogen was discovered to be the impurity which caused the difference: Type I stones have nitrogen in them, Type II stones do not. Further work led to the proposal that, since Type II stones showed some differences in luminescence and photoconductivity within the class, they should be further divided into Types IIa and IIb. Type IIa stones would be those which have no nitrogen in the crystal lattice. They are rare and show a dark to light brown colour; stones such as the Cullinan (a Type IIa stone) are exceptions. Type IIb stones are thought to contain some boron; they are usually blue and have semiconducting properties. All natural blue stones are Type IIb (including the Hope diamond).

In 1965 Type I stones were also divided into two classes. Type Ia stones have nitrogen up to 0.1 per cent, forming platelets (the majority of natural stones); Type Ib stones also contain nitrogen but it is dispersed through the stone rather than segregated into platelets. Most synthetic stones are believed to be Type Ib, which otherwise is not a common classification. To complete the record, Type III stones (which do not concern this study) are those with a hexagonal rather than a cubic crystal structure. Some are found in meteorites and some are man-made. When nitrogen is concentrated into platelets (Type Ia stones), absorption takes place in the ultra-violet rather than in the visible. The result is to give the stones a white appearance and they are obviously the most desirable commercially.

High Pressure Annealing

Another colour enhancement technique is reported by Chrenko et al in 1979. They show that high temperature and high pressure annealing of diamond can be used to increase the mobility of the dispersed nitrogen in a Type Ib stone, thus allowing the nitrogen to accumulate in the platelets which are the main feature of Type Ia stones. The platelets only absorb light at the ultra-violet end of the spectrum, unlike the dispersed nitrogen which gives the yellow in Cape stones. General Electric workers report that, after heating for long periods (from hours to days), the deep yellow of a Type Ib had faded considerably. The General Electric team suggest that large yellow Ib stones could be turned into colourless ones by appropriate annealing at high pressure.

Instruments for testing Diamonds

In recent years, a number of instruments designed to detect diamond and its possible substitutes have been devised. Several of these make use of the surface tension of diamond which differs, due to the atomic structure, from that of its possible imitations. Based on the report by Nassau (1978), Shaw (1978) reports on an instrument devised by the Gemological Institute of America which spreads a liquid on diamonds and 'beads' it on other substances. The 'pen' is quite simple and contains a viscous liquid made up of a non-drying fluid. The pen forms part of a kit which also includes a polishing compound that ensures that the surface to be tested is clean and flat. Care should be taken with the softer imitations. The pen should be held vertically above the cleaned facet and drawn straight across it, pressing slightly. With a diamond, the line should appear straight, perhaps spreading a little. With other stones, the line will appear as a series of beads along the path taken by the pen.

The Gem Diamond Pen reviewed by Read (1979) is like a draughtsman's pen with a similar dispensing head and ink container. The ink itself is a non-drying viscous fluid containing inert chemicals and a blue dye to aid visibility. The pen comes in a kit which includes a pair of stainless steel locking tongs, some polishing powder, a felt cleaning pad and a supply of the ink. The stone is cleaned by placing powder on the pad and rubbing the table facet on it. Excess powder should be removed and then the pen is used to see whether a clear line of ink can be drawn across the surface. If this can be done the stone is a diamond since with imitations the ink will bead. It is vital that the surface be adequately cleaned and that the ink in the pen flows freely. Paste, quartz and spinel all allow a line to be drawn with greater ease than with diamond.

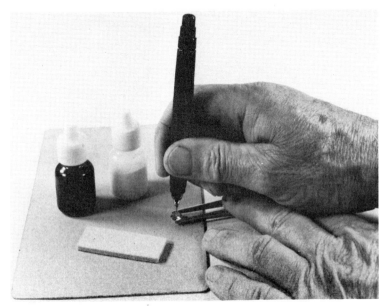

Fig. 8.5. The Gem Diamond Pen in use.

THE 'GEMPRINT'
Although a number of workers have suggested that individual diamonds might be identified by comparing the reflection patterns of light passed through the stone, the systems have never really been taken up by the diamond trade. One system suggested recently (Miles, 1978) was to use laser light (the laser had already been used to remove some types of inclusion from diamond). One invention, called the 'Gemprint', was devised by Isaac and presented to the Weizman Institute of Science in Israel. It consists of a recording camera and a low-powered laser light source; this is usually a helium neon gas source, less dangerous than some other types. The laser beam passes through a pinhole opening in a Polaroid film, through a lens and thence into the diamond. The beam

strikes the table facet which is at right angles to it and is then reflected directly back to the film. There it is recorded as the strongest reflection point in the pattern. The laser light, which is reflected from the back facets, is recorded as weaker points. For each stone the pattern is unique and depends upon the cutting and the nature of the stone.

The report by Miles includes a table in which diamond shows a random pattern of reflections, as does zircon (the most like diamond in this respect), synthetic rutile, YAG and zirconia. Synthetic corundum shows a semi-concentric pattern with brush-like structures; synthetic spinel shows a semi-concentric pattern; strontium titanate shows a modified cut corner ribbon or cube-like pattern; and a doublet, with strontium titanate pavilion and a synthetic spinel crown, shows a spoked wheel pattern. The images shown by these stones vary much more than the patterns; diamond shows a sharp star-like image; the star-like image produced by zircon is doubled; synthetic corundum shows an image resembling fish vertebrae; synthetic spinel shows a rather fuzzy fingerprint-like image. The image shown by synthetic

Fig. 8.6. The Gemprint of a strontium titanate stone.

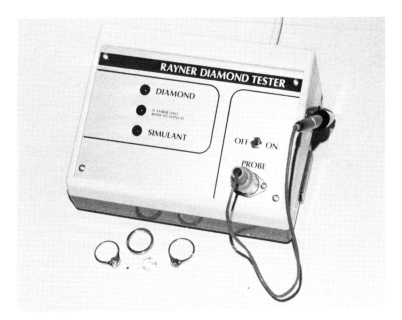

Fig. 8.7. The Rayner Diamond Tester which uses a thermal probe to identify diamonds.

rutile resembles that shown by zircon but is larger and less distinct; while strontium titanate gives random images like horsetails. YAG gives pulled-out stars and triangles; GGG also gives triangles with some patchy images. Zirconia gives an image like the tail of a comet with vague fingerprints; the doublet described above gives images at random resembling knife-slashes.

It should be possible with this method to show whether or not a stone has been recut. Another use would be to check the stones in a piece of jewellery after it has been sent for repair so that any substitution can be detected. Prints could be used to supplement laboratory reports for insurance purposes and the dealer could record the prints of all stones in his stock.

THE DISTILLED WATER TEST
It has been suggested that the angle made by a drop of water on the surface of a stone could be utilized in testing that stone. Diamond, being notably averse to being 'wetted', can be distinguished from its imitators by this means. However the test needs to be carefully carried out. A

report by Nassau (1978) shows that distilled water can be used as a contact medium. The stone needs to be clean and dry and given a rinse in trichlorethane which should then be shaken off or blotted. It should then be placed so that the table is exactly horizontal; then a drop of distilled water placed on the flat surface. The drop must be round and not touch the edges of the facet; lastly the angle between the drop and the surface is measured. This should be done as soon as possible after the drop has formed so that evaporation or contamination has little time to take place. Grease or other contaminant may cause too high a reading to be given; contaminated water may cause too low a reading. Stones should be checked also to ensure that they are not composites.

The angle in the report quoted was measured with the aid of a telescope with cross-hairs; one of these was fixed horizontally, while the other was attached to a calibrated rotating scale. A table gives the contact angle of a number of natural and synthetic stones.

It is interesting to note that irradiated stones gave inconsistent readings. It is thought possible that a polymeric layer is formed on the surface on irradiation and that this is not thick enough to affect the refractive index. Such a layer could be removed by light repolishing and the normal contact angles should then be obtained.

THE THERMAL DIAMOND PROBE
Diamond can be tested by using a thermal diamond probe. The tester applies the point of the probe to the stone and observes the deflection of a meter needle or a flashing light. The probe measures the thermal conductivity of the stone. So far as is known, readings are unaffected by surface coatings. It is interesting that breathing on a diamond can be helpful as the moisture from the breath will evaporate more quickly (because of the greater thermal conductivity) from diamond than from imitations. Ceres (U.S.) and Rayner (U.K.) make such probes.

Reports on Individual Cases from the Literature
A brown diamond had been bombarded and annealed; it showed the absorption band at 592nm with an additional band at 575nm. There was an orange fluorescence under long-wave ultra-violet light. An irradiated pink diamond is reported as turning to brown after irradiation with X-rays. This is thought to be caused by continued phosphorescence. The original colour returned after gentle heating. Brownish-pink stones, known to have been irradiated, showed absorption bands at 637nm with a pair at 620 and 610nm in conjunction with the band at 592nm.

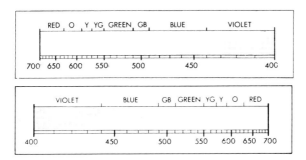

Treated pink diamond spectrum in UK (top) and US readings.

A German report stated that X-rays do not affect colourless stones but may improve the colour of yellows; green Brazilian stones may become bluish or a purer green. Brown stones may turn violet.

A report in *Gems and Gemology* stated that some irradiated stones which fluoresced before irradiation, were inert after it. A stone accidentally dropped into the cyclotron and left there for two weeks, was found to have turned a ruby red; it altered to brown on the cessation of radioactivity. Four stones subjected to alpha-particle bombardment for five minutes with a beam current of 2 microamperes and 40,000,000 volt energy, showed an increase in the whiteness of two of the stones; the other two turned brown. On increasing the current to 15 microamps and with a four minute exposure time, another stone became tourmaline green. Ten stones bombarded with deuterons from 10 to 15 microamps at 20,000,000 volts gave colours ranging from olive green, tourmaline green, bluish zircon green, and light to dark brown. The colours remained after recutting.

Diamonds exposed to electrons from a Van de Graaff generator sometimes turn pink; a blue colour occurs at energies around 500kV and blue-green to green at about 1.2MeV. Neutron bombardment gives a greyer colour though, on heating, a new range of colours may be obtained. These include light yellow to deep reddish gold (this can be obtained by heating from about 1600° to 1900°C for about five minutes). Excessive irradiation gives a very dark green or black.

A summary of reports on some coloured diamonds was given in the *Journal of Gemmology* (July 1969). A bright yellow jonquil-coloured stone was inert to radiations, non-phosphorescent, opaque to 253.7 and gave absorption bands at 493, 451 and 430nm. Carbonized inclusions were found in the stone, which proved to be natural.

A straw-yellow diamond was a weak bluish-green under X-rays but showed no phosphorescence; it showed a medium green under long-wave ultra-violet light. The absorption bands were at 594, 504, 498, 484, 478, 465, 415.5 and 401.5nm. This was a treated stone with a 'Cape' spectrum.

A straw-yellow stone with medium intensity of colour was inert to X-rays and showed a weak yellow under long-wave ultra-violet light. Absorption bands were seen at 594, 504, etc, as with the previous stone. Colour was induced by irradiation.

A deep orange stone showed no luminescence and was opaque to short-wave ultra-violet light. Absorption bands were noted at 594, 568, 504, 498, 500, 620-590nm. The stone passed some orange when viewed in light which had passed through a copper sulphate solution. The colour was induced.

A steel-blue stone was weakly fluorescent under X-rays but showed no luminescence under ultra-violet light, being opaque to short-wave rays. Absorption bands seen at 478, 415 and 400nm showed that the stone's colour was induced.

A pale green stone was bluish-green under X-rays, and gave a bluish luminescence under long-wave ultra-violet light. It was opaque to short-wave and showed absorption bands at 478, 465, 451, and 415nm. The colour was induced.

A dark moss-green stone had a weak fluorescence under X-rays and a faint yellow under long-wave ultra-violet light. There was a yellow luminescence and phosphorescence under short wave. Absorption bands appeared at 700, 670, 620, 504, 498, 482, 478, 465 and 420nm. The line at 504nm was strong.

A blue treated diamond examined by the G.I.A. showed no fluorescence but did show an emission band at about 504nm. It is possible that pink diamonds fluorescing orange to yellow-orange were faint pink before treatment with an orange fluorescence. Many of these stones show a band at about 575nm. A blue-green stone, treated, was tested by the G.I.A.; it had no fluorescence but showed a strong emission band at about 505nm.

A red-brown stone, known to be treated, showed a band at 640nm but not one at 592nm. The use of cryogenic techniques with a recording spectrophotometer helps to show the nature of coloured diamonds; it also alleviated some of the anxiety felt when it was announced that re-heated yellow treated diamonds lost the band at 592nm. The band at 640nm is one of a series running into the infra-red.

Two radium-treated diamonds are described in Gems and Gemology (Winter 1978/79). The stones were dark tourmaline-green in colour and no internal imperfections were noticed under 10 × magnification. There was a bluish-white fluorescence under X-rays, but none under ultra-

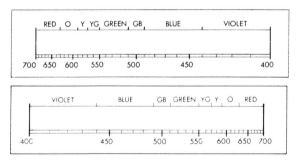

Treated yellow diamond spectrum in UK (top) and US readings.

violet light. No trace of the 'umbrella' marking around the culet could be seen, as is common with stones treated in a cyclotron. No bands characteristic of treated diamonds could be seen in the absorption spectrum. Each diamond was then placed in contact with unexposed film and, after an exposure of 72 hours, autoradiographs were produced. There was no sign of the brown, disc-like spots often seen in radium-treated stones, although the autoradiographs proved that they were in fact treated in this way.

A radium-treated diamond was examined by the G.I.A. New York Laboratory and reported in 1972. It was yellow-green and weighed about 6ct. Under magnification, dark spots on the surface could be seen which indicated treatment with radium bromide. Placed in a film for 15 minutes in the dark, an autoradiograph was obtained.

Nu-Age Products, an American firm, offers a diamond treatment service; light zircon-like blue is one of the colours seen.

A diamond with an orange-brown colour was shown to the Los Angeles Laboratory of the G.I.A. in 1980. The orange-brown colour was common in the early days of cyclotron-treated diamond (in which the induced colour was surface only) but is less commonly observed today when stones treated in atomic piles and with colour throughout are more usual. This stone did not show the absorption band at 592nm, probably because the colour was skin deep only. However intense colour was observed along the edges of the facets on the crown and around the culet.

An interesting accident probably befell a dark blue-green diamond which appeared watery from the side, suggesting surface treatment. There was no 'umbrella' around the culet nor were there any dark zones on the star facets or table. It was decided (by the two G.I.A. laboratories) that the stone probably fell from its holder during treatment. When viewed through the upper girdle and bezel facets, a grid-like penetration zone could be seen on one side of the pavilion only.

9. The Simulants of Diamond

Glass is the oldest and probably still the commonest simulant of diamond; it is covered in Chapter 21. This chapter deals with other simulants – synthetic rutile and strontium titanate – and with the high-temperature oxides: YAG, GGG and cubic zirconia. At the time of writing, the first two are still frequently seen. Strontium titanate melée and doublets were still being made in 1979. YAG lacked something and was quickly superseded by cubic zirconia.

Rutile

Rutile was synthesized by the Linde Air Products Company and the Titanium Division of the National Lead Company, as described in a report by Liddicoat which appeared in 1947. The refractive index was 2.62 and 2.90 for the ordinary and extraordinary rays respectively; the hardness was 6-6½ and the specific gravity 4.3. The main feature distinguishing rutile from diamond is the very high birefringence of 0.28. The dispersion, of about 0.3, is so much greater than that of diamond that there can be little possibility of confusion. Red, blue and brown stones have been produced; the yellowish colour of the stone most frequently offered as diamond is due to a strong absorption band in the deep violet. Some synthetic blue rutile is electroconductive and is thus so far similar to blue diamond. The effect appears to be stronger in a direction parallel to the optic axis.

Rutile is grown by the flame-fusion method, originally using an oxy-acetylene torch with two nozzles inclined at 45 degrees. This had the disadvantage that it helped the loss of oxygen, a serious problem to the crystal grower. When oxygen is lost, the ratio of titanium to oxygen alters from the required 2:1 to about 2.02:1. Oxygen-deficient material is very dark blue or black so that, to use the stones, they need to be heated

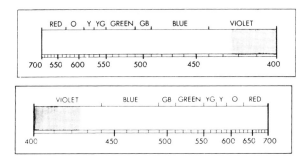

Synthetic rutile spectrum in UK (top) and US readings.

in an oxydizing atmosphere for a few hours at 800°C to 1200°C. The use of a three-tube burner helps to reduce oxygen loss. As with ruby, rutile powder is carried down the oxygen stream in the central tube, but a separate flow of oxygen is maintained around the tube and helps to prevent the reducing of the material from the hydrogen in the intermediate tube. Although it should be possible to grow large crystals of rutile by the flux-melt process (small ones are regularly obtained) it is difficult to overcome the preferred needle-like habit.

Feed powder is prepared from ammonium titanium sulphate. Addition of niobium pentoxide Nb_2O_3 in a concentration of 0.05 per cent, of Ga_2O_3 or Al_2O_3 between 0.005 per cent and 0.05 per cent gives a more nearly colourless crystal. Cr_2O_3 or V_2O_5 in a concentration of about 1 per cent gives red. Low concentrations of cobalt oxide (CoO) give yellow, but with an increase in concentration (to about 0.1 per cent), an amber colour is obtained which becomes reddish with further increase. Yellow can also be obtained from NiO at low concentrations; again an increase in NiO gives amber and deep red. Molybdenum, tungsten, uranium or beryllium oxides give bluish-white when the concentration is below 0.005 per cent. Light or dark blue stones can be obtained by increasing these dopants up to about 1 per cent and blue-black stones are obtained with higher concentrations. Addition of MgO in a concentration of 0.2 to 1 per cent gave a star stone (made by the National Lead Company). The oxidized boule needs to be heated to between 1100° and 1500°C to precipitate the MgO.

Strontium Titanate

Strontium titanate, a man-made analogue of the natural mineral perovskite ($CaTiO_3$), has the composition $SrTiO_3$. It was made in the 1950s by the National Lead Company and, at one time, was given the trade name 'Starilan'. 'Fabulite' has also been used as a name. The hardness is near 6, while the Knoop microindenter hardness is 5.95. The dispersion is about four times that of diamond. The refractive index is 2.409, and the specific gravity is 5.13. The melting point is 2080°C; it is opaque to X-rays and there is no fluorescence. It can be marked with the point of a needle and sometimes shows ladder-like inclusions. Photographs by Tillander (1960) show faint but distinct scratches on every face (dark-field illumination will show this clearly).

Strontium titanate has been grown by the flux-melt method; the fluxes used were potassium fluoride mixed with lithium fluoride. Alternatively strontium borate mixed with lithium borate has been used. There is some slight birefringence (due to strain) in the Verneuil-grown material; but this does not occur in the flux-melt grown stones. It is interesting to note that strontium titanate behaves in an unusual way (structure alteration) at low temperatures so that work on it is still proceeding.

It is grown by the flame-fusion method using a three-tube burner as for rutile. Melting point is 2050°C and the flame is kept at 2110° to 2130°C. Powder used is obtained by heating strontium titanate oxalate with strontium chloride at 500°C. Crystals of up to 20g (0.7oz) have been grown. Although black on leaving the furnace, they are made colourless by heating in an oxidizing atmosphere for 12 to 180 hours at temperatures between 1700°C and 650°C. Addition of strontium oxide helps the formation of perfectly colourless crystals. High quality crystals have been grown by adding 3.8 per cent excess of strontium carbonate to the starting powder and using a growth rate of 20-26mm (0.8-1.02 in) per hour.

Colours of strontium titanate vary with the addition of certain elements, although coloured stones are rarely seen. Chromium gives yellow to dark brown if 0.001 to 0.005 per cent is added; dark-red to red-brown to black if the amount is increased to 0.005-0.02 per cent. More gives black. From 0.005-0.02 per cent of cobalt gives a yellow to topaz colour; this increases to reddish if the amount of additive is increased to 0.02-0.1 per cent. More than this gives black. From 0.005-0.02 per cent of iron gives yellowish brown and the same amount of manganese gives yellow which alters to orange as the amount is increased. Similar amounts of nickel give yellow to topaz colours and smaller amounts of vanadium give a darker yellow.

BARIUM TITANATE

Although barium titanate could be used as a gem having, like its strontium analogue, a high dispersion (though it is soft), the preparation

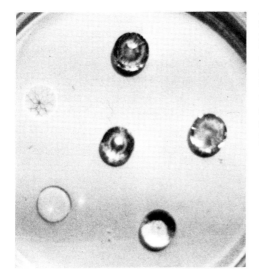

Fig. 9.1. The refractive liquid test showing how the diamond in the centre compares with some imitations. Clockwise from the top: strontium titanate, synthetic rutile, zircon, synthetic white spinel, paste.

of single crystals is more difficult than with strontium titanate. Barium titanate decomposes on melting and crystals can only be pulled from a melt which contains an excess of titanium oxide. Such a difference in composition between crystal and melt slows down the rate of growth and makes production less economic.

Lithium Niobate

Lithium niobate has an interesting and important combination of piezoelectric and optical properties which have made it of some importance to the industrial and research world over the past few years. Single crystals were reported by Ballman (1965); growth was by the Czochralski crystal-pulling technique. First reports of the material came in 1928, but only with the advent of the Czochralski material did its gem significance appear. Lithium niobate does not exist in nature. At the time of writing, work on surface acoustic waves is being carried out; and lithium niobate is important for these studies because it is second only to quartz as a single crystalline piezoelectric.

From the gemmological aspect, the constants of lithium niobate are specific gravity 4.64; refractive indices 2.30 and 2.21; birefringence 0.090; hardness just over 5 and dispersion about 0.120. The author's collection contains material in several colours; a fine stone with polished girdle (lapidary, George Harrison Jones) shows great brilliance and attractive dispersion. As a fairly short-lived diamond simulant, the material had the trade-name 'Linobate'.

The first crystals, produced in the 1960s, came out brown from the growth apparatus but could be bleached by annealing in oxygen. The brown colour was due to some form of impurity – a case which can be paralleled with other materials. Water-clear crystals with gem application are grown from a starting powder of Li_2o_5 and Nb_2O_5. It is relatively easy to grow the crystals, which have a melting point of about 1265°C: a number of heating methods can be used. The crucible material is platinum and there is no need for special atmospheric control. It is rather more difficult to grow crystals with a diameter of considerable size, although diameters of 50mm (1.97 in) or more are regularly made. Cracking of lithium niobate crystals presents a major problem and heat shields of considerable efficiency are essential. The shape of the furnace (tubular is preferred) is critical in this respect.

Doping of lithium niobate is regularly carried out. Rare earths are the commonest dopants, neodymium giving the typical lilac colour with the characteristic absorption spectrum. Lithium niobate crystals have been coloured by Cr_2O_3 to give green; and by Fe_2O_3 and $FeTiO_3$ to give red. Co_2O_3 and $CoTiO_3$ are used to give blue; while MnO_2 and $MnTiO_3$ give yellow. NiO and $NiTiO_3$ are also used to give yellow.

Lithium niobate shows a very strong photorefractive effect. Roughly this means that the refractive index changes with a change in the nature of the incident light. In this case, the phenomenon can be used for the storage of information within the crystal. The effect can be enhanced and made more complex by the addition of various dopants to the crystal. It is interesting to note, however, that lithium niobate doped with Nd could only be used for laser action for a very short time, because damage was caused to the crystal which then needed to be annealed at 200°C. Such disadvantages illustrate why many crystals with an initial appeal as gemstones do not really get to the commercial market; it is because their industrial potential has been found to be so limited.

Yttrium Aluminium Garnet (YAG)

YAG has already been mentioned in the context of crystal growth (Chapter 4). Although referred to as a 'garnet', it resembles that family only in structure, as, having no silica, it differs in composition. YAG is a member of a group of substances, none having a natural counterpart, which are grown without too much difficulty, because the absence of silica prevents the too-easy formation of glass.

YAG can be doped with Mn to give red; with Ti to give yellow; with Cr for green; and with Co for blue. The commonest rare-earth doping is with Nd, which gives the characteristic lilac colour, and also the two

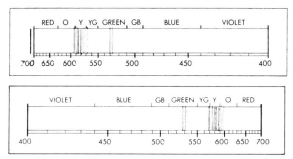

YAG spectrum when doped with a rare earth in UK (top) and US readings.

groups of fine lines in the absorption spectrum. YAG has a hardness of 8 or just over; a specific gravity of 4.55; a refractive index of 1.83; and dispersion of 0.028 (compared to the 0.044 of diamond). The chemical composition is $Y_3Al_5O_{12}$.

YAG is isotropic but somehow the stones never overcome a certain lifelessness, even when compared to the analagous material GGG which is less hard. There is no cleavage and only a slight brittleness. Elongated drops of the melt will identify pulled crystals and those grown by the flux-melt technique will show feather-like structures made up of drops from the melt.

Gadolinium Gallium Garnet (GGG)

These are some of the most perfect single crystals being produced at the time of writing. They are used for magnetic bubble devices which have rigid requirements of perfection because they operate by the movements of magnetic domains through a thin epitaxial magnetic garnet layer grown on a non-magnetic, rare-earth, single crystal, garnet substrate. The crystals must be virtually free from defect with a lattice parameter closely matching that of the magnetic film. GGG is made commercially with diameters up to 75mm (2.95 in). It has also some application in the field of lasers, being a possible laser host as a substitute for yttrium aluminium garnet (YAG). The chemical composition is $Gd_3Ga_5O_{12}$.

GGG has been grown by a variety of techniques, although most crystals are grown by the Czochralski method. This method allows for quick growth with a high degree of perfection. The desired purity of the starting material needs to be at least 99.99 per cent. The growth atmosphere most commonly used is 2 per cent O_2, though some growers have used N_2. The rotation rates vary according to crystal size with a rate of up to 50rpm for 25mm (1 in) diameter crystals. A pulling rate of 15mm (0.6 in) per hour will give crystals of 25mm (1 in) diameter without observable defects. The crucible material has to be iridium, as the melting point of GGG is 1750°C. It is the reaction of the garnet material with the crucible material which is the source of most of the defects seen in the finished product. The crucible is heated by induction by radio frequency and an automatic diameter control is normally employed. When sufficient growth is achieved, the crystal is removed from the melt by rapidly increasing the pull rate and then the furnace is slowly cooled to room temperature over several hours. Boules rejected are remelted and used to grow new crystals.

The commonest inclusion in GGG comes from the crucible material and consists of triangular and hexagonal platelets of iridium, lying in the growth plane. It is thought that a reaction occurs between gallium and the crucible wall. The incidence of this type of inclusion can be controlled by careful adjustment of the melt geometry and the thermal gradients.

Although GGG crystals are grown to be free from colour, a number of conditions cause unwanted tints. These include a deep burgundy colour which is the result of impurities in gadolinium oxide; europium and terbium are also common colour-causing impurities which do not degrade the quality of the GGG for substrate use. As a laser host, colour is more definitely undesirable, however; and colour from centres formed by exposure to ultra-violet light are sufficient to make a crystal unusable for this purpose.

The author has several coloured GGG crystal groups in his collection; some of a very attractive dark red, are thought to be coloured by manganese; the blue ones are probably coloured by cobalt.

The author (O'Donoghue, 1973) was the first to describe crystals of the new material in gemmological terms and to note the various types of luminescence observed. A truncated cone of colourless or faint straw-coloured GGG showed a fluorescence spectrum under both short-wave ultra-violet light and under X-rays. A strong absorption in the red is accompanied by an emission line; the sodium doublet shows an emission and there are two distinct bands in the green and two in the blue. Some of the effects observed may have been due to the reflection of some of the mercury emission of the lamp by the stone, except that the stone examined was rough-surfaced. Under long-wave ultra-violet light, the stone gave a very pale straw colour and under short-wave a peach colour. Under X-rays, there was a lilac fluorescence similar to that sometimes displayed by YAG. No phosphorescence was observed. Various figures are given in the literature for the specific gravity and refractive index of GGG; average constants are a specific gravity of 7.05;

and the refractive index is 7 (isotropic). The hardness is about $6\frac{1}{2}$; the dispersion 0.038. This is quite close to that of diamond at 0.044. Most stones are very clean, although small bubbles were observed in at least one cut stone (Webster, 1974).

Cubic Zirconia

Zirconium oxide (zirconia, ZrO_2) is probably the best simulant of diamond yet to appear on the market, at least at the time of writing. Although ZrO_2 has been found in nature, it appears there as the monoclinic baddeleyite; it has also been grown in the cubic form for ceramic use and even single crystal forms have been known for some years.

The cubic form of zirconia, which is the material used as a diamond imitation, is not stable and needs to be 'supported' by a stabilizing agent; this may be either calcium or yttrium. In its pure form zirconia is stable only at high temperatures; below about 2300°C it changes to the tetragonal form and below about 1100°C into the monoclinic form (these two forms are polymorphs of ZrO_2). Stabilization by the addition of small amounts of metallic oxide (in practice about 15 mol. per cent CaO, MgO, Y_2O_3 or Yb_2O_3) causes the crystal to remain cubic and of one phase only. Zirconia has been grown using fluxes of borates ($Na_2B_4O_7$), carbonates (Na_2CO_3), phosphates, fluorides (PbF_2) etc. Usually, however, the monoclinic or tetragonal form results from flux growth.

Stones stabilized with yttrium differ in some respects from those stabilized with calcium and the table (page 110) from a recent study of zirconia (Bosshart, 1978) shows them in a convenient form. It will be seen from the table that in the calcium-stabilized stone, no inclusions in cuttable material can be seen; in the stones stabilized by yttrium, there are some noticeable inclusions. Natural looking 'feathers' can also sometimes be seen in zirconia.

Some time after the first introduction of zirconia to the gem market the author was able to examine some coloured varieties (O'Donoghue, 1978). One was a darkish lilac, the other a brownish-pink. The lilac stone showed a heavy didymium spectrum and this showed at once that it could not be a natural stone. The other stone showed no absorption in the visible region. A further stone, from the U.S.S.R., is a magnificent padparadschah orange. For specific gravity and other constants of cubic zirconia see the table below.

Tests for distinguishing diamond from cubic zirconia include: specific gravity if the stone is unmounted and the recently developed 'ink tests'. On the surface of a diamond, the ink forms a spot with smooth edges; on cubic zirconia and other man-made imitations the ink forms

Identification of Cubic Stabilized Zirconia

Properties	(Zr, Y) O$_{2-x}$		(Zr, Ca) O$_{2-x}$ (ref. 8)
Cut	round brilliant 32/24		brilliant 32/24(?)
Weight	3.86 ct	1.38 ct	—
Proportions			
Table	58%	60%	
Crown	15½%	14%	
Girdle	6%	6%	
Pavilion	45½%	47%	
Symmetry	good	good	
Polish	medium	insufficient	
Colour	weak yellowish	very weak pink (almost colourless)	colourless; according to pigmentation also various hues and degrees of saturation
Refractive Index n$_D$	2.1712 (±0.005)	2.1651 (±0.005)	2.1775 (±0.005)
Dispersion n$_F$—n$_C$	0.0338	0.0336	(0.0376)
n$_G$—N$_B$	0.0591	0.0587	0.0653
Reflectivity R$_{meas}$	13.0% (polish)	12.3% (polish)	—
R$_{calc}$	13.6%	13.5%	13.7%
Fluorescence			
UV-A	none	vw, reddish	none
UV-C	vw, greenish-yellow	w, greenish-yellow	distinct, yellow
Absorption total in the VIS	below 370 nm	below 340 nm	below 310 resp. 360 nm
	no lines or bands		no lines or bands
Inclusions	parallel rows of small, semitransparent, isometric crystal-like cavities extending into hazy stripes of tiny particles	none	in the experimental stage of growth small gas bubbles and individual large ones; in the new cuttable material no inclusions remain
Spec. Gravity (4°C)	5.950 (±0.005)	5.947 (±0.005)	5.65 (5.60 to 5.71)
Cleavage	none	none	none
Vickers Hardness V (500 g test load)	1250 to 1570 kg/mm² (indentation not oriented)		1407 and 1437 kg/mm² (oriented?)
Mohs Hardness			
M$_{dot}$	approximately 8¼		8½
M$_{calc}$	approximately 8.2 (8.0 to 8.5)		(8.2 and 8.3)
Brittleness	more brittle than synthetic corundum but less than Y$_3$Al$_5$O$_{12}$		analogous
External characteristics	roundish facet edges, percussion marks, small chips		analogous
Magnetism	indifferent (diamagnetic?)		
Conductivity	electrical insulator (room temp.)		

beads and withdraws from the surface rather in the way that water does on a greasy surface. The spot should be examined as soon as the ink is applied. Recently some zirconia has been reported as having been

THE SIMULANTS OF DIAMOND

coated by diamond so as to make this test less effective; however light rubbing with a mild abrasive will remove this coating.

The thermal conductivity of diamond is much greater than that of any of its imitations and the Ceres diamond probe behaves very effectively here. Reflectivity meters are probably most used.

Another simple test for zirconia, if a binocular stereoscopic microscope such as the 'Gemolite' is available, is to place the stone table down over the iris diaphragm when the pavilion facets will be seen to show monochromatic colours, red and orange to yellow. A similar effect can be seen at the shorter end of the spectrum. This strong display of colour by pavilion facets has not been reported for diamond.

It is possible that doublets with a thin slice of diamond on the top of a base of zirconia could be found on the market in the future. In such cases, the tester will have to look for as many features of one or other stone as possible.

An imitation· of diamond, manufactured from a polycrystalline ceramic, has been given the trade name 'Yttralox'. It consists of Y_2O_3, stabilized to a cubic form by the addition of thorium oxide. This is then followed by hot pressing. The hardness is 6.5; the refractive index is 1.92; and the dispersion is 0.039 (diamond is 0.044).

10. Corundum

Since almost all corundum manufactured for gem use is made by the flame-fusion process, considerable details have already been given in Chapter 3 which deals with that method. Rubies may show dichroism through the table facet since there is no reason to orient the stone in any particular way. The greatest possible yield from the rough is required so that almost all table facets will lie parallel to the optic axis. Curved growth lines and gas bubbles will be seen in the ruby, blue sapphire and particularly well in the 'alexandrite' imitation. The last is coloured by vanadium and gives its true nature away by a prominent band at 475nm. It is sometimes not very easy to see curved growth lines, especially when the stone is small. On these occasions a photograph taken while the stone is immersed in a liquid of lower refractive index (for example monobromonaphthalene, R.I. 1.6) will show up the lines very well. It should always be remembered that the bands in natural corundum are straight and angular, never curved.

From time to time small cabochon rubies are encountered which resemble a button; these can show a fan-like structure quite unlike the curved lines seen in the commoner synthetics. These stones appear to be products of either an early development of the Verneuil process or of a process similar to it. When in their rough form, a stalk gives their true nature away.

A quick examination with a 10× lens will often show markings near the junction of facets. These markings, resembling wave patterns on the sand, are called 'fire marks' or 'chatter marks' and are the result of hasty polishing. More care would be taken with fine natural stones. An examination of the bubbles in a Verneuil-grown ruby will show that, while the smaller isolated ones are spherical, those ranged in groups tend to show distortion. They have a liking for their own kind and so form 'clots'. Sometimes they show hose-like shapes, while some others resemble flaming grenades or bombs – in a group of such bubbles, all the

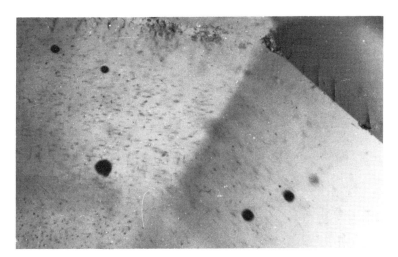

Fig. 10.1. Fire or 'chatter' marks in a synthetic ruby (top right).

tails will point the same way (see Plates 1-4).

If a corundum shows light throughout a complete revolution between crossed polars, it is more likely to be a natural stone, because such an effect would be due to lamellar twinning.

Since synthetic rubies are more transparent to short-wave ultra-violet light than natural ones, a stone immersed in a dish of water, table facet down and exposed to the radiation for a few seconds (the lamp should be held about 45cm (18 in) above the dish) will show a dark body with a white edge when the film has been developed. Natural stones will appear white. Since synthetic rubies phosphoresce after exposure to X-rays, this can be a useful if expensive test. Other properties of synthetic corundum are indistinguishable from those of the natural material, although the luminescence and the absorption spectrum may be stronger.

Hydrothermal Corundum
Hydrothermal ruby is described by Gübelin in a report of 1961. The process is similar to that used for making quartz, although corundum is somewhat more difficult on account of the various modifications (gibbsite, boehmite and diaspore) in which aluminium oxide can occur. The autoclave is a steel cylinder. The nutrient — poorly crystallized gibbsite ($Al(OH)_3$) or corundum — is placed in the cylinder at the bottom of a silver tube. The rest of the tube is filled with sodium carbonate. Seed crystals of natural or synthetic ruby are placed in the top of the

apparatus, suspended from a silver frame. The assembly is heated to 400°C from below and growth on the seed plates takes place by convection. Growth is slow and a run may take one or two months (Plates 7-9).

Some hydrothermal rubies made by Chatham had a refractive index of 1.76 to 1.77 with a birefringence of 0.008. There was little phosphorescence after X-ray exposure but, if the seeds had been made from synthetic ruby, this might have been more obvious. Natural inclusions in the seed could deceive, although a careful examination showed that they stopped at the junction. The coating had profuse minute gas bubbles. Chatham ruby crystals intended for the lapidary appeared on the market in the U.S.A. in 1966. The stones were a rich purple-red with a noticeable seed crystal inside. A transparency test with short-wave ultra-violet light showed up these cores well; they were also more transparent to this form of radiation than are natural rubies (Plates 10-13).

Corundun by the Czochralski Method

Rubies grown by the Czochralski method are more expensive to make than those grown by flame-fusion. Power for heating usually comes from a radio-frequency induction heater. This uses several kilowatts of energy at a frequency of about 100 kilocycles per second in a water-cooled copper coil several inches in diameter and length. Since the current through the coil changes at high frequency, power is induced in a conducting material near the coil. With the Czochralski method, power is coupled into an iridium crucible in which the molten alumina is contained, via an outer crucible called a 'susceptor' which is made from a less expensive material. The alumina is kept at a temperature above its melting point and a seed crystal is lowered into it so that the lower end is below the surface of the melt. The upper end of the seed, cooled by the conduction of heat through the seed holder, is below the melting temperature and stays solid. Rotation of the seed avoids temperature variations around its circumference. Pulling from the melt extends the crystal.

Czochralski stones may show growth bands which are caused by the unstable convection in the melt or by the rotation of the crystal. To avoid the thin plates typical of the Czochralski growth habit of corundum, some workers found that modifications to the after-heater were needed. Another modification involved the alteration of the floating-zone apparatus to give a controlled atmosphere; this prevented oxidation of the heater strip. Tyndall scattering is much reduced by these modifications and crystals up to 100 × 15mm (3.9 × 0.6 in) have been obtained, probably with blue sapphire. Synthetic rubies with cracks induced by quenching were reported by the G.I.A. New York Laboratory in 1975.

Corundum by the Flux-Melt Method

Synthetic ruby grown by the flux-melt method on a seed of Verneuil-grown ruby has been seen from time to time and is reported from the Gem Trade Laboratory in Santa Monica in 1976. Another example can be seen in the Geological Museum, London. The stone can be recognized by the curved striae in the Verneuil part and by the flux inclusions; additionally a purplish dividing line could be seen between the two sections.

Ruby and blue sapphire grown by the flux-melt method have been seen on the market in the last few years, the main manufacturer being Carroll F. Chatham. A group of Chatham blue sapphire crystals from the author's collection was shown to the Precious Stone Laboratory of the London Chamber of Commerce in 1976 and reported, with some remarks on ruby from the same manufacturer, by Scarratt (1977).

Examination of the blue sapphire crystal groups showed that they were made up of tabular plates arranged randomly. Colour was concentrated in the tips of the crystals, the rest were colourless. The blue was medium dark ranging to very pale and appeared in markedly angular bands. Dark angular platelets, perhaps metallic, could be seen in the crystals and twisted veil-like structures were prominent, proving the flux-melt growth of the stones. Under long-wave ultra-violet light, the sapphires glowed an overall yellow with dark blue and greenish patches; under short-wave they were an overall blue, though parts of the surface and the junction area of some of the crystals were yellow.

The rubies also were platy crystal groups, each of which had a larger number of individual crystals than the sapphire groups. The colour was a strong carmine red seen in depth, otherwise it was a pale pink. Dark, angular, probably metallic platelets could be seen as with the sapphires, also the characteristic twisted veils. The absorption spectrum was normal for ruby. The absorption spectrum of the sapphires showed the 450nm band clearly with a hand spectroscope (this is the reverse of the case with the Verneuil stones where it would be exceptional to see any absorption in this region). In addition, the bands at 460 and 471nm can be faintly seen.

The sapphires showed red between crossed filters and yellow with a hint of green under X-rays; here there were also some dark blue patches. Some of the colourless areas and some of the pale blue areas discoloured to a deep green or yellow. These colours were not permanent since a patch of deep green induced by X-rays lightened to a medium green after exposure to a 40-watt bulb for five minutes. After exposure for 8½ hours, the green had almost disappeared; the same happened to a crystal which had turned yellow under X-rays. It is interesting to note that in both cases the blue portions of the crystals remained unaffected.

Photographs of the Chatham synthetic rubies show that they are equidimensional rather than plate-like and this suggests that the flux was a tungstate or a molybdate. Ruby tends to grow as plates and the rate of lateral spread can exceed the rate of thickening by as much as 100:1. As this tendency appears to be stronger at lower temperatures, these can be increased to about 1200°C or above. The addition of about 0.5 per cent lanthanum oxide to the solution can also reduce the incidence of plate-like crystals. The stones are more transparent than natural stones to short-wave ultra-violet light.

Earlier work on flux-melt grown rubies used lead fluoride or a mixture of this substance with lead oxide or boric oxide. Crystals were grown by cooling the solutions from about 1300°C to 900°C at 2°C per hour. Work done by G.E.C. in 1965 involved a seed crystal suspended from wires in the middle of the solution with small ruby fragments at the bottom to act as source material.

Sahagian (1966) gives a table of corundum colours and the elements needed to obtain them:

Colour	Element
gold	copper
pink	manganese
purple, varying with the incident light	vanadium
greyish-green	cobalt
yellow	nickel
grey	iron
yellow	titanium
blue to red	chromium with vanadium
pale blue to red	cobalt with vanadium
maroon	cobalt with chromium
blue-green	iron with titanium

The fluorescence of the ruby groups was a strong red under long-wave ultra-violet light except for a few small inert areas; under short-wave, the colour was a strong pinkish-red with pale blue in the crevices on the bases of the groups. Under crossed filters there was a strong flame-red; and under X-rays, a very strong red with a strong persistent phosphorescence, as one would also expect with the Verneuil type of ruby. After irradiation times of between 10 seconds to 10 minutes, the phosphorescence varied from two to twenty minutes. A small area discoloured to an orange-red after a four-minute exposure but this was not easily perceptible. With one of the ruby groups, examination by room lighting after exposure to both long- and short-wave ultra-violet light showed that the crystals had turned to deep purplish-red from carmine-red. This could not be repeated with other groups and it was not possible to return the stones to their original colour.

The flux-grown 'Kashan' ruby was reported by the London Laboratory (Anderson, 1972). The report showed that 'paint-splash' inclusions were prominent and that they were flattish, elongated with parallel sides and rounded ends (compared to a moccasin print). They were arranged in parallel formation in parallel groups. This stone was made by Ardon Associates of Dallas, Texas.

What are probably later Kashan products than the one mentioned above are described in *Jewelers Circular-Keystone* (January 1981). Some Kashan rough has been found mixed with genuine rough in Bangkok. The cut stones show tiny inclusions reminiscent of dust or raindrops. 'Cigarette smoke' is a sure sign of flux-melt origin and an effect like heat shimmer faintly echoes the twinning lines seen in many Thai rubies. Dichroism is notable, with one of the colours being a strong orange or brown. Sometimes these two colours can be seen concentrated in parts of the stone (see Plates 15-18).

Many synthetic rubies are more transparent to short-wave ultra-violet light than natural stones, but a recent report (Brown, 1981) suggests that Kashan stones, at least, may have had iron added to them, since a number of them do not transmit short-wave ultra-violet light and are virtually opaque to the rays. These particular stones are noticeably dark and show some iron bands in the absorption spectrum.

Star Corundum
Star-stones began to be produced by the Linde Division of Union Carbide Corporation in 1947. The asterism is caused by tiny crystals of aluminium titanate Al_2TiO_5 which are aligned in sheets at 60 degrees to each other. The effect is produced by adding rutile to the feed powder. On cooling this separates out, not as rutile, but as aluminium titanate, due to reaction with the alumina. According to Linde, the best stars are produced when the rutile is from 0.1 to 0.3 per cent of the total feed powder and when the boules are kept at 1100° to 1500°C for several hours to crystallize out the needles.

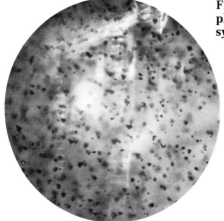

Fig. 10.2. Triangular two-phase inclusions in a synthetic star ruby.

One problem is to ensure that the star occupies the whole top of the stone. If the oxygen flow is altered so that the temperature can be made to fluctuate regularly, this problem can be overcome. At the lower rate of flow, the needles spread out over the whole width of the stone; at higher rates, the needles are concentrated in the outer zones only.

Linde also produced surface stars by polishing rutile-free stones cut en cabochon and then diffusing them in rutile to form a layer of needles before the final polish; these stones are more transparent than those grown by the commoner method. Star stones produced before 1952 had much greater transparency than later products. The stars, too, were much less clearly defined. However curved striae were also more prominent with these productions.

Linde stars have been produced in purple, green, pink, yellow and brown as well as in ruby and blue sapphire colours; they were graded A, B and C according to their colour depth. Curved colour banding and characteristic bubbles show the true nature of the stones. One of the dichroic directions of the ruby is more inclined to yellow than in most natural stones.

'Reconstructed Rubies'

A report by Benson (1952), showed that the bottom tips of boules of synthetic ruby had, from time to time (at least) been sent to certain parts of the world for cutting. They contained few of the tell-tale signs present in the upper portions of the boule, so they may have escaped notice and be masquerading as natural rubies. The report dealt mainly with the story that, in the 1880s, some 'reconstructed rubies' were made by fusing together small particles of natural ruby with melted silica. The variable hardness of such stones, together with their lack of extinction under the polariscope, would make them stand out from other stones. However, none have been reported. Between 1880 and 1890, 'Geneva' rubies were said to have been made from ruby sand, but again they have never been reported. In any case some (non-gem) synthetic corundum was being made as early as 1877. Gem-quality material was said to have been on the market by about 1886. It is unlikely therefore that much effort was put into 'reconstructing' stones.

Nassau (1973) refers to a story that synthetic corundum was made at the town of Hoquiam, Washington, by a former assistant of Verneuil, who was invited to the town by two lumbermen. Several hundred carats of boules were produced during the short time that the venture went on. The boules were generally small, so that a 2ct stone would be perhaps the largest stone that could be cut from them. Exceptionally large quantities of gas bubbles are a feature of all known boules examined. There is no possibility that ground rubies were used as part of the feed powder, as has sometimes been suggested. The colour distribution varied a good deal within the boules. It is possible that the bubbles were caused by coarse or uneven feed powder, or by irregularities in the method of melting it.

Fig. 10.3. Inclusions in an early synthetic ruby. Approx. 25x

Plato Lines

'Plato' lines in synthetic corundum can be found by turning the stone so
that the optic axis lies in the optic axis of the polarizing microscope; the
black cross of the optic axis should be at the centre of the field. Parallel
polarized light will show single, double or triple systems of straight
lines as the stage is rotated. The second and third groups are at 60 or 120
degrees to the first system. In colourless corundum, fine straight lines
can sometimes be seen in a direction perpendicular to the optic axis. If
they are screened by a diaphragm, they can even be seen in ordinary
light, but on even a slight rotation of the stone they disappear. The
thickness of the lines or striations has been estimated at about 70
microns.

In a few cases, polysynthetic twinning similar to that frequently seen
in natural corundum, has been observed in its synthetic counterpart.
This occurs parallel to the face of the primitive rhombohedron (10$\bar{1}$1).
These latter striations cannot be taken as an indication that a stone is
synthetic.

**Fig. 10.4. The 'plato' effect in a
small colourless synthetic
sapphire taken between crossed
nicols down its optic axis.**

Reports on Individual Cases from the Literature

An attempt to imitate a cluster of blue sapphire crystals was reported by
the Gem Trade Laboratories in New York and Los Angeles. It consisted
of a number of synthetic sapphires cut to resemble hexagonal prisms
and then cemented together. A typical cobalt spectrum came from the
cement used, which was presumably dyed.

Some blue sapphires bought in Sri Lanka proved to be poor quality (colourless to milk-white) stones which had been improved by heat and possibly chemical treatment. Some stones with a dark watery appearance tested by the G.I.A. showed a greenish fluorescence rather like that shown by some synthetic blue sapphires. Another (inert) stone showed a weak iron band, but the remainder did not. Ten of the 13 stones had cracks or fractures radiating from included crystals or liquid inclusions. There was no obvious evidence of heating.

The practice of heating heavily rutilated corundum, to reduce the amount of included matter and to enhance the colour, was first carried out in Thailand. Cloudiness (due to the rutile inclusions) which gives a greyish overall colour, is dispersed by the heating and the titanium from the rutile is reincorporated into the crystal lattice. This aids the improvement of the blue colour which arises from intervalence charge transfer between iron and titanium.

Orange corundum can be produced by heating natural sapphire in a powder which will give the desired colour by the migration of atoms into the lattice of the stone. The coating will fluoresce while the rest of the stone remains inert.

Coloured varieties of synthetic corundum can often be quickly checked by simple gemmological tests: crossed filters (two pieces of Polaroid so arranged that no light passes through them) will show a red for green synthetics, and for the 'alexandrite' imitation. No bands will be seen in the absorption spectrum of green synthetic corundum nor in the yellow variety. A yellow corundum which shows no absorption spectrum and no luminescence, is almost certain to be synthetic. Some yellow synthetic sapphires show a reddish luminescence under X-rays with some phosphorescence; a variety of synthetic corundum imitating amethyst showed red under long-wave ultra-violet light and a bluish white under short-wave.

A ruby reported by Schiffmann (1976) weighed about 3ct, had a violet-red colour, was quite bright, and showed violet-reddish and orange dichroic colours. The refractive index was 1.772 to 1.764 with a double refraction of 0.008; the specific gravity was about 4.02 with a typical absorption spectrum for ruby. Fluorescence colours under both long- and short-wave ultra-violet light were medium red. No phosphorescence was observed after exposure to X-rays, although the fluorescence was a strong red, a little weaker than that shown by Verneuil stones and about equal to that shown by flux-melt ruby.

Under high magnification (40× to 240×) tiny particles (possibly cavities) could be seen irregularly distributed along roughly parallel-seeming planes. They appeared bright under reflected light. During faceting, some of the cavities were opened and showed as tiny holes on some of the facets. Coarser cavities, some with a dumb-bell shape, were observed, as were some straight needles, one ending in a fork shape. In the direction perpendicular to the optic axis, when the stone was immersed, growth structures were seen forming a wavy plane of colour saturation. Traces of parallel growth planes could be seen also throughout the whole stone under immersion. The tiny particles in one place were concentrated in a structure somewhat like that of the flowing tail of a comet. This has not been seen in any ruby other than synthetic ones.

Some good quality rubies were examined at the Gem Trade Laboratory of the G.I.A. at Los Angeles. These showed uniform parallel growth planes which did not intersect; they were said to resemble the lamellar twinning planes seen in some natural rubies. Wispy veils, angular inclusions of flux (some appearing white, some black) could also be seen.

A blue sapphire examined by the G.I.A. and reported in 1980 showed fingerprint inclusions throughout the stone but with a concentration near the culet. Curved colour bands could be seen under immersion. The fluorescence was a chalky-green and no iron line could be seen in the absorption spectrum. This stone was believed to be a treated Verneuil synthetic. Later on, a visitor said to a G.I.A. staff member that it was now possible to introduce fingerprint inclusions into Verneuil-grown stones. It was stated that boules were cut into bipyramids, treated to introduce the fingerprints, and then cut. See Plates 19-22.

Further notes on the heat treatment of corundum are also supplied by the G.I.A. It is thought that cloudy rough of mediocre quality (from Sri Lanka) is chosen for the treatment and it is interesting to note that the price of this kind of material has been steadily rising, due to Thai visitors to Colombo buying it. It is rumoured that the government of Sri Lanka has now ruled that any heating must be done over Ceylonese fires. Apparently the rough is sealed in clay and porcelain crucibles which are then packed in 250 litre (55 gallon) drums placed in charcoal. Heating reduces the incidence of rutile needles. Other reports say that very dark Australian sapphire will retain its green dichroic colour after heating. Generally it would seem that the process is in no way pre-dictable.

Chatham blue sapphire has recently been reported as a cut stone. Early products were sold as groups of thin bladed crystals, all of which showed strongly marked angular banding and which were heavily

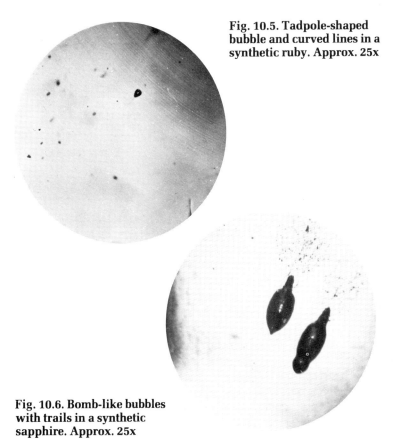

Fig. 10.5. Tadpole-shaped
bubble and curved lines in a
synthetic ruby. Approx. 25x

Fig. 10.6. Bomb-like bubbles
with trails in a synthetic
sapphire. Approx. 25x

included. The cut stones examined by the G.I.A. were in the 2ct range
and were dark blue. The specific gravity fell between 3.98 and 4.06 and
the refractive indices were close to 1.763 to 1.772 in all cases. The
double refraction was 0.009. Platinum crystals were observed in the
stones as splinters and flakes and residual flux in fingerprint patterns
could be seen. This flux was white and resembled smoke veils. A vague
band at 415.5nm could be seen, but could not be counted as diagnostic.
X-ray fluorescence ranged from pale white through bluish-white to
yellowish-white. No phosphorescence could be seen. A dull brownish
fluorescence under short-wave and a moderate whitish-yellow under
long-wave ultra-violet light was observed. In two stones, bright yellow
fluorescent patches could be seen under both forms of ultra-violet light
(see Plates 23-25).

Some yellow sapphire, whose colour has been deepened by various methods of irradiation, will fade at temperatures as low as 250 to 300°C. Some natural yellows may fade at this temperature.

A list of colours produced by a leading manufacturer of flame-fusion corundum, may prove interesting.

Numbers	Djéva Synthetic Corundum Colours
1	ruby: topaz light rose
1A	ruby: topaz rose
1dark	ruby: topaz rose
1¼	ruby: topaz rose
1bis	ruby: topaz rose
2	ruby: topaz dark rose
3	ruby: light rose
4	ruby: rose
5	ruby: dark rose
6	ruby: garnet colour (light)
8sp	ruby: dark red or dark garnet
8	ruby: dark red
12	sapphire: white
20sp	sapphire: lemon yellow
21sp	sapphire: gold yellow
22sp	sapphire: orange yellow
25sp	sapphire: topaz of Brazil
30	sapphire: bluish of India
31	sapphire: Ceylon light blue
32	sapphire: Ceylon dark blue
33	sapphire: Kashmir blue
34	sapphire: Burma blue
35	sapphire: Burma dark blue
44	alexandrite: light for big stones
45	alexandrite
46	alexandrite: dark
47	alexandrite: greenish
50sp	danburite
55sp	padparadshah
61	kunzite
65	sapphire: 'pourpre'
75	corundum: Djéva green

sp indicates homogeneous colour inside the boule.

An unusually bright yellow-orange sapphire was reported in New York. The stones showed no iron absorption and only a weak red fluorescence in long-wave ultra-violet light. Many stones showed evidence of high-temperature treatment: many had stress fractures and most had multi-plane girdles which appear to be typical of treated sapphire. The stones often had surfaces which had not been completely repolished.

A pink sapphire examined by the G.I.A. Laboratory in Los Angeles had two different structural surface patterns on each side of the cabochon. On one side, a hexagonal pattern could be seen by transmitted light; on the other it had a star-like appearance with an irregular number of rays. The stone was synthetic.

A pale brownish-orange brilliant-cut stone shown to the G.I.A. proved to be synthetic corundum but with a refractive index of 1.755 to 1.763. No inclusions could be seen.

Grey tablets used as cuff-links and made of sintered synthetic corundum were reported from the U.S.A. in 1962. They had a refractive index of about 1.77 and a specific gravity near 4.00 with a hardness of 9.

A synthetic white star sapphire examined by the G.I.A. showed a very strong star. On the base was a transparent colourless patch in the shape of a hemicylinder with layers apparently cylindrical and concentric through a rod which ran parallel to the base all the way across, and was at right angles to the optic axis of the cabochon. Needle-like inclusions appeared similar to those in a Linde star sapphire. The base seemed more transparent than the rest of the stone and from the side the whole piece seemed to be layered from the base to the top. A large group of bubbles could be seen.

Some synthetic star-stones were examined by Breebart (1957). German-made stones showed air bubbles appearing as tiny pinpoints throughout the stone and radiating from the centre of the stone towards the girdle. The rutile crystals appeared to be coarser and longer than in stones made in the U.S.A.

A simulation of star sapphire consisted of a pinkish star quartz with a blue backing. The blue coating can be scratched quite easily and the scratches might appear to be inclusions when the stone is examined from above. A star sapphire backed with a natural rough sapphire, the whole set in a closed setting, has also been reported. In this case the top was also genuine sapphire but presumably without the star. Reflection from the separation plane is a good method of testing such stones.

A number of doublets were examined by short-wave ultra-violet light. In all cases, the garnet and glass doublets could be distinguished by the greenish-yellow fluorescence from the glass backs.

A new synthetic ruby has been grown by Professor Knischka of Steyr, Austria. It is described by the grower and Dr. E. J. Gübelin (1980) and the author has two interesting specimens, one by courtesy of the grower. The ruby is of gem quality. The author has not seen a cut stone so far, but they would be of very fine colour and good clarity. The rubies were grown from the melt. Without doubt, the most interesting feature is the cubic habit that some of the crystals adopt. Not all of the crystals adopt an isometric habit: those that do show faces (0001), $(00\bar{1}5)$, $(10\bar{1}9)$, $(01\bar{1}2)$, $(10\bar{1}1)$ and $(22\bar{4}3)$. From above, there is a hexagonal outline and from the side the crystals appear something like a parallelogram. The forms whose indices are listed above are, respectively, the basal pinacoid, the positive rhombohedron $(10\bar{1}1)$ and $(10\bar{1}9)$; the negative rhombohedron $(01\bar{1}2)$ and $(01\bar{1}5)$, and the hexagonal dipyramid $(22\bar{4}3)$. Twinned crystals have also been grown. Chemical analysis of one of the rubies shows the presence of 0.073 Fe; 0.043 Zn; 0.031 Ni; 0.03 Au; 0.025 Co; 0.199 Pb and 1.585 Cr.

From the gemmological point of view, the colour of the new stones approaches that of the best Burma stones (the so-called 'pigeon's blood' colour). On the DIN Farbenkarte (the West German colour standard) the references are 10:7:3 for the red colour and 10.5:6.5:4 for the violet (pleochroic) colour. The absorption spectrum shows the chromium lines at 468.5, 5.475, 476.5, 659.2, 668, 692.8 and 694.2nm. The pleochroic colours are purple-red and orange-red. Under long-wave ultra-violet light, the rubies turn a carmine red and this colour is repeated with X-rays. There is a strong phosphorescence after irradiation with X-rays, as is the case with other man-made rubies. The length of this very long period of phosphorescence is attributed to the lack of iron which is contained by most natural stones. The refractive index has been calculated at 1.760 to 1.761 for the extraordinary ray and at 1.768 to 1.769 for the ordinary ray. This gives a birefringence of 0.008. The specific gravity was measured at 3.976.

Under the microscope, a number of inclusions could be seen. These were zoning of colour, two-phase inclusions and black negative crystals. Liquid-filled structures could be seen forming a widely spaced network. With the two-phase inclusions, large bubbles could be seen and these are thought to be gas-filled. Alteration of luminescence and striation of colour has been attributed to the content of the dissolved gas in the melt in the case of rubies grown by using lasers as the source of energy.

A sapphire of emerald green colour was produced using an apparatus similar to the Verneuil furnace. Constituent materials included the normal corundum feed powder with the addition of cobalt oxide, vanadium oxide and nickel salt. The proportions were roughly 98.6 per cent aluminium oxide, 0.986 per cent cobalt oxide, 0.119 per cent vanadium oxide and 0.295 per cent nickel salt.

A sapphire from Chimwadzulu Hill, Malawi, was heat-treated (Rutland, 1971) to see if the colour (a pale greenish-blue) could be improved. Heating over a range 500°C to 700°C had no visible effect; heating for five hours at 800°C caused the blue colour to become paler; in the range 900°C to 1200°C all residual blue was eliminated and the stones became pale green. Pleochroism for the unheated stones was distinct, a very pale green for the extraordinary and an aquamarine colour for the ordinary ray. Heating to 900°C and above virtually eliminated the blue in the ordinary ray which then showed as a pale, slightly greyish-green. No change in the absorption spectrum could be seen on heating the stones and there was no change in refractive index or weight. In this case it can be seen that no improvement of colour on heating is possible; this is the reverse of the case with aquamarine.

Australian workers isolated three types of synthetic yellow sapphire. Type 1 is coloured by iron and manganese and is a pale yellow; type 2 is coloured by manganese and chromium and is inclined to orange; type 3, with varying hues of yellow, is coloured by iron and vanadium.

Type 1 is inert under both forms of ultra-violet light, shows yellowish-green through the colour filter, is inert through crossed filters and shows a negligible absorption spectrum.

Type 2 fluoresces deep red under both forms of ultra-violet light, shows a strong glow and some red through the colour filter and a strong red through crossed filters. A bright line is shown in the red of the absorption spectrum.

Type 3 fluoresces orange under short-wave ultra-violet light and a deep red under long-wave. It is yellow-green through the colour filter, inert with crossed filters, and shows weak iron lines in the absorption spectrum.

A flux-grown (possibly Chatham?) stone which weighed more than 5 carats, showed flux fingerprints and angular silk-like banding visible to the eye. The stone was well cut and fluoresced strongly. Another ruby, seen at the G.I.A. New York Laboratory, was a Verneuil-grown stone which showed both curved striae and fingerprints.

Some sapphires have recently been heated after cutting, to diffuse colour into the surface. This practice seems to be taking place in

Bangkok. Most of the stones show a patchy fluorescence under short-wave ultra-violet light.

A paper published recently outlined an evaluation of transmission behaviour in the ultra-violet region between natural and synthetic rubies. It is said that the behaviour of rubies under short-wave ultra-violet light can be used to separate natural from synthetic stones.

A ruby presumably manufactured as an experiment was reported by the author (O'Donoghue, 1975). The specimen examined was tabular and showed uneven upper and lower pinacoids, pyramids, rhombohedra and prism forms. Some of the faces showed striations and two pieces of wire protruded from it, which gave sufficient proof of its unnatural origin! The colour varied with the direction from orange to dark red. Through some of the faces, the colourless seed could be seen and, in this particular direction, the colour was much more reminiscent of ruby. The dark red suggested iron and the absorption spectrum, lacking emission lines, appeared to bear this out. The inclusions were those typical of flux-melt material; 'paint-splashes', twisted veils and a haziness from those parts of the crystal adjacent to the seed. The refractive index was 1.764 to 1.766.

A report in the March 1982 issue of *Jewelers' Circular-Keystone* gives some notes on the Kashan synthetic ruby. Characteristics listed include solid-filled very coarse negative crystals with high reflectivity: clusters of parallel rod-like negative crystals, also solid-filled; networks of solid-filled negative crystals; wispy patterns resembling rain or, sometimes, a tailed comet; straight growth lines. Some Kashan stones are reported to be inclusion-free up to magnifications of 126x.

Orange corundum has recently been placed on the market by Chatham. It is currently being sold as single crystals or, more commonly, as crystal groups. The colour varies from orange to reddish orange and there is marked colour zoning as in the crystals groups of blue sapphire from the same manufacturer. Some inclusions appear white to the eye. The microscope shows that a coating is present and the manufacturer states that a liquid silica-based deramic glaze is applied to the backs of the crystal groups. The refractive index is between 1.762 and 1.770; the double refraction was 0.008. The absorption spectrum shows three sharp narrow lines; at 468.5nm, and a close doublet at 475 and 476.5nm. Broad absorption obscures all the violet and some of the blue, all the green and yellow. Orange crystals show a strong reddish-orange fluorescence with zones of chalky yellow – this under long-wave ultra-violet. Much the same phenomenon showed under short-wave ultra-violet. X-ray fluorescence gave reddish-orange to orange.

◀ **1. Verneuil Ruby:** Incompletely calcinated, so the stone contains impurities within, between the curved layers. 30x

▼ **2. Verneuil Ruby:** Curved striae and a swarm of gas bubbles. 30x

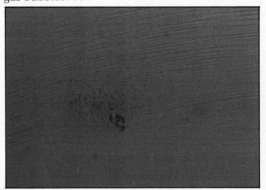

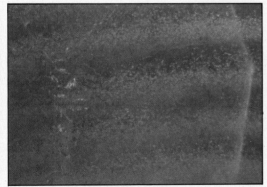

▲ **3. Verneuil Ruby:** Broad curved zones of tiny gas bubbles. 20x

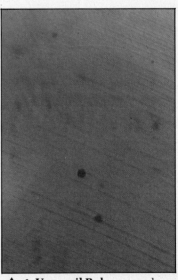

▲ **4. Verneuil Ruby:** curved striae with discrete spherical gas bubbles. 20x

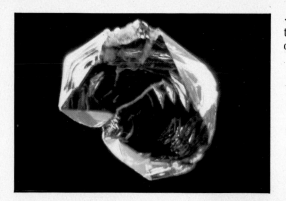

◀ **5. Frémy Ruby:** Typical triangular inclusions, the so-called 'coat hangers'. 10x

▶ **6. Early Hydrothermal Ruby:** Natural seed ruby with polysynthetic twin lamellae surrounded by synthetic coat (mantle). 5x

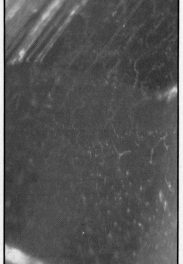

▲ **7. Early Hydrothermal Ruby:** Telltale features in the synthetic coat, formed by gas bubbles. 40x

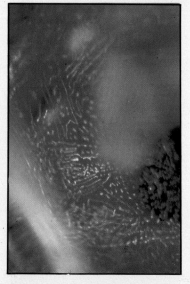

▲ **8. Early Hydrothermal Ruby:** Deceiving liquid 'feather' (fingerprint inclusion) in the mantle. 40x

▼ 9. Chatham Ruby: Fingerprint inclusion, highly reminiscent of liquid feathers in natural ruby. 25x

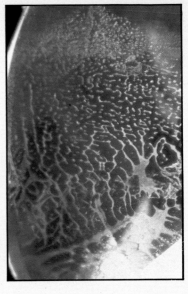

▲ 10. Chatham Ruby: Highly characteristic, lacelike 'feather' (fingerprint inclusion). 10x

▼ 12. Chatham Ruby: Typical liquid 'feather' (fingerprint inclusion), easily confused with natural ruby. 10x

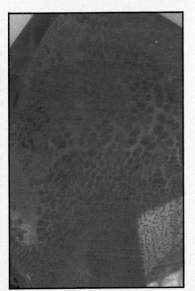

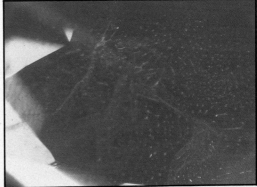

▲ 11. Chatham Ruby: Netlike inclusion with dense and narrow meshes. 10x

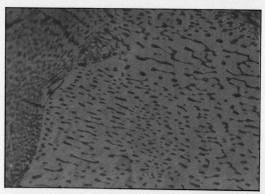

◀ **13. Chatham Ruby:**
Variously shaped individual
drops and different patterns of
'feathers'. 20x

▶ **14. Chatham Ruby:**
Disseminated platinum
platelets. 35x

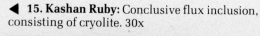

◀ **15. Kashan Ruby:** Conclusive flux inclusion,
consisting of cryolite. 30x

▶ **16. Kashan Ruby:** 'Hoses'
and flux-drop inclusions, in
parallel alignement and forming
zones. 25x

▲ **17. Kashan Ruby:**
Gossamer-fine veils of flux
inclusions. 15x

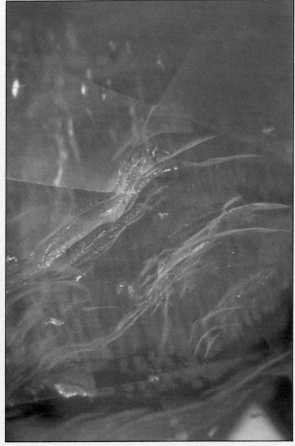

◀ **18. Kashan Ruby:**
Typical fog and cloudlike
inclusions, affecting the
clarity of the stone. 32x

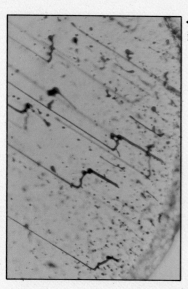

◀ **19. Verneuil Sapphire:** Gas bubbles and irregular 'hose' gas inclusions. 10x

▲ **20. Verneuil Sapphire:** Curved growth zone emphasized by numerous tiny gas bubbles. 20x

▲ **21. Verneuil Sapphire:** Strong interference colours betray the Plato-Sandmeier effect between crossed polars. 10x

▼ **22. Verneuil Sapphire:** The Plato-Sandmeier effect between crossed polars. 10x

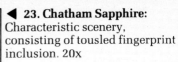
23. Chatham Sapphire: Characteristic scenery, consisting of tousled fingerprint inclusion. 20x

24. Chatham Sapphire: Dense accumulations of fine liquid films and feathers. 15x

25. Chatham Sapphire: Concentration of typical platinum inclusions. 15x

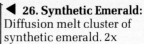
26. Synthetic Emerald: Diffusion melt cluster of synthetic emerald. 2x

▶ **27. 'Igmerald':** Typical inclusions, forming veils and wisps. 10x

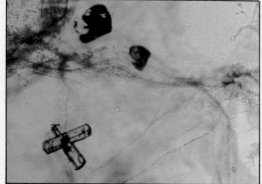

▲ **28. 'Igmerald':** Veils and wisps, accompanied by phenakite crystals (two in a crosslike position). 30x

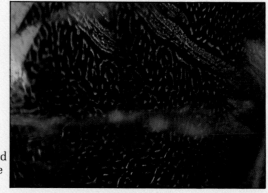

▶ **29. 'Igmerald':** Typical and conclusive pattern of veil-like inclusions. 35x

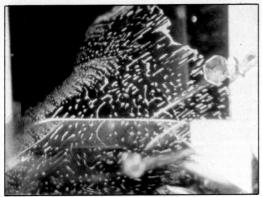

◀ **30. Chatham Emerald:**
Telltale fingerprint veil in
contact with a phenakite crystal
(under dark field illumination).
15x

◀ **31. Chatham Emerald:** As No. 30 but
photographed in bright field illumination. 30x

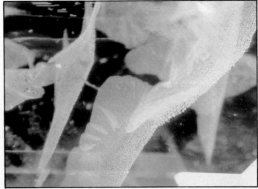

▲ **32. Gilson Emerald:** Typical veil inclusions,
forming 'flying' banners. 10x

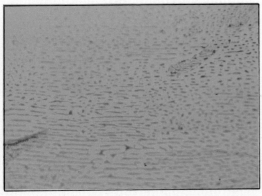

◀ **33. Gilson Emerald:** Note the
conspicuous directional
orientation of drops and 'hoses'
forming a large veil. 40x

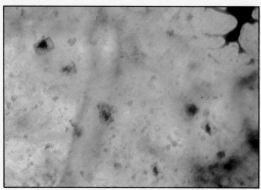

◀ **34. Lenix Emerald:** Survey of affiliating inclusion scenery. Note the strongly-dichroic, green, guest crystals and the curious splashes. 50x

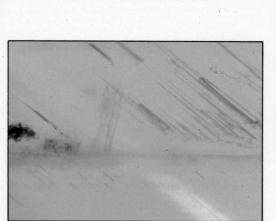

◀ **35. Linde Hydrothermal Emerald:** Thin seed crystal; on either side, cuneiform two-phase inclusions dart out at an oblique angle to the surface of the seed plate. 50x

▲ **36. Zerfass Emerald:** Typical veil inclusions form a honeycomb pattern. 20x

▲ **37. Zerfass Emerald:** Cuneiform two-phase inclusions in parallel alignment, starting from tiny phenakite crystals. 25x

▶ **38. Synthetic Emerald from a Melt:** Strong magnification of a section of one of the typical wispy veils. Note the solid impurities in the drops and tubes. 200x

▲ **39. Lechleitner Emerald:** The surface displays a dense pattern of fine fissures. 5x

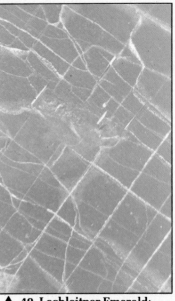

▲ **40. Lechleitner Emerald:** Strong magnification displays the nature of the fissures, which form a narrowly-meshed net in the synthetic mantle. 50x

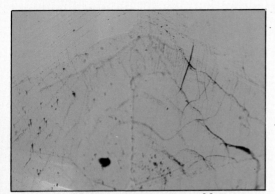

▲ **41. Lechleitner 'Emerita' Emerald:** Two systems of netlike fissures meet along the facet edges of the pre-cut core. 30x

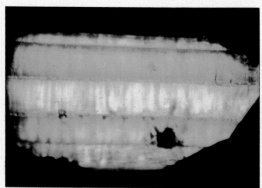

◀ **43. Verneuil Spinel (aquamarine blue):** Note the gas-filled 'hoses' and the negative crystals. 30x

▲ **42. Lechleitner 'Sandwich' Emerald:** Lateral view of the central colourless beryl and the synthetic crown and pavilion, which impart green colour to the whole. 5x

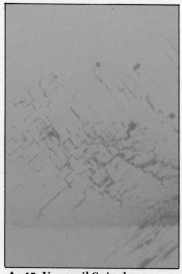

▲ **44. Verneuil Spinel (red):** Note the curved growth layers (striae). 20x

▲ **45. Verneuil Spinel (tourmaline green):** Spherical gas bubbles and a system of cracks follow the isometric directions of the cubic crystal system. 35x

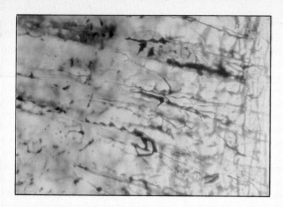

◄ 46. Verneuil Spinel (lime green): A dense concentration of fissures and gas-filled 'hoses' (highly irregular formations). 35x

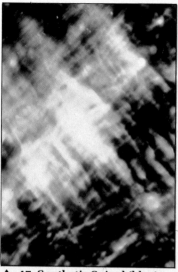

▲ 47. Synthetic Spinel (blue): The irregular pattern of anomalous double refraction in this synthetic spinel. 20x

▲ 48. YAG (imitating Demantoid Garnet): The irregular flux residues bear no resemblance at all to the byssolite fibres in natural demantoid garnet! 30x

► 49. YAG (green): Large freeform flux inclusions. 30x

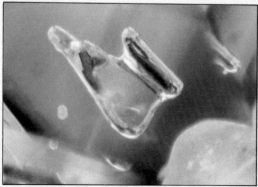

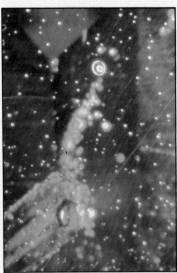

◀ **50. Paste (green glass):** Discrete large and small air bubbles are accompanied by myriads of pinpoint air bubbles. 20x

▼ **51. 'Goldstone':** A dense accumulation of copper crystals. 10x

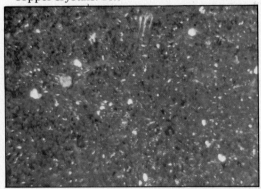

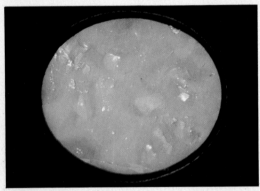

▲ **52. 'Slocum Stone':** Low magnification displays only colour patches; note their sharp contours. 5x

▼ **53. 'Slocum Stone':** High magnification reveals the discrete cuttings of aluminium foil which reflect interference colours. 50x

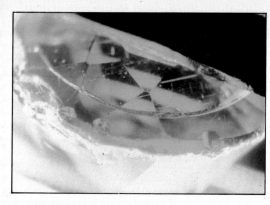

◄ 56. Doublet: Red reflections along the rim of the crown and fractures below the girdle betray this doublet with an almandine crown and glass pavilion. 10x

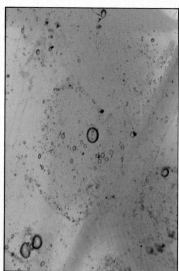

▲ 54. Paste (imitating Jadeite): Large and small bubbles and irregular colour patches are seen in this green glass. 25x

▲ 55. Doublet (imitating Emerald): Lateral view showing the beryl crown and green glass pavilion. 5x

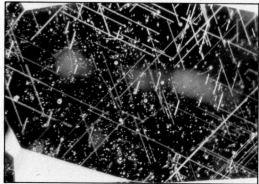

▲ 57. Doublet (imitating Emerald): Rutile needles in the almandine crown are in focus; air bubbles in the cement layer are blurred. 10x

▶ **58. Doublet (imitating blue Sapphire):** Hexagonal zoning in the natural sapphire pavilion; gas bubbles in the synthetic sapphire crown. 20x

▲ **59. Doublet (imitating whole natural Ruby):** Straight parallel lines (edges of polysynthetic twin lamellae) in the natural ruby crown; spherical air bubble in the cement layer above the synthetic ruby pavilion. 10x

▲ **60. 'Naftule' Doublet:** Synthetic colourless corundum crown is attached to the strontium titanate pavilion below the girdle. Note the fine separation line. 12x

▲ **61. Diamond Doublet:** Natural mineral inclusion in the diamond crown. Note the demarcation line inside the girdle, marking the separation rim between the crown and the imitation pavilion. 10x

11. Emerald

Synthetic emerald is probably the most dangerous of all the coloured stone synthetics, because a considerable degree of skill is needed to identify the stones. Testing on a refractometer is not conclusive nor is the absorption spectrum nor specific gravity. However those who are practised with the 10× lens will find that it serves the purpose very well, except for the smallest stones.

The first synthesis of emerald was reported by Hautefeuille and Perrey in 1888. 18.75g (0.60 oz) of the constituents of beryl were dissolved with 0.6 per cent chromic oxide in 92g (3.25 oz) of lithium molybdate in a platinum crucible. The lithium molybdate was first melted with the furnace at a dull red, then the temperature was raised over 24 hours to 800°C which was kept up for five days. This gave about 15g (0.53 oz) of small crystals. Larger crystals up to 1mm (0.09 in) in diameter were obtained later and involved a heating period of 14 days.

In late 1979, it was generally laid down by trade associations (at least in the United Kingdom) that a stones must be shown to contain chromium to qualify for the name of emerald.

Means of Identification
Early synthetic emeralds could be more easily recognized than most of the productions on the market today. Specific gravity readings were all below 2.70 and the refractive index was around 1.560 to 1.563. Only a few natural emeralds will show figures as low as this; 1.570 is a more characteristic figure. Similarly the birefringence of synthetic emerald is low, at about 0.003, compared with 0.006 in many natural stones. Although the Chelsea colour filter is still useful, its use is now a little more limited than in the early days when almost all synthetic emeralds showed a notably bright red through it. If necessary apparatus is

available, it is most instructive to test the transparency of a suspected emerald to short-wave ultra-violet. Almost all natural stones are opaque to wavelengths of 300nm or lower, whereas Chatham stones at least will transmit the rays down to about 230nm.

X-ray topography can be useful in the study of synthetic emerald, as reported by Schubnel (1971). When a beam of X-rays, prevented from spreading by a slit, impinges on a crystal, it can be separated into plane waves. Each of these in the crystal have two propagation directions spread between the incident and the reflected directions; these waves interfere. If in a crystal the lattice planes are slightly misorientated, the interference phenomena may be suppressed or modified. A 'dynamic image' will be seen in the trace of the beams. Where the planes are misorientated, they will be able to reflect part of the direct beam; areas with the greatest slope of misorientation will reflect most. In this way a 'map' of the crystal can be obtained which will show the topography of the disturbed area in the crystals. If the crystal and the photographic plate are moved simultaneously, the map will extend through the whole of the disturbed area. The defects themselves cannot be observed in this way but only the effect that they have upon the crystal lattice.

The topography of a synthetic emerald was studied in a slice cut perpendicularly to the c-axis and 1.5mm (0.06 in) thick. Subgrains, due to very strong internal tension, could be seen and there was a mosaic of juxtaposed grains misorientated with each other, each grain itself being curved. A natural stone from Muzo showed zonings related to growth spirals.

Early German Experiments

Work on the growth of emerald ('Igmerald') at the German firm of IG Farbenindustrie began in 1911 and from the start the main problem encountered was that of multinucleation: i.e. that a large number of crystals formed on the melt. Espig of IG Farbenindustrie found that a chemical reaction between two of the constituents of the crystal (silica and beryllium oxide) assisted growth. BeO and Al_2O_3 dissolved in the flux of lithium molybdate, but the other main constituent (SiO_2) floated on the surface of the solution. Since flotation rather than sinking was necessary, the density of the flux had to be near 2.9. To prevent crystals from floating up to grow with the silica (which gives poor crystals), a platinum screen separated the two. The reaction had the silica dissolving in the flux and diffusing to a part of the crucible when the concentration of all the ingredients was high enough for emerald to crystallize. Once a few crystals had started to grow, multinucleation is less likely so long as the silica arrives slowly enough for it to be used up in the reaction. The process is slow and would take a year to produce a reasonably-sized emerald. Espig said that the best colour was obtained when another element (unnamed) was added with the chromium. This could have been vanadium since, many years later, the Crystals Research Company of Melbourne, Australia, made emerald with this element but no chromium.

The 'Igmerald' was presented to a few people and never placed on the commercial market. Striae parallel to the basal plane were observable and the dichroism was weaker than that seen in natural emeralds. This was in contrast to earlier synthetic material in which the dichroism was noticeably strong. The absorption spectrum showed, in addition to the expected emerald lines and bands, two additional bands at 594 and 606nm. Both of these showed more clearly in polarized light. The specific gravity fell in the range 2.497 to 2.702. Wisp-like inclusions, showing tiny bubbles in each separate liquid patch under high magnification, were grouped in broad swarm-like lines which crossed the stone in slightly curved directions. The rod-like inclusions, seen in some earlier products, were not so pronounced in the Igmerald. See Plates 27-29.

Synthetic Emerald Grown by R. Nacken

Although many gemmological textbooks state that emeralds grown in Germany in the 1920s by Professor Richard Nacken were of hydro-thermal origin, Nassau (1978) has shown that this is not true and that the emeralds were grown by the flux-melt process. The misunderstanding arose from several factors; firstly, that Nacken's work on crystal growth centred round the hydrothermal growth of quartz; and secondly, that reports of a team interviewing German scientists after the war mentioned emerald during a report which dealt largely with the growth of quartz, while not mentioning the process by which the emerald was grown. Research into the true nature of the stones was therefore more or less left until recently when it was noticed that the inclusions shown by Nacken emeralds were more typical of the flux-melt process.

In the research carried out by Nassau several crystals were examined. The crystals had no attached material or places showing where they might have been attached to something, so that it is reasonable to assume that they had grown on the surface of a melt. Infra-red spectra showed that some of the crystals contained water as hydrothermal and most natural stones – but not flux-melt grown stones – do; not all Nacken crystals, however, showed the bands attributed to water. Those crystals that did show the water bands showed them in two forms denoting two types of water. This showed that there was some alkali in the crystals and spectra of this kind had been previously observed only in natural material.

On examination it could be seen that growth had taken place on a seed of colourless natural beryl. The natural seed explained the presence of water. The pale centres of the seeds could be seen at the correct angle. Inclusions were the characteristic veils, twisted to resemble cigarette smoke; plus cuneiform nail-like inclusions caused by the nucleation of a phenakite crystal with a tapering inclusion extending from it. These tapers all pointed to the surface of the nearest basal pinacoid which suggested that the growth parallel to the vertical crystal axis was quicker than that following other directions. Two-phase inclusions could also be seen and appeared to be fluid with a gas bubble; small groups of crystals, probably phenakite, could be seen and some tapered inclusions, apparently polycrystalline and dark brown in colour.

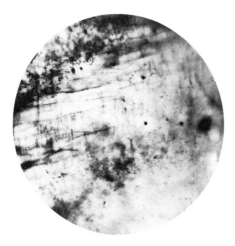

Fig. 11.1. Inclusions in a Nacken emerald, made in 1930. 22x

An energy-dispersive analysis of one crystal showed that molybdenum and vanadium were present which indicates that a flux of MoO_3 and V_2O_5 (perhaps combined with Li_2O but lithium cannot be detected by this method) was used.

One of the two-phase inclusions was exposed by thinning down the crystal and the contents which were transparent, solid and isotropic gave a spectrum typical for beryl plus Mo and V. This seemed to indicate that the contents were trapped flux of beryl composition with extra chromium, but in a vitreous state. Growth in a hydrothermal alkaline medium is impossible for emerald, though it is possible for beryl; this is because chromium will precipitate in any media but acid ones.

Emerald (also quartz and some feldspar) has been grown by placing seed crystals in a loosely packed powder matrix, consisting of a gel with the same composition as the respective silicate. The temperature for growth is well below the melting point for each silicate and growth time is over three weeks. First the gels transform into metastable phases with accretion on to the surfaces of the seed crystals. Then these phases transform into the silicates. Adhesion to the surface of the seeds takes place and euhedral (well-shaped) single crystals are formed. Growth layers of the single crystals show a mosaic structure composed of a number of single crystals arranged with preferred orientation. The stones show an abnormal anisotropy, while quartz and emerald show a biaxial interference figure.

Chatham and Gilson Production
The bulk of the emerald production today comes from the firms of Chatham in San Francisco and Gilson in the Pas-de-Calais, France. Both use a flux-melt method; that adopted by Chatham is still almost completely secret, while Gilson does advertise some of his methods.

Gilson stones reported by Webster in 1964 had a specific gravity of 2.65 and a refractive index of 1.562 to 1.559 with a birefringence of 0.003. Dichroism is distinct with yellowish-green and blue-green as the two colours. Stones showed a dull red through the colour filter and the absorption spectrum was strong and typical for emerald. Through crossed filters, the stones showed red; under long-wave ultra-violet light they showed mustard-yellow and under short-wave an orange colour. Under X-rays the stones glowed a very dull red. Some phosphorescence after irradiation by X-rays was noticed (this is also the case with Chatham stones). The Gilson stones appeared to transmit ultra-violet light to about the same extent as natural stones, but not so far into the ultra-violet as do the Chatham stones. Inclusions are similar to those found in other synthetic emeralds: twisted veils and groups of euhedral phenakite crystals (see Plates 30-33).

Gilson crucibles are divided into two compartments: one is for the actual crystal growth; the other contains the molten salt solvent which replaces that lost by evaporation during the growth period. The raw material is said to be poor quality emerald from Madagascar and Brazil, so that the process can be said to be one of recrystallization rather than one involving a chemical reaction as in the IG Farben method. Seed crystals of 40×1mm (1.5×0.04 in) are mounted on a frame of noble

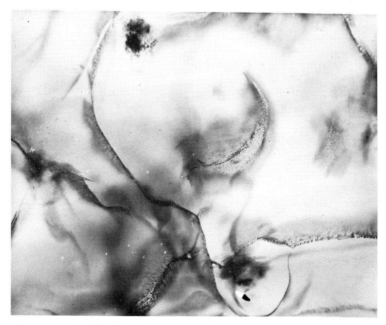

Fig. 11.2. Veil-like 'feathers' in a Gilson emerald.

metal. The growth rate is about 1mm (0.04 in) a month for nine months. Each seed crystal will give about 200ct of emerald and about 500 to 100ct are obtained from each run.

A report (Duyk, 1965) suggests that a simple test to identify Chatham and Gilson synthetic emerald is to immerse the stone in benzyl benzoate (R.I. 1.569) and observe the facet angles. Should the stone be synthetic, the angle will light up if the focus is raised. Another test is to prepare a liquid (bromoform diluted with xylol) in which a piece of rock crystal will just rise to the surface on immersion. Synthetics will float and natural stones will sink. If the stones are examined between crossed polars on the stage of a microscope while immersed, the synthetics will show bright colouration (due to internal stresses?) while natural stones show the normal chromatic polarization. However, since different kinds of synthetic emerald are constantly appearing, it is probably better to rely first upon the microscope, leaving the other tests as back-ups.

Emerald-coated Beryl
A report by Gübelin in 1961 examined emerald-coated beryl. Stones

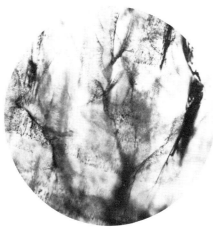

Fig. 11.3. Feathers in an American synthetic emerald.

marketed at that time under the name 'Emerita' had a core of natural beryl with a thin coating of hydrothermally-produced emerald. Herr Lechleitner was asked to produce a blue and a yellow beryl with an emerald coating; in both cases the green was unaffected by the underlying colour. The refractive indices were 1.578 to 1.590 and 1.571 to 1.583 for the ordinary and extraordinary rays respectively; the birefringence was 0.007. These figures are high for man-made emerald. The specific gravity was between limits of 2.676 and 2.713. Parallel lines were characteristic and resulted from an internal fracture at the junction of seed and overgrowth. Another set of lines running at right angles – these lines were parallel to the basal plane (0001) – gave the stone a

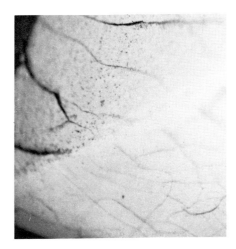

Fig. 11.4. Crazing in a Lechleitner 'Emerita' (emerald-coated beryl).

crackled appearance. The junction plane seemed to be covered by tiny dust-like particles which were of euclase or phenakite. A wedge-shaped two-phase inclusion orientated parallel to the main growth direction was characteristic of these stones and with the parallel lines gave a clear indication of their nature. It is interesting to note that Lechleitner, on occasion, has caused tiny gold octahedra to appear in the emerald overgrowth; these are only examples of gold in a man-made crystal of which I know. See Plates 39-41.

Lechleitner emeralds had previously been reported in Gems and Gemology (Spring 1960). The report mentions the presence of well-formed crystal faces on cabochons which had not been polished. First- and second-order hexagonal bipyramids were noticed.

An emerald by Lechleitner was reported in the Journal of Gemmology by Eppler (1968). This stone had a core of natural beryl, over which was placed a very thin coating of synthetic emerald; over this again was a covering of colourless beryl which protected the green coating. Because the colourless synthetic beryl had a much faster growth rate than the emerald with chromium, it was possible to obtain a thick-layered stone with more weight by this method. In Lechleitner stones at this time, the core was polished before it was covered so that the overlay also needed to be polished. During this process, it could happen that some of the facets lost their coloured part. This was the reason for the second coating described above.

In 1964, Lechleitner produced a 'sandwich' emerald in which the seed plate of colourless beryl (natural or synthetic) was covered by a layer of emerald during a hydrothermal run. The 'joint stone' was then enlarged by further hydrothermal growth, though this later stage was again colourless. Examination from the side while the stone is immersed will show the process well. See Plate 42.

Lechleitner has at various times attempted to produce a complete synthetic emerald; his first trial stones were a dark green with many imperfections. Later on he was able to produce a seedless emerald which had a good colour, was fairly transparent and which showed a weak, dark red fluorescence. Microscopic examination showed that this stone had been grown from a seed plate of synthetic emerald, which itself had been grown on a piece of natural beryl. This was sawn off after it had reached a thickness of about 0.5mm (0.002 in). This piece of synthetic emerald must have been placed in the autoclave more than once, since this would be the only way that the supersaturation could be kept up. But a striation pattern unlike that seen in any other synthetic emerald, may have been due to slight changes in the composition of the melt on each immersion. It was also possible to see an effect similar to the anomalous double refraction shown by synthetic spinel; features resembling cracks have been shown to have different refractive indices between various parts of the stone. Rounded brass-coloured inclusions could also be seen: each was the origin of a cuneiform growth tube. The specific gravity of these stones is 2.70, the refractive index was 1.574 and 1.569 with a birefringence of 0.005. Constants for the emerald overgrowth on beryl were a refractive index of 1.581 and 1.575, a birefringence of 0.006 and a specific gravity of 2.695. For the synthetic 'sandwich' emerald, the refractive index was 1.570 and 1.566, the birefringence was 0.004, and the specific gravity was 2.678.

A paper by Flanigen et al (1965) described the Linde hydrothermal emeralds. The crystals were usually tabular, parallel to two opposing dipyramid faces, and were bounded by first and second order prism faces. The basal pinacoid, though always present, was very small and sometimes a second order dipyramid had developed. Generally the stones were faceted with the table parallel to the first order pyramid and a distinct dichroism could be seen in this direction. The refractive index range was 1.566 to 1.572 for the ordinary ray and 1.571 to 1.578 for the

Fig. 11.5. Nail-like inclusions in a Linde emerald.

extraordinary ray. The birefringence was 0.005 to 0.006 and the specific gravity was 2.67 to 2.69. The stones were said to have appeared to be flawless under 10× magnification; under a 400× magnification, two-phase inclusions could be seen, consisting of an aqueous fluid and a gas bubble. These were concentrated at the interface of seed and overgrowth; the cavities were tube-like and the bubbles elongated. Some, but not all the stones, had phenakite inclusions. The colour and brilliance were notable and a bright red was displayed through the colour filter. See Plate 35.

Linde synthetic emerald was reported by Anderson (1972) as showing a specific gravity of 2.70 and refractive indices of 1.570 to 1.576 – this was rather higher than those recorded for previous stones from this firm. There was a strong red fluorescence under crossed filters and some fluorescence under both long- and short-wave ultra-violet light. The most characteristic inclusions were seen to be (as in older material) groups of pointed hollow tubes, in parallel formation and each containing a bubble.

Emeralds produced by the Hydrothermal Method

Relatively fewer emeralds have been grown by the hydrothermal method than by the flux-melt method. Some of the most successful were those made by Johann Lechleitner which appeared on the market in the early 1960s. This product was marketed in the U.S.A. by Linde, and by Sturmlechner in Austria, using the trade-names 'Emerita' and 'Symerald'. The first complete hydrothermal emeralds were made by the Linde Division of Union Carbide Corporation from 1965 to 1975. Production ceased in 1970 with a lot of unsold stones; some at least of the trouble was over the marketing of these emeralds in the Corporation's own line of jewellery; cracking was also said to be a problem.

Patents show that hydrothermal stones could be grown in a neutral alkali medium with mineralizers such as alkali or ammonium halides; and that iron, nickel or neodymium could be used as colouring agents. Chromium, of course, was the colouring agent. The pressure needed to grow a typical stone varied between 10,000 and 20,000 p.s.i. at temperatures of 500°C to 600°C from a fill of 62 per cent. Aluminium came from gibbsite, silica from crushed quartz crystals, beryllium from $Be(OH)_2$, and chromium from $CrCl_2 .6H_2O$. As with flux-melt growth, it was found necessary to keep the silica away from the other components and to prevent multi-nucleation.

A recent paper on Lechleitner emerald demonstrated that the refractive indices of the overgrowth on the beryl seed show a linear

correlation with the chromium content of the coating. In a sample with
the refractive index of 1.580 and 1.572, a Cr content of 3.99 per cent was
found. In another stone with a Cr content of 10.01 per cent, the refractive
index was 1.610 and 1.601.

A later patent (1973) showed that, in a new process, a very acid
medium was used. This gave growth rates of 0.8mm (0.03 in) per day.
Too fast a growth gave too many inclusions. The growth started on a
beryl seed but it was then cut away from the original seed and used as
the seed for subsequent growth. When growth slowed down, the
crystals would be removed and replaced until up to three periods of new
growth had been carried out. Generally a thickness of about 6mm (0.24
in) was produced on a 12×12mm (0.47×0.47 in) seed plate.

An emerald from the U.S.A. has clearly been produced by the
hydrothermal method. Marketed under the name of 'Regency Created
Emerald', the stones are manufactured by Vacuum Ventures of New
Jersey. The publicity material states that stones are made using patents
originally taken out by Union Carbide. In the crystal, the seed can be
seen. Characteristic inclusions seen by the author (O'Donoghue, 1979)
were growth tubes emanating from phenakite crystals and all pointing
in the same direction. The specific gravity and refractive index were in
the range expected for synthetic emerald. The stones were bright red
through the colour filter and there was a weak reddish fluorescence
under long-wave ultra-violet light. The absorption spectrum showed a
strong band at 477.4nm (using an Eickhorst 'Kaltlicht' spectroscope
assembly with polarizing and blue filters); there were the expected
bands in the red with their characteristic accompanying regions of high
transparency.

The manufacturers gave the hardness of the product as 7½ to 8; the
specific gravity as 2.67 to 2.69, and the refractive index as 1.570 to 1.576
with a double refraction of 0.005 to 0.006. There is no transparency to
X-rays, nor do the stones luminesce. The infra-red spectrum and
absorption spectrum are similar to those shown by natural emeralds.

An emerald, reported to have been made hydrothermally in the
U.S.S.R., had a specific gravity of 2.70 to 2.71; a refractive index of 1.583
to 1.586 for the ordinary ray and of 1.577 to 1.579 for the extraordinary
ray; with a birefringence of 0.006 to 0.007. Through the Chelsea filter,
the colour was either not present or was dark orange with a dull red near
the seed plate. A zonal structure could be seen, plus gas-liquid
inclusions. Reddish-brown platy crystals were present, but phenakite
was only rarely seen. Some of the seed plates were of natural beryl. A
dull, dark red fluorescence was present under long-wave ultra-violet light.

Emeralds coloured by Vanadium

A man-made emerald coloured by vanadium then by chromium was reported in 1967 (Taylor, 1967). The makers were the Crystals Research Company of Melbourne, Australia. The stones are said to be made by the hydrothermal method and can reach 10ct in size, from which faceted stones of up to 2ct have been obtained.

Whether or not the stones ought to be called emeralds can be left to those who spend time and paper on such controversies but the stones looked like emerald and had the constants of beryl, with a refractive index of 1.571 to 1.575 for the ordinary ray and 1.566 to 1.570 for the extraordinary ray. The birefringence was about 0.005. Marked colour banding could be seen when the stones were immersed in a liquid of similar refractive index (such as benzyl benzoate R.I. 1.569). Later production showed the banding much less prominently. The specific gravity was 2.68, which was slightly higher than that typical of flux-grown emerald. In this case, the difference was attributed to the water content of the hydrothermal production. No fluorescence could be detected with ultra-violet light or with X-rays. The colour of the stones was a warm grass-green with a trace of yellow, with less suggestion of blue than in other emeralds.

Dichroism gave a yellow-green for the ordinary ray and green for the extraordinary ray. Through the colour filter, the stones appeared greyish-green to dull pink. A polaroid used in conjunction with the filter showed that the ordinary ray is green and the extraordinary pink.

Absorption spectra over the range 1000 to 350nm were recorded on a Beckman DK-2 spectrophotometer at C.S.I.R.O. Polarized radiation was passed through a polished plate of the emerald cut parallel to the optic axis. The ordinary ray showed strong absorption of the violet with an edge about 460nm and a weaker band in the orange centered at 610nm;

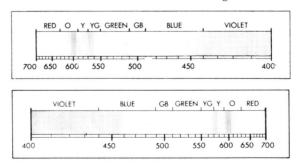

Spectrum of an emerald coloured with vanadium in UK (top) and US readings.

there was another band in the infra-red at 764nm. The maximum transmittance was at 510nm. In the extraordinary ray, there was also strong absorption of the violet, while the central band in the orange-yellow was wider and more assymetrical than that for the ordinary ray. The maximum was at 600nm with a shoulder at 575nm and an overlapping band at 632nm. The band in the near infra-red was at 850nm; maximum transmittance was at 520nm and 750nm. Crystals were grown on seed-plates fashioned from already grown crystals which were 1mm (0.04 in) or less in thickness. They were inclined to the c-axis. The interfaces of the seed and overgrowth could be seen on immersion. There were no phenakite crystals or other characteristic inclusions.

Reports on Individual Cases from the Literature

An emerald examined by the G.I.A. Los Angeles Laboratory had apparent gas bubbles when other features proved that it was grown by the flux-melt method where such bubbles are not usually seen. Magnification was 126×.

A pale green natural emerald gave a red fluorescent line at about 680nm and had red transmission under the spectroscope light.

Dyed quartzite has been offered as an imitation of emerald ('Emerald Nova'). The stones appeared as cabochons with a variegated green and white colouring. Quartz was shown by tests and the absorption spectrum showed a band at 670nm. No change could be seen through the colour filter and there was no fluorescence. Hydrochloric acid did not affect the stones in any way. Heating in the acid, however, destroyed the green colour leaving the stone almost opaque and black.

Dark green emeralds set in a ring with diamonds, and examined by the G.I.A. Los Angeles Laboratory, were found to have been set in a closed setting, the inside edge of which had been covered with a hard black enamel. This gave the emeralds their dark colour.

Emerald beads have been imitated by inserting a green plastic in the drill hole of beryl beads. The concentration of colour in the hole was obvious (reported by the G.I.A. in 1961).

Emerald imitations, consisting of pale green beryl with a surface layer of green enamel, which had apparently been baked on, was reported by the G.I.A. in 1975. The enamel chipped, so alerting the purchaser.

An emerald, made in France under the trade name of 'Lenix', has a specific gravity of 2.62 to 2.63 and a refractive index of 1.562 to 1.566. Two-phase inclusions resembling feathers and particles of flux have been seen. A strong red can be seen through the Chelsea filter (Plate 34).

Fig. 11.6. Two well-shaped phenakite crystals in a synthetic emerald. 80x

An emerald examined in 1969 (Anderson, 1969) weighed about 2ct and was mounted in a ring. Two-phase feathers brought to mind the productions of Chatham and Gilson (the feathers showed the characteristic twisting) but the refractive index was 1.574 to 1.580 and specific gravity 2.72. These figures were more suggestive of natural emerald. Through the colour filter there was very little red glow and the absorption spectrum showed that chromium was present. However the band at 427nm, ascribed to iron, could be clearly seen and this would account for the lack of fluorescence.

At this point the stone was sent to Bell Laboratories who discovered that there was no set of bands in the infra-red spectrum; these bands show the presence of water which is virtually always seen in natural stones. It was thus confirmed as a flux-grown synthetic. This was the first time that the 427nm band had been noticed in an emerald.

An emerald manufactured in Germany and reported by Schlossmacher (1959) was said to have a noticeable profusion of small, wrinkled and entangled feathers and to have a refractive index lower than that of benzyl benzoate. The fluorescence was a weak red. This was probably the production by Zerfass of Idar-Oberstein, reported more fully in 1963 (Schlossmacher, 1963). It had a specific gravity of 2.66 and a refractive index of 1.555 and 1.561 with a birefringence of 0.006. A crystal and a cut stone in the author's collection display profuse twisted veils; and the crystal shows interesting and rather attractive hexagonal crystallites growing from the hexagonal faces of the main crystals. The colour is a pleasant somewhat yellowish-green, without the trace of blue shown by Chatham and even more by Gilson stones. See Plates 36-37.

Stones which have had their appearance enhanced by the addition of a light oil (which permeates any cracks and thus minimizes them), may show yellow in the cracks when examined under ultra-violet light. Heating will bring out the oil to show as a film on the faces of the stone.

An apparent emerald examined by the G.I.A. was fair in quality when looked at with overhead lighting. It turned out to be a nearly colourless beryl with some green and smaller amounts of yellow dye in surface fractures when the stone was placed on a translucent white plastic and examined by transmitted light.

A glass imitation of emerald reported by the New York Laboratory of the G.I.A. in 1976 showed confusing flaws and a layered effect reminiscent of the calcite often seen in natural emerald. No clear gas bubbles could be seen. Another emerald imitation consisted of green plastic which showed red through the colour filter; a 'matrix' consisted of an earthy micaceous material bonded with some kind of cement.

Some triplets imitating emerald have a cement that glows red through the colour filter. The colour (green) is also quite convincing. Another imitation of emerald is pale green beryl coated with plastic which shows red through the filter.

An imitation of emerald crystals on matrix has been encountered in the U.S.A.; one was a painted quartz crystal. A better-quality imitation was also painted quartz fixed into the matrix by non-fluorescing plastic mixed with powdered matrix. This matrix must be sedimentary since fossil material could be seen in it – wrong, of course, for emerald matrix. 'Captured emerald' was the name given to a hollow rock crystal cabochon with birefringent material embedded in a green plastic. On dissolving the plastic the fragments were found to be beryl.

An imitation of emerald reported in Japan consisted of a dyed quartzite, some of which showed biotite inclusions. The colour was slightly bluish-green. A similar material was used to simulate jadeite. The colour of this latter material could fade if exposed to an alcohol flame for two minutes.

Emeralds said to be from Japan were tested by Keith Mitchell who found that their chromium absorption spectrum was clear and that they had a refractive index of 1.568 to 1.564. A dull khaki fluorescence showed under both forms of ultra-violet light. One stone showed an apparently crystalline incrustation (possibly of flux) between long two-phase tubules. The stone showed only a dull red through the Chelsea filter and was much less bright than the red shown by a Chatham stone used for comparison. Another synthetic emerald had a similar dull glow; in this case double refraction was 0.004 (which pointed towards artificial origin). The stone was of fine quality and clean with some growth lines unlike anything seen in a natural emerald.

12. Beryl

Apart from emerald, the members of the beryl family are less often synthesized. There are sound commercial reasons for this, as the value of aquamarine, yellow and pink beryls is so much less than that of emerald. Most imitations of these stones are either synthetic corundum or synthetic spinel. Beryl crystals can be doped with various elements to give different colours, but apart from emerald, this is not widely done; mainly because the expense would not be justified. Nickel gives a pale green; manganese a greyish-green; cobalt a pinkish-brown; copper a pale blue; and iron a deep blue.

Blue Beryl caused by Neutron Irradiation

A good deal of trouble has been caused by the alteration of colour in the blue varieties of beryl. For many years the trade has found that blue aquamarines are more acceptable than the green stones that would result if no action was taken to heat the rough material. This is normal trade practice and does not come within our scope. Much more serious is the relatively new practice of irradiating blue beryls to turn them a darker blue. This blue is unstable in most cases.

Supposedly-irradiated blue beryl was described by Nassau and Wood in the *Journal of Gemmology* (Nassau and Wood, 1973). Before the publication of the report, several dealers had been questioning a beryl of an unusually dark blue (rather similar to the topaz on the market in 1979), which was found to fade after a very short exposure to daylight. Thoughts naturally turned to a naturally-occurring dark blue beryl – first noted as long ago as 1917 – which was also dark and which also faded in much the same way. This material showed anomalous dichroism in that the ordinary ray was more blue than the extraordinary ray. It had an unusual absorption spectrum in which bands could be seen in the red and the yellow. The colour was lost by bleaching or exposure and could be recovered by gamma-ray irradiation, only to be lost again, and so on. Out of 23 faceted stones examined by gamma-ray spectroscopy, three were found definitely to have been coloured by neutron irradiation; the history of the others was less certain. The writers used the term 'Maxixe-type' for any dark blue beryl with blue in the ordinary ray, anomalous dichroism, a narrow-band absorption spectrum for the ordinary ray and with colour fading on exposure to light. The trade-name is 'Halbanita'. The name 'Maxixe' was given to stones from the Maxixe mine in Minas Gerais, Brazil.

Experiments with four deep blue stones, deep blue and green rough and part of the natural Maxixe rough showed that, after exposure for one week to daylight with intermittent sun or to a 100-watt frosted tungsten light bulb at a distance of 15.25cm (6 in) in an air-conditioned room, all the stones had faded significantly finishing with about half or less of the original colour. After exposure, the stones were bleached by heating to a maximum of 235°C for 30 minutes; after that they had turned yellow or pale pink. Natural aquamarine is heated to around 400°C to improve the colour (which is stable). Stones were also examined by gamma-ray spectroscopy apparatus which showed that caesium-134 was present in three of the faceted stones. This has a half-life of two years and is not present in nature. It must therefore have come from neutron irradiation, since it is produced by neutron irradiation of natural caesium-133. The remainder of the stones, which did not show this, had probably not been treated by neutron irradiation but by some other method.

After heating one of the partially bleached stones to 150°C for 30 minutes, there was no further change in colour. After 30 minutes at 200°C, only a pale pink colour remained. Neutron irradiation (this was 15 minutes at 10^{13} neutrons/cm²/sec) returned the stone to an even deeper blue than it was originally. A similar stone was bleached to pale pink in less than 30 minutes at 95°C; it was exposed to gamma-rays (2 × 10^7 rads from cobalt 60) and also turned deep blue. The stone bleached again in around 15 hours.

Heat Treatment of Green and Yellow Beryl
Many green and yellowish beryls are heated as a matter of course, with aquamarine blue as the desired end. Two Fe ions, one giving yellow and the other blue, combine to give green. Heating removes the yellow component leaving the stone coloured by the Fe ion which causes the blue. Irradiation by gamma-rays will bring back the original green colour which is stable. Whether this is done, depends on the colour attained by the first irradiation; on occasion it is not commercially acceptable.

Green material bleached by exposure to sunlight to a deep yellow could be returned to green by neutron irradiation and to a weak bluish-green by X-rays. However, gamma rays from Cobalt 60 had little effect and the material could be bleached again by exposure to light. Thirty minutes' exposure to heat at 150°C changed the green to yellow; while heating to 400°C removed the yellow. A further neutron irradiation would return the stone to green from the colourless state. A high iron content was found in the green stones but virtually none in the original sample from the Maxixe mine. It is therefore believed that a colour centre plays some part in the phenomenon. Nassau thinks that any blue or green beryl with the characteristics mentioned above should be known as 'Maxixe-type' and that it should not be offered for sale without some mention of its propensity to fade.

Electron Paramagnetic Resonance (EPR)
EPR uses microwaves which are non-destructive and will reveal energy differences which are much smaller than those in optical spectra and which relate to the energy states of unpaired electrons. Normally, in ions and chemical bonds, electrons are paired but such events as irradiation can remove one of the pair, leaving the unpaired electron to form an entity detectable by EPR. These entities with unpaired electrons are often the colour centres familiar to us as the colouring agents in a number of gemstones. Ions of the transition metals often have unpaired electrons in their inner shells and, when they occur in materials which have not been irradiated, they can be detected by EPR. Cr^{3+} was detected as the impurity causing the colour in some synthetic yellow sapphire (Barrington, 1975) when it was previously thought that Fe^{3+} was responsible.

In the case of the dark blue beryl (Maxixe and Maxixe-type), spectra were obtained with the magnetic field at right angles to the vertical axes of the crystals. To allow for differences in individual apparatus, the frequency is divided by the resonance field and multiplied by a constant to give a characteristic value for the EP resonance (this is called the g-value). G-values are 2.021 for Maxixe beryl and 2.015 for Maxixe-type beryl when the magnetic field is perpendicular to the c-axis. At right angles to this direction, the g-values are 2.004 and 2.005 respectively. Subtracting the g-values from that of the free electron (2.002) gives an indication of the material with which the unpaired electron is associated. In this case similar values have been found for NO_3 (where the g-values are 2.023 and 2.003) in an irradiated KNO_3 and for CO^{-3} (g-values 2.016 and 2.005) in irradiated calcite.

EPR spectra of the 'Halbanita' material and of a Maxixe-type beryl obtained by X-ray irradiation from morganite show that, in both cases, the blue colour arose from a CO^{-3} ion with its plane normal to the vertical crystal axis and placed in the largest part of the empty central channel of the beryl. As the blue colour in both true Maxixe and Maxixe-type beryl is known to be caused by NO_3 and CO^{-3} respectively, it is presumed that the centres responsible are created by the loss of an electron or when a hydrogen atom is removed from HNO_3 and HCO^{-3}. This loss can easily occur when substances are exposed to X-rays or gamma-rays.

A report (Bastos, 1975) on the 'Halbanita' stones states that they have not been exposed to either X-rays or gamma-rays. A 'Halbanita' stone bleached by heat was subjected to ultra-violet irradiation in the range 230 to 330nm for a few minutes. After a short time, the CO^{-3} signal could be seen in the EPR spectrum and, after two hours' irradiation, a weak blue colour began to appear and the EPR signal was much stronger.

Only those beryls which contain CO^{-3} or NO^{-3} impurities can be coloured blue or green. For the colour to remain, the electrons need to be securely trapped and the strength of the trapping varies from stone to stone. Most electrons in the Maxixe-type beryl are trapped together with protons to form atoms of hydrogen. Maxixe beryl was found to be the same in this respect. Many electrons in the Maxixe-type beryl are trapped by centres which are at present thought to be CO_2 impurities which form CO^{-2} associated with different alkali metal ions. EPR signals of NO_2 can be seen in the Maxixe beryl. Heating shows that the stones with CO^{-2} signals are the least stable and that the colour decays at a fast rate. Stones which give a hydrogen signal have a colour which disappears more slowly.

Later work on the electron paramagnetic resonance of similar material (Anderson, 1979) showed that the colour arose from different impurity ions which have lost one electron, probably by irradiation, to form CO_3 colour centres in the Maxixe-type beryl and NO_3 colour centres in the Maxixe beryl itself.

Red Beryl

Synthetic red beryl coloured by cobalt was reported in 1967 (Taylor, 1967). This is made hydrothermally and coloured light brown to a reddish-purple (ordinary and extraordinary rays respectively). Beryls coloured deep blue (from Fe) and light blue (Cu) have also been made. The best colour for this stone was obtained when the table was parallel

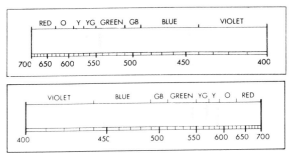

Spectrum of synthetic red beryl coloured by cobalt in UK (top) and US readings.

to the optic axis. The purple colour, which belonged to the extraordinary ray, could only be seen at its best with the aid of the dichroscope or with Polaroid, because to the eye it was always diluted by the ordinary ray (a similar case occurs with aquamarines from Madagascar).

With the colour filter, the ordinary ray showed green and the extraordinary ray was bright red. With a Beckman DK-2 spectrophotometer, the following absorption bands were recorded for the ordinary ray:

561.2nm, weak

544.7, weak

525.6, weak

447.5, strong

For the extraordinary ray, measurements were:

586.0nm, strong

567.0, strong

543.0, strong

The strong dichroism seen in the stones was due to the dissimilarity between the spectra of the ordinary and extraordinary rays. The brown ordinary ray absorbed strongly in the violet and weakly in the green, whereas the extraordinary ray transmitted all the violet and showed the characteristic cobalt bands in the yellow-green.

In beryl, Be^{2+} and Si^{4+} are in tetrahedral sites and Al^{3+} in octahedral sites. Cobalt could be located in either type of site (theoretically) as Co^{2+} or Co^{3+} but hydrothermally-grown crystals favour the divalent form, due to the reducing nature of the process. Most compounds with Co^{2+} in tetrahedral sites are blue, while those with it in octahedral sites are pink because the absorption bands are thereby moved to shorter wavelengths. It looks as though cobalt in these stones is divalent and substitutes for Al in the octahedral sites.

13. Alexandrite

The nature of alexandrite is so intriguing, that it is not surprising that many efforts have been made both to synthesize and to imitate the stone. Almost all 'synthetic' or even natural 'alexandrites' offered by the public are in fact synthetic corundum coloured by vanadium. This can be detected by the tell-tale absorption band at 475nm even if the strange colour (purplish-mauve) does not give it away. One of the reasons why these quite interesting stones get away with their imposture is that relatively few people know what a true alexandrite looks like. A rarer imitation is a dark green spinel with flashes of red (which was originally made to imitate green tourmaline).

Although true alexandrite (i.e. chrysoberyl) has been attempted many times using a variety of techniques, success was slow in coming. In some instances, chromium preferentially crystallized with the lead of the flux to give lead chromate. It is now clear that some other flux has been found. At least two and probably more firms are now producing alexandrite by the flux-melt method and by pulling.

Reports on Individual Cases from the Literature

Synthetic alexandrite, reported by the G.I.A. in 1973, was manufactured by Creative Crystals Inc. of Danville, California. The stones had a strong colour change, more reminiscent of the stones from the U.S.S.R. than those from Sri Lanka. The colour change was from a violet-red to a bluish-green. There was no resemblance to the synthetic corundum so frequently offered as 'alexandrite'. The refractive index was 1.746 to 1.755 and the specific gravity was 3.73. A layer of dustlike inclusions parallel to the seed face could be seen and there was also quite a strong banding. Wispy veils ('cigarette smoke') could be seen as in most flux-melt grown stones. At the time the report was made, stones were being

Fig. 13.1. A typical pattern of wisp-like feathers, consisting of fluid-filled channels, in synthetic alexandrite. 20x

offered at US$150 per carat for sizes under 1ct and at $250 per carat for stones over 1ct.

An 'alexandrite' glass simulant was reported by the G.I.A. in 1965. In this case, the stone showed red and green from different angles but was, in fact, made from a piece of red and a piece of green glass joined together. The pieces were separated by a plane of minute bubbles. No change in colour with change in type of light occurred.

Glass with a change of colour similar to that in alexandrite-like corundum (a daylight colour of steely-blue and a amethyst colour under incandescent light) is reported by the G.I.A. (1973). Apparently such glass has been known since the beginning of the nineteenth century. Tiny crystallites could be seen under a magnification of 63×.

A patent taken out in the U.S.A. by Cline and Patterson – the founders of Creative Crystals – and dated 1975, involves the slow cooling of a solution of BeO and Al_2O_3 in a flux of Li_2O+MoO_3 from 1200°C at 1°C per hour. About 4 per cent of the melt is made up by beryllia and alumina and iron oxide Fe_2O_3 and Cr_2O_3 make up about 1 per cent. Seeds of synthetic or natural chrysoberyl are mounted in a platinum frame and lowered into the melt before cooling begins. Growth takes from seven to nine weeks; the crystals are then cut from the seeds. There is also a mention in the patent of growth by pulling; stones of up to 400ct,

152

ALEXANDRITE

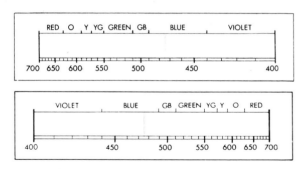

Spectrum of synthetic corundum, coloured by vanadium, imitating alexandrite in UK (top) and US readings.

76mm (3 in) long and with a diameter of 19mm (0.75 in) have been grown.

Alexandrite grown by the Czochralski method is described by Liddicoat (1975). The stones were very transparent and coloured a bluish-green to greenish-blue in daylight with a change to purple to violet in incandescent light. The refractive indices were 1.740 to 1.749 with a birefringence of 0.009. The stones were biaxial positive and their specific gravity was 3.715. A strong red fluorescence could be seen under both long- and short-wave ultra-violet light and under X-rays. The stones were much more transparent to ultra-violet light than are natural alexandrites; stones grown by the flux-melt method were more transparent than the pulled stones. Some randomly oriented needles could be seen in the stone, together with some lath-shaped crystals.

Alexandrite is grown by the Kyocera Company of Kyoto in Japan and occurs in quite large flawless crystals pulled by the Czochralski method. They have the trade-name of 'Crescent Vert Alexandrite' and are marketed in the U.S.A. as 'Inamori Created Alexandrite'.

Another alexandrite, of origin at present unknown, has constants as for the natural stone and is remarkably clear; the colour-change is excellent. Although alexandrite is known to have been grown in the U.S.S.R. and in Japan, it is not certain that the stone (which is in the author's collection) is from either of those places.

14. Spinel

Virtually all synthetic spinel is made by the Verneuil flame-fusion process. While spinel itself is not of great importance as a gemstone, the colours available can imitate a large number of better-known and more valuable stones: topaz, aquamarine and peridot, plus blue sapphire imitations are frequently produced. The white variety can easily, at first glance, be mistaken for diamond; especially when the stones are small and set as surrounds to a larger stone. As we have seen in Chapter 2, the first attempt resulting in a spinel was one involving a supposed blue sapphire. The addition of cobalt required the further addition of magnesium as a flux, but this gave a spinel rather than a corundum composition (see Plates 43-47).

Curved growth lines like those in synthetic corundum are not seen in synthetic spinel. Bubbles are also rarer, because the boules grow more slowly. The bubbles which are seen sometimes resemble hoses in parallel arrangement; and some, according to Anderson, resemble furled umbrellas. As shown by Gübelin, these can look very natural as they have the shapes of negative crystals which look hexagonal when viewed from the end. They are also grouped at right angles to the trigonal axis of the boule lattice; the grouping also has a hexagonal pattern. Tiny flat cavities containing a bubble either of liquid or gas are sometimes joined by a tube to a similar flat cavity parallel to and below the first. The study of synthetic spinel bubbles is a rewarding one.

However, in most cases, the gemmologist will find that the refractometer will give the game away when one of these stones is encountered. Owing to the incorporation of extra alumina to give a composition of $Mg3Al_2O_4$, the refractive index will reach 1.728 as against 1.718 for the natural stones; similarly the specific gravity will be 3.64 as against 3.60. Between crossed polars, there will be the characteristic anomalous

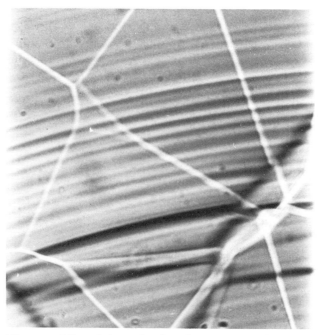

Fig. 14.1. (Above) Curved striae, characteristic of ruby red synthetic spinel.

Fig. 14.2. (Below) A synthetic spinel between crossed polars, showing the tabby extinction.

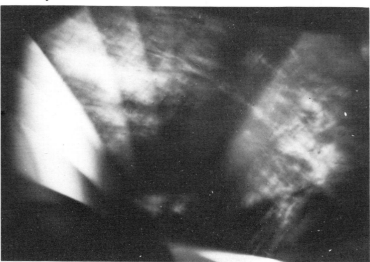

Fig. 14.3. Hexagonal crack pattern in synthetic spinel.

double-refraction stripes resembling those on a tabby cat and familiarly known as 'tabby extinction'. Where small white stones are involved, an immersion of the piece will show that diamond is not a candidate because the spinels will show lack of relief; the liquid used could be methylene iodide.

Blue synthetic spinels intended to imitate blue sapphire will show the absorption spectrum of cobalt rather than that of iron. The cobalt shows as three broad bands in the orange, yellow and green; the central band is the widest of the three. In some very dark blue stones, almost the whole of the orange to green is absorbed. It is also easy to check dark blue stones with the colour filter because cobalt passes a good deal of red; blue sapphires will remain dark.

Pink spinels coloured by iron (to imitate pink beryl or perhaps kunzite) and a pale yellowish-green variety (coloured by manganese) will show a strong green fluorescence under ultra-violet light. The yellow stones show two absorption bands in the violet. White synthetic spinels will glow a bluish-white under short-wave ultra-violet light.

Some authorities state that some light blue spinels are coloured by the addition of cobalt and chromium and that some yellowish-green stones contain manganese with vanadium.

Colours of the range of synthetic spinel produced by Djévahirdjan.

Number	Colour
100	white
101	bluish-white
105	aquamarine: green
105 bis	aquamarine: blue
105 ter	aquamarine: blue
106 light	aquamarine: light blue
106 dark	aquamarine: dark blue
108	aquamarine: bluish
108 bis	aquamarine: dark blue
109	aquamarine: bluish dark
111	Ceylon colour
112	Burma blue
114	azurite: light
115 bis	azurite
116	Cyanithe (Kyanite)
118	aquamarine: bluish (dark colour)
119	aquamarine: dark blue
120	zircon: blue
122	zircon: green
130	chrysolithe: greenish-yellow
135	Brazil emerald: green (Erinite)
136	Brazil emerald: dark green
140	rose
149	tourmaline: light green
152	tourmaline: dark green

Reports on Individual Cases from the Literature

Synthetic red spinel in the form of octahedra was described by Crowningshield and Holmes in Gems and Gemology (Winter 1950-51). The presence of a wire showed that the crystal was man-made. Triangular markings could be seen on the crystal, both by optical methods and with the electron microscope. The markings were not symmetrical and also included a rosette-like structure. The interior of the crystal showed numerous liquid feathers and flattened liquid bubbles. The hardness appeared to be greater than that of flame-fusion synthetic spinel since it scratched topaz easily and could even scratch synthetic ruby when some pressure was applied. The specific gravity was found to be greater than 3.63 but less than 3.98. There was a marked

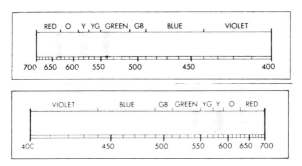

Spectrum of a synthetic spinel, coloured by cobalt, imitating blue sapphire in UK (top) and US readings.

zoning of colour. The refractive index was measured at 1.75. A strong fluorescent doublet could be seen in the red and a broad absorption zone began in the orange in about the same place as the similar zone in ruby; in natural red spinel, the broad absorption zone is more towards the green. There was almost complete absorption of the violet. An X-ray powder diffraction pattern showed that the crystal was indeed spinel. Chromium was detected by an emission spectrograph. Later work showed that it may have been rich in zinc: this would explain the higher refractive index. It was clearly grown by the flux-melt process.

Spinel, presumably made by the Verneuil flame-fusion process, was reported with apparent two-phase inclusions (Brinck, 1955). The stones were yellow-green in colour; the inclusions showed negative crystal faces in a number of cases, with needle-shaped forms predominating. Magnification up to 500× was necessary to distinguish the different parts of the inclusion, although they were visible at lower magnifications.

Synthetic red spinel thought to have been grown by the flame-fusion method, was reported by Gübelin in 1953. Because at least some of the material was found as octahedra, it may be thought – in the light of present knowledge – that the stones may well have been manufactured by the flux-melt method. There are now a number of crystals of spinel, both red and in other colours, known to have been made in that way. However the stones described in the paper were known to have been cut from a boule. Some of them showed numerous cracks which accorded with similar markings in a whole boule in my own collection. X-ray powder tests showed that the synthetic material did not differ from the natural and that both had the same crystal lattice.

The specific gravity was in the same range as natural spinel and the refractive index also coincided closely. In the absorption spectrum, the group of emission lines was not seen; rather there was one brilliant and broad band extending from 685nm to 690nm with a faint narrow red line at 678nm. Gas bubbles of tadpole shape could be seen; these were more reminiscent of synthetic corundum than the usual type of synthetic spinel. Distinct curved striae could also be seen curved more strongly toward the bottom of the boule. Almost complete extinction could be seen in one specimen showing that it was pure.

A red stone which proved to be synthetic spinel, was reported by Eppler (1956). It appeared to be part of a boule grown by the Verneuil process. The specific gravity was determined as 3.599 and the single refractive index was 1.720. From these figures Eppler estimated that this particular stone was equimolecular in composition, rather than having the excess of alumina usually shown by other synthetic spinels. Under the microscope, curved lines could be seen. These were not parallel but somewhat distorted. Gaseous inclusions, in the form of round cavities and hose-like channels, could be seen. Some dark spots proved to be two-phase inclusions; some represented negative crystals filled with hydrogen and water.

Verneuil-grown spinel was examined by Schiffman (1972). An early report of the successful synthesis of the red type was made by Michel (1926) and a later report in 1932 mentioned that the stones had no excess of alumina such as is found in the other colours of spinel. Chromium and manganese were mentioned as colouring agents; however all these early productions were said to have the propensity to crack which we now know can scarcely be avoided.

A boule of red spinel examined by Schiffman did not show the usual rectangular/squarish outline shown by most spinel boules; instead it looked as though the material had 'run over'. The same effect can be seen in a boule in the author's collection. Surfaces are striated by arc-like markings as a result of the uneven deposition of the melt. The upper end of the boule examined by Schiffman had a frosted appearance and was a paler red than the remaining part. The frosted appearance was shown under a higher resolution, to consist of skeletal formations which were caused by the rapid fall in temperature after the cut-off of the flame. The manufacturer stated that chromium with traces of titanium had been used as a colouring agent. Similar formations have been reported on colourless, green and blue spinel boules.

A cut stone (from the same boule) was prepared and found to contain numerous cracks due to internal strain. The weight was 5ct, the refractive index was 1.726, and the specific gravity was 3.60. The spectroscope showed some ill-defined lines in the red. One, at about 694nm was an emission line; while two broad and strong bands were situated at

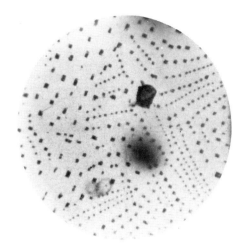

Fig. 14.4. Octahedral
inclusions in a synthetic
purple spinel. 36.5x

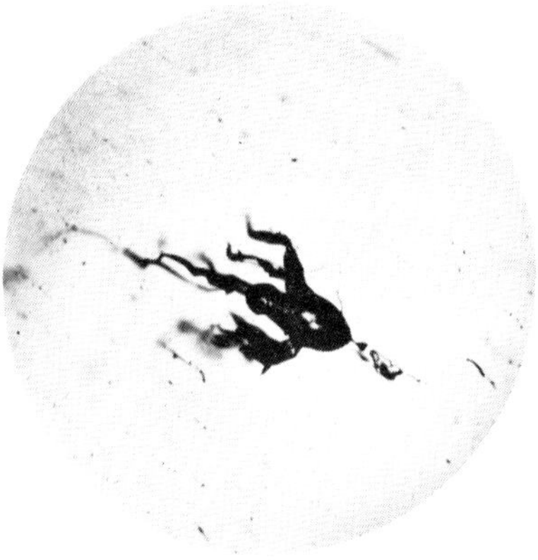

Fig. 14.5. Oddly-shaped gas
bubble in synthetic green
spinel. 23x

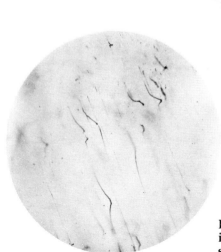

Fig. 14.6. Drawn-out bubbles
in synthetic greenish-yellow
spinel.

Fig. 14.7. Tension fissures following the direction of the cube in synthetic spinel.

610 to 490nm and from 465nm to the end of the spectrum. There was some transparency left in the blue at about 490 to 465nm: this is the cause of the purplish colour shown by the stone. No lines in the blue could be seen. Under long-wave ultra-violet light, there was a weak, dark red fluorescence; a similar effect appeared under short-wave.

Stones cut from near the centre of the boule showed curved growth lines like those seen in Verneuil corundum. Unlike the corundum, however, they were not even and showed some irregular distribution of colour with arcs meeting at an angle. Thin elongated bubbles could also be seen.

Some red flux-melt grown spinels had a specific gravity of 3.592 and 3.598 and showed a fluorescence spectrum with a line at 685.5nm. There was a red fluorescence under ultra-violet light of both types and a more purplish glow under X-rays, with a persistent phosphorescence.

A group of blue crystals made by the same method showed the characteristic cobalt spectrum with a bright red through the colour filter. There was very little luminescence under ultra-violet light or under X-rays. This is unlike the Verneuil-grown blue spinels, which

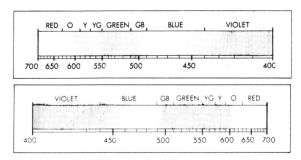

Spectrum of Verneuil-grown red spinel in UK (top) and US readings.

will give red under long-wave and a greenish white under short-wave.

A yellow crystal had a specific gravity of 3.609, no distinctive absorption spectrum, but gave a green glow under long-wave ultra-violet light. This was quite vivid under X-rays, but there was no phosphorescence. Pale green crystals with a specific gravity of 3.601 and 3.589, had no definitive absorption spectrum but showed a dull green glow under X-rays.

Crystals with a bluish-green colour had a specific gravity of 5.7. They showed a fine line in the red with indeterminate lines in the yellow, which was perhaps due to rare earth dopants. They showed a strong yellow under both ultra-violet light and X-rays.

Two-phase inclusions were noticed in a yellow-green synthetic spinel. They appeared to show distinct crystal forms, perhaps negative crystals, and to be accompanied by elongated gas bubbles. The inclusions appeared also to lie in a curved zone, perhaps following the curved top of the boule.

A green synthetic spinel showed a greenish-yellow surface effect under short-wave ultra-violet light and a rich red under long-wave. This indicated the presence of chromium and, with a strong ray of white light

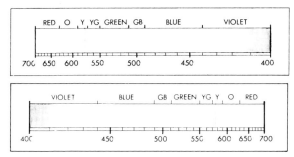

Spectrum of synthetic green spinel in UK (top) and US readings.

shining on it, the stone showed some red. Chromium lines in the absorption spectrum settled the matter.

A synthetic green spinel examined by the G.I.A. had, in the absorption spectrum, a faint band between 550 and 540nm, a stronger band between 580 and 570nm and a more diffuse band with a centre about 620nm. All these were seen by transmitted light. In reflected light, there was a fluorescent spectrum with a bright line near 680nm and a sharp dark line at 678nm.

A synthetic spinel with a colour similar to that of a pale aquamarine was examined by the G.I.A. in 1974. The absorption spectrum showed a fluorescent line near 690nm which may have been due to chromium. A strong red fluorescence could be seen under long-wave ultra-violet light and a bright orange-red fluorescence under short-wave. There was also a very noticeable anomalous double refraction with interference colours visible. The refractive index was normal for synthetic spinel at 1.73. Tiny gas bubbles could also be seen.

A moonstone-coloured spinel was reported by Breebart (1958). The colour was in a range from nearly colourless to bluish and the refractive index was 1.728. Specific gravity values ranged from 3.63 to 3.66; the latter was rather high for synthetic spinel. Inside the stones, air bubbles could be seen; these took the irregular forms and patterns characteristic of synthetic spinel. Between crossed polars, colours could be seen – notably yellow, blue and green – and, on rotation, the typical stripes of anomalous double refraction could not be seen. It is thought that the moonstone effect is due to interference at minute fractures running through the stone. The manufacturer was reported as saying that the boules had been subjected to heat treatment to give the moonstone effect.

A white schillerized spinel has been used to imitate moonstone. The spinel showed a strong blue under short-wave ultra-violet light; under this, moonstone is inert.

15. Garnet

Synthetic garnets have the same structure as natural garnets. The substitution of elements which takes place is the same as that which takes place in the natural stones. Examples are Y^{3+} and Al^{3+} for Mn^{2+} and Si^{4+}. Grossular garnet, for example, has 24 total positive charges (i.e. $3Ca^{2+} + 2Al^{3+} + 3Si^4$). Total negative charges ($12 \times {}^{-2}$ on the oxygens) makes up an electrically-balanced crystal. Si makes the crystal difficult to grow; it has a charge of 4+ which no other ion has. Although atoms of the same charge and of suitable size substitute readily, and a difference of up to 30 per cent can be tolerated, the charge balance needs to be maintained to achieve an electrically-neutral crystal. This can be achieved by coupled substitution where two ions are replaced at the same time by two others, one with a higher and one with a lower charge. Al^{3+} remains with a size of 0.50Å; it is only one unit out compared with the Si^{4+} that we want to replace. Substituting Al for Si, we can get 21 positive charges ($3Ca^{2+} + 2Al^{3+} + 2Al^{3+}$). To get the three extra positive charges needed, one each can be added to the three Ca^{2+}; therefore an ion of about the same size as Ca but with a 3+ charge is needed. Yttrium fills the bill as the size is very close to that of Ca. The end result is $Y_3Al_5O_{12}$.

Similar substitutions can take place with other elements; for example gadolinium and erbium can replace calcium and gallium replace aluminium. It is also possible to make mixed rare-earth garnets. Most of these materials are grown by the Czochralski method (which is best suited to larger crystals); the smaller ones can be grown by the flux-melt method.

Garnets containing Nd, Ho, Er, Tm or Yb show fluorescence and may be used in lasers. For this application, the combinations $Y_3Al_5O_{12}Nd$ and $Y_3Al_5O_{12}Nd$-Cr are the most important.

Garnet-type synthetic stones, according with the general formula $X_3Y_5O_{12}$, have been regularly grown for a number of years for a variety of industrial and research purposes. They can be doped with rare-earth elements which, in many cases, will lend the stones an attractive colour. Most of these crystals have specific gravities and refractive indices outside the range of the natural materials they may imitate from time to time. For stones doped with yttrium, which gives a green colour, the constants are 4.60 and 1.834. For those doped with other elements in the same series, the constants are as follows:

terbium	pale yellow	6.06 and 1.873
dysprosium	yellow-green	6.20 and 1.85
holmium	golden yellow	6.30 and 1.863
erbium	yellowish-pink	6.43 and 1.853
thulium	pale green	6.48 and 1.854
ytterbium	pale yellow	6.62 and 1.848
lutecium	pale yellow	6.69 and 1.842

Several other colours, including some shades of blue, are also made. The blue, in particular, could easily be mistaken for aquamarine, were not the constants so clearly wrong for that stone.

YAG

However it is as a diamond simulant that yttrium aluminium garnet ('garnet' from the garnet-like structure of this cubic material – true garnets are silicates) is best known. Since the introduction of zirconia, it has lost ground, but it is still on the scene. As there is no dopant needed for a colourless stone, the constants are lower than those quoted above, being about 4.57 with a refractive index of 1.834. The dispersion is about 0.028 compared with the 0.044 of diamond. To my mind the stones never look really exciting; life seems to pour out of them as they are tilted away from the light source. With some specimens, a yellow fluorescence under long-wave ultra-violet light has been noted, with a similar but weaker effect under short-wave. A bright mauve was shown by these stones under X-rays. The fluorescence spectrum showed a discrete band in the yellow.

Some green stones are coloured by chromium and show the appropriate absorption spectrum and red through the colour filter. Others show a complex line spectrum due to the rare-earth dopants. Inclusions seem to be mainly natural-looking feathers and particles of flux which may look angular. A 'treacly' appearance has been reported from some chrome-rich green stones. See Plates 48-49.

Analogous substances, such as yttrium iron garnet and yttrium gallium garnet, have been made but have not reached the gem market. Yttrium iron garnet is black and opaque, although it provides some very well-shaped crystals which would be interesting to the collector. Gadolinium gallium garnet is treated separately, see Chapter 9.

Reports on Individual Cases from the Literature

An attractive green stone was reported in 1967 (Mitchell, 1967) and was first described as a 'fine green garnet'. The stone weighed 2.94ct and the attempt to obtain the characteristic absorption spectrum of demantoid garnet met with an unexpected reverse, when a spectrum of about 10 strong lines accompanied by about 20 weaker ones was observed. The stone was, in fact, a YAG which had been doped with rare earths, certainly including didymium. There was a strong red fluorescence under both long- and short-wave ultra-violet light; under X-rays there was an orange fluorescence with strong phosphorescence. Even with visible light, some red could be seen through the green. A strong red could be seen through the colour filter.

A light yellow garnet-type stone was reported by the G.I.A. in 1969. It had fine absorption lines at 590nm, with more fine lines near 540nm and another group near 475nm. Further lines were seen in the violet and deep violet; in this region particularly prominent lines could be seen at 412 and 405nm. There was a weak absorption of the near red.

Another stone, also yellow, was known to owe its colour to europium. There was absorption in the red, two groups of fine lines centered at about 650 and 545nm with the remainder of the spectrum absorbed from about 500nm.

A light blue-green 'garnet' showed an absorption spectrum with faint narrow absorption in the deep red with a band in the red-orange centered at about 660nm with a stronger line at about 667nm. There was also a faint band centered at about 610 and the remainder of the spectrum was absorbed from about 440nm onwards.

16. Quartz

Quartz is so plentiful in the natural state that it is scarcely worth making it artificially for gem purposes. Much quartz is made by the hydro-thermal method, but this is intended for the industrial and research market, as the predictability of the material is greatly in its favour in these fields. In recent years, one or two manufacturers have embarked upon a course of making and selling citrine and amethyst, but there can be very little commercial success (I should have thought) from such activities. They are much more likely to be an ingenious way of disposing of material which, through twinning or some other undesirable feature, is found to be unsuitable for industrial purposes. When man-made quartz is encountered, problems of identification are likely to be severe – or would be if the material was not so relatively inexpensive – as neither amethyst nor citrine can be distinguished satisfactorily from the natural stone.

Colours of Synthetic Quartz

blue	add cobalt and reduce by heating
brown	add iron
dark brown	add aluminium and irradiate
green	add iron and reduce by heating
violet	add iron and irradiate
yellow	add iron
yellow-green	gamma irradiation plus heating

The brown colour may be due to either Fe^{3+} ions or to iron silicate finely dispersed in the quartz rather than in the crystal lattice. Green stones are produced by heating the brown ones so that the ferric iron ions are reduced to ferrous Fe^{2+} again, either in the lattice or as dispersed particles. Dark brown smoky quartz crystals owe their colour to colour centres brought about by sodium or lithium and aluminium impurities which need to be irradiated. In the synthetic stones the colour is enhanced by adding small amounts of germanium, then irradiating.

Violet is produced by using some radioactive source, such as cobalt 60, which produces colour centres. It is believed that Fe^{3+} ions are required for amethyst-type colour centres. To obtain them, a fairly high energy is needed at a low temperature. Radioactive particles are suitable for this task; better than high temperatures since in those circumstances the colour centres would not form as the electrons could return to their original orbits. Since the colour is destroyed when the stones are heated, this would seem to bear out these observations.

Crystals of synthetic quartz, when removed from the pressure vessel, are easily recognized by the cobbled structure which appears on some faces. This structure arises from impurities in the crystals.

Reports on Individual Cases from the Literature

The author has described a fine citrine (O'Donoghue 1973) from Sawyer Research Products, Ohio, U.S.A. The stone weighed 49.28ct and gave the characteristic constants for quartz; there was no zoning of colour and the only inclusions visible were tiny groups of crystals resembling breadcrumbs. It is suggested that these crystals are of the mineral acmite, a sodium-iron silicate. In nature, acmite forms slender brown monoclinic crystals; in the hydrothermal process, it may be formed by the reaction of iron with sodium and silica in the solution.

In many quartz crystals grown by the hydrothermal process using a seed, it is possible to see an effect which has been called 'heat shimmer'. This is an area of discontinuity where the seed and overgrowth meet. In the cut citrine, no such region was visible, but this may simply be that the stone was cut from a very large crystal and this distinctive area was avoided by the cutter. The seeds from which such quartz is grown by this manufacturer were also examined by the author. They show one set of faces at the ends where growth is slow and different forms where growth is more rapid. The manufacturers claim that they can make smoky quartz by subjecting the crystals to an ionizing radiation of 10^6r. This activates the colour centres which produce the well-known smoky effect.

The same manufacturers produce a green stone and, in the example in the author's collection, the seed area can clearly be seen. The colour would not successfully imitate any other known gemstone.

Synthetic quartz manufactured by Sawyer Research Products of Eastlake, Ohio is further reported in *Gems and Gemology* (Crowningshield, 1972). Breadcrumb-like inclusions from the area of the seed are prominent in some examples, although faceted stones would, presumably, be cut from clear areas.

A quartz crystal from the U.S.S.R. had been grown from a plate of clear quartz which had two wire loops attached. The colour of the whole crystal varied: next to the seed on either side was a layer of colourless material followed by a band of green and finally by a band of a brown colour. A similar crystal is in the author's collection.

Blue quartz apparently manufactured in the U.S.S.R. is described by Anderson (1969). The stone in question was bright blue and mounted in a ring; the constants were those of quartz. Bands ascribed to cobalt could be seen, but the central band was rather narrower than its counterpart seen in cobalt blue spinels. The owners of the piece said that they had also obtained a ring set with a piece of synthetic green spinel which also emanated from the U.S.S.R.

A synthetic green quartz made in the U.S.S.R. was bi-coloured yellow and green with breadcrumb inclusions (Crowningshield, 1977).

Synthetic amethyst from the U.S.S.R. was seen at the G.I.A.'s New York Laboratory and reported in 1978. Apparently this has been appearing in large quantities. Some of the material gave a weak greenish fluorescence (but this could be seen in some of the paler examples only and not in all of them). Darker stones were virtually inert, while some natural amethyst gave a similar weak fluorescence. No characteristic inclusions could be seen, although there was some indistinct colour banding. Probably the material was cut from a region well away from the seed crystal (the amethysts are grown hydrothermally like all quartz). The colour varied from pale brownish-purple to a deeper purple while still retaining the brown tinge. This seems to agree with the author's report (O'Donoghue, 1978), see below.

Two synthetic amethysts were examined by the author (O'Donoghue, 1978); both were presumed to have been manufactured in the U.S.S.R. Since writing the paper quoted, I have been able to examine some rough amethyst both in Moscow and later on here in Great Britain. Both the cut stones were of fine colour and nothing about them suggested anything amiss, at least to casual observation. There was a trace of a mauve-brown colour in one direction in both stones which I had not seen so prominently in natural amethyst. On the other hand, there was no sign of the characteristic colour bands or stripes so typical of natural stones. These two cut stones were presumably made by the hydrothermal process but, as quartz made by this method (which involves a seed), is normally cut well-away from the seed area, no trace of the discontinuity which results in 'heat-shimmer' or 'breadcrumbs', could be seen. These phenomena can usually be detected when material from the area where seed and overgrowth meet is incorporated into a cut stone. Neither stone transmitted short-wave ultra-violet light, although some synthetic quartz has been known to do so.

I have heard from more than one source that these stones are unlikely to find much favour on the market, especially as the price of good natural amethyst is not especially high. As identification would provide quite a difficult problem, were it called for, this seems just as well.

Some amethyst can be heated to give a leek-green colour. This material is sometimes offered in its rough state.

Amethyst-citrine quartz was reviewed by Kurt Nassau (April 1981) in *Lapidary Journal*. Various names for this material (which consists of amethyst- and citrine-coloured quartz together in a single crystal or cut stone) have been proposed but some at least are unsuitable. Nassau feels that 'amethyst-citrine' quartz is to be preferred.

Iron causes colour in quartz in a number of ways. One is where it occurs on its own to give yellow (ferric iron) or green (ferrous iron) – the latter can also be produced by heating amethyst. So long as the temperature does not rise above about 450°C, heating has no effect on colours so caused. If the yellow or green quartz is then irradiated by, for example, gamma rays, a light-absorbing colour centre forms in much of the material. The colour produced is the amethyst colour which can be driven off at temperatures of around 300-500°C (when the yellow or green colour reappears). The critical temperature can vary to some extent with the specimen.

The amethyst colour comes from a radiation-induced colour centre associated with the iron. Ferric iron atoms enter the quartz structure, perhaps by substituting for silicon atoms (with a necessary charge compensation), or by occurring interstitially in the gaps between the tetrahedra of SiO_4 also with some charge compensation. One of these types of iron gives the citrine colour and the other the amethyst colour, after irradiation.

Growth conditions dictate how much iron enters the quartz at any given place. Most natural amethyst growth is under the positive rhombohedron where polysynthetic twinning is frequent. If growth takes place under the negative rhombohedron, then the colour is paler or even smoky. This shows that much less iron has entered the crystal.

The amethyst-citrine crystal examined showed amethyst towards the tip and the rest of it was citrine-coloured. It was grown hydrothermally. When the crystal was immersed and viewed, colour was seen to be amethyst in the major rhombohedron regions and citrine in the basal pinacoid growth region (this form is very rare in natural quartz). The crystal was grown from an iron-containing solution and had then been irradiated to give the amethyst colour. Various patents bear this out.

Natural amethyst-citrine quartz, in which six regions of alternating colours have been described, can be seen to have come about in a similar way. The colours correspond to the same parts of the crystal and both materials show dichroism. Polysynthetic twinning is noted by a number of writers in the amethyst parts alone and Brazil law and Dauphine twinning is also reported. It is possible that the natural material may have been formed by amethyst-forming iron entering the major rhombohedra and the citrine-causing iron under the minor rhombohedra. Irradiation would finish the task. It is also possible that at first the amethyst colour was present in all parts and that the crystals then passed through some form of heat in which the minor rhombohedron amethyst was bleached. Another way would be if heat followed by irradiation coloured some parts only.

Various experiments were tried and showed that sectored (Brazilian) amethyst on moderate heating gave the change which could be reversed by irradiation; stronger heating followed by irradiation and a gentle heating also produced the change but it was impossible for the colour to be returned to all-amethyst. No tests to separate the natural from the synthetic material are possible.

17. Opal

As a most beautiful and desirable stone, opal has been simulated by a variety of materials over many years. Most of these simulants were of glass. Although attempts at a simulation of the opal-like effect (play of colour) were partially successful, it was only when the true nature of the cause of the play of colour was comprehended in the 1950s that a synthetic opal could be produced. The glass imitations were usually heated and then introduced into dye-containing water; the same process was often applied to rock crystal. In neither case could the resulting colour effect really look like opal. By far the best effort at imitating the true opal is of course the composite stone, doublet or triplet. These will be dealt with in Chapter 22.

The discovery of the cause of the play of colour was quite soon followed by the first attempts at synthesis. One of the first was by Iler of Wilmington, Delaware, U.S.A., who achieved the play of colour but whose pieces had to be enclosed in plastic to give the required stability. The later productions by Gilson and others are very like the true opal and give the complete range of colours whereas the Iler material only gave blue and green.

The Structure of Precious Opal

Precious opal is made up of uniformly-sized silica spheres which are stacked to form a regular array. The voids between the spheres are also spaced regularly and these voids cause diffraction since they give a break in optical continuity. The wavelength of the light depends on the radius of the spheres and also on the type of stacking. In volcanic opal, the voids between the spheres are small and thus give a greater transparency to the stone. The particles, being more uniformly oriented, give broad colour bands instead of the pattern of patches seen in other types of opal. The opposite is true of opals formed in a sedimentary environment.

A method which aimed to reproduce the structure of spheres and voids was described by Darragh and Perdrix (1975). They first attempted to use sodium silicate as a starting material but this proved to be too slow a method because the spheres had too large a range of particle size distribution. In addition, in many cases the silica cross-linked to form sheets and needles rather than spheres. Another method, using silicic acid, was too slow to be of serious value.

A method developed by Stöber, Fink and Bohn (1968) used a silicon ester (either tetraethyl orthosilicate or tetramethyl orthosilicate) as a starting material. This gave uniform droplets of silicon ester suspended in a water-alcohol mixture. These drops were then hydrolyzed by a mild alkali, such as ammonia, and formed spherical particles of hydrated silica. The size of the droplets – and hence the size of the spheres – can be controlled (by the amount of water and ammonia in the system). When the silicon ester was added slowly over a period of several minutes to a gently agitated mixture of the other reagents, more uniform spheres were obtained. To obtain the degree of stacking needed to diffract white light, the particles were allowed to settle over a period of several weeks.

Hardening of the mass was more difficult to achieve. One of the methods tried was to impregnate the array with plastic; this would produce an imitation, rather than a synthetic opal. When the shrinkage of the plastic on polymerization is small, this method can be successful but not otherwise. If impregnation is by silica, the extra silica tends to shrink away from the spheres. If partial sintering by heating is attempted, the spheres and voids tend to shrink and a fair hardness and strength can be obtained at about 500°C to 800°C. Over 800°C, a change to tridymite takes place (i.e. from an amorphous to a crystalline structure). When Gilson opal was investigated non-destructively, it proved to have a lower water content than most natural opals. Many healed cracks were observed and these may be due to stresses set up during manufacture rather than from dehydration.

One of the earliest attempts at the synthesis of opal was made by Iler and Sears (1965). They prepared particles of silica of about 0.1mm (0.004 in) in diameter and found that there was a layer of colour between a white concentrated region below and a diluted region above. The addition of hydrochloric acid to the solution produced the formation of thin solid plates showing a colour range from red to violet. The silica spheres settled to form a conglomerate which was then heated to 900°C so that they could bond together. It was necessary to add water or butyl alcohol to the material so that the colours could be seen.

Workers in Australia used tetraethyl orthosilicate which was suspended as droplets in a mixture of water and alcohol. This produced silica spheres of uniform diameter when ammonia was added to the solution and stirred. The spheres were compacted by heating between 500°C and 800°C.

Slocum Stones

The Slocum stone is one of the best imitations of opal to be seen on the market. It does not really look very like opal but is quite attractive in its own right. In any case, however easy it is for the gemmologist to dismiss such products by eye examination alone, those less familiar with gemstones may easily mistake such products as Slocum stone for the real thing. Slocum stone is named for its creater Mr John S. Slocum and is made from a silicate glass containing calcium, sodium and magnesium. In the publicity material sent with the stones, they are said to be made in shades of white, amber, semi-black and black. There is also a 'crystal' variety. Some of this material has been used in doublets.

The stones are transparent by transmitted light and the bodies which cause the colour can be seen suspended inside. Seen from above, the colours (which include all those in the spectrum) appear to change with the angle of viewing just as in opal. It is important to note that there is one direction in which the play of colour is seen much better than in any other direction; when seen from the side the play of colour is much reduced. Another important diagnostic feature is that, when the stone is viewed with transmitted light at right angles to the direction in which the play of colour is best seen, a patchwork of very small green splotches may be observed. No such array can be seen in opal (see Plates 52-53).

The specific gravity (this and other findings by Dunn, 1977) was 2.47; the refractive index was 1.514. It is amorphous and appears kaleidoscopic between crossed polars. There is no fluorescence or phosphorescence under any form of radiation and X-rays are not diffracted coherently. Slocum stone is not affected by heating. The stone is very tough and quite hard (5½) and is resistant to chipping. Analysis showed that there was a negligible water content compared to that of opal.

Observation of a polished surface showed that there was an irregular suturing between the adjacent grains of the glass. This suggests a lamellar or granular texture with a grain size of up to 1.5mm (0.06 in). The nature of the inclusions which give rise to the play of colour is still conjectural, but Dunn found that two separate textures – one fine-grained and the other micro-granular – could be seen on a fracture surface. It may be that colour arises from the junction of these two inhomogeneous materials.

Gilson Opals

Although there have been many imitations of opal, mostly involving glass, it was not until the productions of Pierre Gilson appeared on the market in the mid 1970s that detection of synthetic opal became a serious task for gemmologists. A stone in the author's possession was examined in 1976 (Jobbins et al, 1976); this showed broad colour bands, roughly parallel, extending in the long direction of the oval stone. These bands showed fine striae along their length and some 'herring-bone' patterns could be seen between adjacent bands. Where these bands could be seen at the girdle, they showed an equidimensional mosaic pattern characteristic of the later Gilson production. On the surface of the stone, small blemishes could be seen; they resembled evaporated water on the surface of a glass. There was a dark-brown body colour by transmitted light.

Later in 1974 (it is supposed) white opals appeared which showed an 'equigranular' texture in which some of the grains were about 0.75mm

Fig. 17.1. The surface structure of a Gilson opal.

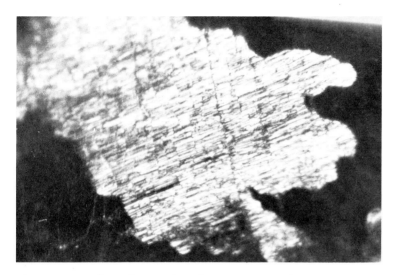

Fig. 17.2. An enlarged view of a Gilson opal colour patch.

(0.03 in) across. Others were in the range 0.5 to 1.5mm (0.02 to 0.06 in.). The side elevation showed a columnar structure which was even more pronounced in the large unpolished pieces being offered for sale to lapidaries in 1979. The general colour by transmitted light was pinkish-buff, but some of this came from the matrix; patches of a paler pink, greenish-blue and yellow could also be seen. Natural opals examined by transmitted light do not show these colours in general but rather very pale yellow to brownish-orange. The mosaic pattern of these earlier opals seemed to remain static as the angle of viewing altered. At some angles, almost the whole surface appeared to be one colour. This was the reverse of the normal appearance of natural opals.

Those requiring a quick guide to the testing of Gilson opal should note firstly the hexagonal patterning shown in each colour patch, and secondly the lack of phosphorescence after irradiation with long-wave ultra-violet light. Some Gilson opals become transparent when immersed in chloroform.

A Gilson opal examined in 1972 by the G.I.A. had a refractive index of 1.44 and a specific gravity of 2.02 to 2.08. The hardness was 4½, lower than for natural opal. The phosphorescence was much shorter (after long-wave ultra-violet light exposure) than for natural material.

Fairly recent Gilson opal sold as 'preforms' for lapidaries, showed the colour patches going over the edge between table and side. There was a change in colour at this point but not in the size of the patch, which suggested a columnar structure. As with other Gilson opals, a broad sweep of one colour could be seen to flood over the whole surface and the size of the colour patches was uniform. Some of the patches showed no colour at any angle of viewing and the appearance of the whole thing was somewhat glassy; the colour appeared to float just below the surface.

Gilson opal was selling (1979) for $15 to $33 per carat for white and $95 to $154 for black. In these ranges, prices narrowly differ according to the quality of the material. Faceting-grade opal (mostly for triplets) costs just over $2 per carat.

Reports on Individual Cases from the Literature

Opal which had been treated is reported by Gübelin in 1964. It showed a pattern of granular black dots which could be seen quite easily with the 10× lens. The dots did not seem to penetrate very deeply into the stone but were concentrated in a layer just below the surface. In translucent specimens the white of the original stone could be seen shining through this darker layer so that, if such a stone is repolished, the colouration may disappear. The black was concentrated into cracks and was much less apparent in more porous areas. Some areas did not appear to have taken the dye and remained light in colour; these could have been some form of agate. A report from the G.I.A. stated that the black could be removed quite easily with warm sulphuric acid.

A paper in *Gems and Gemology* (Rose, 1974) explained the method of treatment carried out on opal to obtain the black background so characteristic of treated opal matrix. The stones were selected as being reasonably porous and shaped to the final shape but without the final polish. The stones were then placed in a sugar syrup; 375g (13.25 oz) of table sugar to 1 litre (1.76 pints) of water worked well. The sugar was dissolved in the water and brought to a light boil; it was then allowed to cool and the stones were placed in it. They were left there for about two weeks and then removed but not washed. The stones were then placed in a glass container and covered with concentrated sulphuric acid. After 24 hours, the stones were removed and washed in water. The stones had then taken on a coating of black which was of oxidized sugar. This could be removed quite easily by brushing. Next the stones were placed in a strong solution of sodium bicarbonate for about two hours and washed in clean water for about 24 hours. After this the final polish was given.

An opal impregnated with plastic but showing a play of colour was reported by Manson (1978). The opal came from Brazil and the voids between the spheroids were filled with a plastic resin. In some of the stones mined a dark dye had also been added to give the whole stone the appearance of Australian black opal. The plastic-impregnated opal had a refractive index of 1.45 and a specific gravity of 1.85. Under the scanning electron microscope, it showed typical arrays of silica spheres on a natural fracture surface, but these were embedded in a matrix which filled the interstitial voids. After dissolving part of the spheroid structure, the interstitial material was found to be n-butyl methacrylate.

An opal manufactured entirely from plastic featured in the same report. Infra-red spectroscopy showed that it consisted entirely of a co-polymer of styrene and methyl methacrylate. The plastic duplicated the three-dimensional stacked array of spheroids. The refractive index of the example tested was 1.465. A similar product, also made from plastic, had a refractive index of 1.48 and a specific gravity of 1.17.

'Calcentine' is the trade-name given to a stone assembled from a nacreous layer of fossil ammonites and baculites from Permian deposits. This is cemented in a suitable matrix and sometimes capped by clear quartz. A play of colour occurs through diffraction, but it does not really resemble precious opal.

Some examples of opal from Mexico and Idaho are said to have been treated successfully by impregnation.

Imitation opal with a white opal top cemented to a base of natural ironstone matrix, was noted by Crowningshield (1975). The back of the opal layer was irregular and had been painted black. The cement appeared to be an epoxy with ground-up ironstone particles in it. Gas bubbles could be seen in the cement, but the whole stone could be mistaken (in a closed setting) for a specimen of Queensland boulder opal. A similar piece had a carved white opal top, painted black on the back, and a backing of dark particles mixed with ground-up opal.

An opal imitation found in Australia had a thin top of Slocum stone (see above) cemented to a base of opaliferous ironstone with an epoxy resin adhesive. The join was apparent from the side.

An imitation of opal made from latex has appeared in Japan and has been freely sold in that country for some time. On casual examination it appears slightly glassy and shows a 'blush' of colour – usually pink or red – rather similar to that shown by a number of the Gilson stones. Overall, however, the quality of the imitation is very good and there is a considerable and attractive play of all spectrum colours. Close examination (a 10× lens will do) shows that markings which resemble the bristles of a paint brush when pressed hard down can be seen. These are not confined to any individual patch of colour but straddle more than one of the patches. I have seen nothing like this in the Gilson stones; nor have I seen in this Japanese material the characteristic hexagonal structure within the colour patches which all the Gilson stones seem to have. There is a faint whitish luminescence under long-wave ultra-violet light but this would be of no particular help in testing.

The specific gravity of this substance, as well as that of another imitation opal of Japanese origin (this time imitating a water opal), is very low, only a little over 1.

Opal has been imitated by a glass with a specific gravity of 2.4. It shows a slight milkiness and is white or yellow so the common opal would seem to be its aim.

18. Lapis Lazuli

Lapis lazuli usually gives a specific gravity of 2.7 to 2.9. Stones offered as this material with a lower specific gravity (especially one of around 2.58) should be regarded with suspicion. The commonest imitations are made from stained jasper (with a specific gravity of 2.58). An imitation of lapis lazuli, which has been known as 'Swiss Lapis' for years, is made by staining jasper with a dye made of potassium ferrocyanide and ferrous sulphate. The flakes of quartz might be mistaken for the pyrite so often seen in true lapis. Its density is between 2.38 and 2.60. A blue aventurine glass with spangles of copper has also been used to imitate lapis.

A synthetic spinel coloured by cobalt was introduced in 1954. In this case, gold flecks were added to simulate pyrite. The refractive index was near 1.725 (compared to the 1.50 of true lapis); the hardness was about 8 on Mohs' scale and the specific gravity was about 3.52. A strong cobalt absorption spectrum could be seen. One interesting test is to pass a strong beam of light through this material; it will appear reddish-purple.

A lapis from Chile has been bonded with plastics. (Chilean lapis, with a high calcium content shown as white streaks, is generally regarded as poor quality compared to the lapis from Afghanistan.) This material will give a plastic smell when touched with the hotpoint.

Another imitation which is a cobalt blue, and therefore shows a brilliant red through the colour filter, gives a granular structure with the lens in a good light. There are no pyrite specks in this material, which is about 8 on Mohs' scale, and has a refractive index of 1.725 with a specific gravity of 3.518 to 3.524. Some form of spinel is strongly suggested by these results. From the random pattern of Laue spots, it would seem that it is a polycrystalline material and not a single crystal.

Further research showed that it had a lattice constant of 8.065, close to that for natural spinel, which is 8.09. The cobalt spectrum was somewhat similar to that normally seen in synthetic blue spinel but with the centre band of the three very weak instead of being the strongest. On the other hand, a band at 480nm, which is very weak in Verneuil stones, was here strongly shown. The colour filter provides the quickest test.

Gilson Lapis Lazuli

The firm of Gilson produce an imitation of lapis lazuli which was described by Schiffman (1976). The colour was very close to that of the natural material and corresponded to 16:4:5 on the German DIN 6164 colour chart (this is a set of colour standards). The corresponding wavelength is 469nm. A test for hardness showed that the new material was less hard than the natural stone (about $4\frac{1}{2}$ against $5\frac{1}{2}$). The substitute left a strong blue streak on an unglazed porcelain plate; the natural stone would only show a faint grey-blue mark (or no mark at all). This suggested that the imitation had a lower degree of cohesion. In addition when the test was carried out, the synthetic material gave off a definite smell of sulphur. Natural lapis gives off a similar odour when touched on a revolving grinding wheel.

The refractive index gave only a vague shadow-edge at about 1.5. The specific gravity, over a range of 12 stones tested, worked out at an average of 2.81 for the natural stones; the new material gave an average value of 2.46. Because it is porous, determinations in heavy liquids were subject to some uncertainty. Chemical tests showed that the substitute was more rapidly attacked by sulphuric acid than the natural stone. A reaction with fumes came at once when it was attacked with hydro-chloric acid, whereas with the natural material, gas bubbles on the surface of the stone appeared more slowly.

It is possible that the Gilson lapis is not a true synthetic and should rather be called an imitation. As Anderson found, the inclusions were softer than pyrite and did not have the characteristic cubic shape. X-ray analysis showed traces of quartz and calcite with some iron.

Reports on Individual Cases from the Literature

Imitation lapis lazuli was reported by the G.I.A. in 1974. Under magnification it showed a uniform structure with not much pyrite. A drop of hydrochloric acid discoloured the area on which it was placed and afterwards became white. There was a strong smell of hydrogen sulphide, much more pronounced than that obtained with the natural material. The white spot, under magnification, showed dark blue fragments like those in a breccia. The refractive index was 1.60. There was no fluorescence under short-wave ultra-violet light; the material was more opaque to X-rays than natural lapis. The hardness was just over 3 and specific gravity about 2.35. The hotpoint charred and the area touched decrepitated.

Another imitation of lapis turned out to be dyed howlite; there was an intense orange fluorescence of an area exposed after removal of the dye.

19. Turquoise

Turquoise varies a good deal in composition and constants, and the task of those wishing to imitate it or manufacture a convincing substitute is consequently difficult. The spectroscope will show the tenacious gemmoligist two bands at 460nm and 432nm. These are hard to see and it will be found convenient to employ a blue filter on the spectroscope or to use a copper sulphate solution to filter the light by which observations are made. Such a spectrum is not shown by any known imitation of turquoise; although, somewhat perversely, some of the bonded types may show it quite strongly. The refractive index should be about 1.61 to 1.62; the specific gravity should be in the range 2.75 to 2.81. A supposed turquoise with a specific gravity below 2.6 should be carefully examined.

There are not many synthetic turquoises on the market and only one manufacturer (Gilson) was known to be producing stones in 1979. There are, however, many imitations and alterations about; the latter at least come within the scope of this book. Imitations made by compressing powdered turquoise may have the same chemical composition as the natural material, but the specific gravity will be lower and no absorption spectrum will be seen. Glass imitations will show characteristic bubbles; porcelain, which is occasionally encountered, will show the same and also a sugary fracture. Stained howlite has a lower hardness (4½ against 6) and a lower specific gravity, 2.50 to 2.57. A broad absorption band can be seen in the green and is caused by the dyestuff. The refractive index is about 1.59, lower than for turquoise. Some very powdery turquoises are bonded with polystyrene resin; these are mostly stones from the south-western United States. They may be sectile and burn with a characteristic odour. Their specific gravity is lower than that of the true turquoise. The stones bonded with sodium silicate are the ones which may show the absorption spectrum strongly.

Gilson Turquoise

The firm of Pierre Gilson now produces two types of synthetic turquoise (one with and one without matrix); these were first reported in 1972. An oval cabochon was reported (Anderson, 1973); the colour was pale blue and somewhat reminiscent of much of the turquoise from the U.S.A. The specific gravity by hydrostatic weighing was given as 2.72; the refractive index, obtained by polishing the back of the stone, was 1.604. The line at 432nm was faintly seen, although this is always difficult. Phosphate (but not copper) was detected by microchemical testing using a flame test. Touching with a drop of hydrochloric acid did not yield the yellow colour which is obtained from the 'Viennese turquoise' (a precipitate of aluminium phosphate coloured blue by copper oleate and consolidated by pressing) and from the material 'Neolith' (a German-made mixture of copper phosphate and bayerite, with 'matrix' banding from some iron compound).

Under a magnification of about 30× to 40×, a characteristic surface structure could be seen. This consisted of a mass of angular dark blue particles against a whitish ground-mass. Seventy specimens of the natural stones were examined for a similar effect but none of them showed it. Further examination of 12 Gilson stones showed that they all had this same surface structure. A bulk density test carried out on the same 12 stones, gave a figure of 2.74, while the refractive indices (taken by distant vision on the six larger cabochons) averaged 1.60. In all cases, the 432nm band was very faint. No useful result was obtained with ultra-violet light. A further report (Tisdall, 1973) showed that the figures obtained earlier were not altered but that, if the surface were examined with a strong light (in this case a photoflood 500 watt lamp) and with the lamp at an angle of about 45 degrees, it could be seen that the whitish ground-mass had been etched or polished away. This left a network of minute cracks unlike anything seen in natural turquoise.

Recent examination of Gilson 'turquoise' has shown that some material can be better described as turquoise plus one or two additional crystalline phases. In fact there are two turquoise-like materials produced by this firm; one is a synthetic turquoise or mixture; the other is a turquoise substitute consisting mainly of calcite. X-ray powder diagrams show calcium in the latter material and Cu, Al and P in the former (as for natural turquoise). Lines not observed in natural turquoise are seen, however, and provide a distinguishing test.

Gilson rough turquoise is sold at US$135 to $750 per kg (1979) according to quality; a medium blue is named 'Cleopatra' and a darker, more intense blue is a 'Farah'. A polished bead would be quite cheap per carat.

A Comparison of Synthetic Turquoises

A major report on synthetic turquoise was published in 1977 by Williams and Nassau. They give the composition of the natural material as $CuAl_6(PO_4)_4(OH)_8.5H_2O$. The calculations give 19.90 per cent Al, 15.23 per cent P, 7.81 per cent Cu and 1.97 per cent H with some Fe. Samples of natural turquoise from Nevada; a Gilson Created Turquoise; a 'simulated turquoise' made by the Syntho Gem Company, Reseda, California; a 'reconstituted turquoise' form Adco Products, Buena Park, California; and a 'Turquite' from Turquite Minerals, Deming, New Mexico, were studied and compared.

For the purpose of the study (and also for more general application), one of the authors proposed that the name 'synthetic' should be given to materials which duplicate the natural at the atomic level (in chemical composition and cause of colour, etc.), the X-ray diffraction level (crystal structure); at the electron microscope level (optical effects where present) and at the visual level (as presented to the eye). For the study, the apparatus used included a scanning electron microscope (SEM) with an X-ray energy spectrometer. Elements not accessible by these techniques (in this case carbon and hydrogen) had to be analysed separately by combustion and gravimetry. Pyrolysis was carried out at a rate of 2°C per minute in an inert atmosphere (nitrogen flow); the results were analysed in a UTC-100 mass spectrometer.

Using the SEM in the energy dispersive mode showed that the Adco and Syntho products gave similar curves to the Gilson stone. The Turquite composition was not like that of turquoise since it had little Al but a good deal of S, Si and Ca. The natural stone showed small amounts of Fe and Si. The Gilson stone came the closest in composition to natural turquoise, but had a lower iron content. This is why the weak Fe spectrum seen in the natural material cannot be seen in Gilson stones. The Syntho and Adco products contained excess carbon; Turquite does not fit the turquoise composition.

A study of the powder diffraction data shows that, again, only the Gilson product had the same crystal structure as natural turquoise. Syntho and Adco, although similar to each other, and with the correct chemical composition, do not have the turquoise crystal structure. Turquite does not have the correct crystal structure for turquoise. Examination by SEM and optical microscopes showed that Turquite has a very coarse structure; that of Syntho and Adco is finer. Gilson stones had a grain size of 0.04nm; the material between the grains was thought to be a gel-like aluminium hydroxide cement (Eppler, 1974). SEM mapping showed that the distribution of P, Al and Cu was quite uniform and that no depletion of these elements could be seen in the grain or intergrain regions so that they both have the same turquoise composition.

As it had been a matter for speculation whether or not the Gilson product was bonded, a sample was heated in an inert gas stream and the decomposition products analysed. Only H_2O and CO_2 and their decomposition products, together with a trace of SO_2 were found. There cannot, therefore, have been any binding.

Reports on Individual Cases from the Literature
An infra-red spectroscopic study of natural and synthetic turquoise was reported by Arnould (1975). The technique can be used to display the transitions of $(PO_4)^3$ radicals whose energy depends upon their cationic environment in the crystal structure. The curves for the natural and the synthetic material differ quite appreciably. In the same way, such substitutes as odontolite and other imitations can be detected.

Turquoise imitations can sometimes be detected by placing a small drop of Thulet's solution (potassium and mercuric iodides) on the specimen. One such imitation sold as synthetic turquoise matrix (previously as natural turquoise) was examined in Germany and found to consist of alum hydrate-copper phosphate (Schlossmacher *via* Benson, 1959). The solution showed a brown spot, whereas on the natural material the spot would have been white.

Chalky-blue material covered with a plastic coating will often show tiny thread-like marks from the application process. The coating will often be cracked. The specific gravity will be below 2.62.

A turquoise offered to lapidaries was said by the seller not to be dyed. Apparently the material had been put through a fracture sealer to offset its extreme porosity. A stone examined by the New York Laboratory of the G.I.A. had a grey appearance with a specific gravity of under 2.57. When a drop of water was placed over a thin scratch in the plastic coating, the area beneath was discoloured.

A turquoise of poor quality, examined by the G.I.A. Los Angeles Laboratory, had been impregnated with some substance that melted when the hotpoint was brought close to it. This substance did not immediately resolidify but remained shiny, giving off a plastic-like smell.

The mineral howlite has been used as a simulant of turquoise though it needs to be dyed in some way. It has a hardness of 3½, specific gravity of 2.53 to 2.59, with a refractive index of 1.586, 1.589, 1.605. In the case of the massive material, a single edge would fall at around 1.59. There is a band in the red in the dyed material with another band in the yellow-green. These bands are probably due to the dye and do not correspond to the faint bands in the violet characteristic of turquoise. Under long-wave ultra-violet light, some specimens have a yellow-brown fluorescence in patches. Some howlites will dissolve in dilute hydrochloric acid. Most of the howlite used for turquoise simulation comes from California.

Ivory has been stained with copper sulphate to imitate turquoise. The specific gravity is 1.80.

A strand of beads, advertised as turquoise, turned out to be blue dyed and plastic-coated. An 'orange-peel' effect could be seen on the highlights of one of the beads. When this was scraped away, there was a violent reaction to hydrochloric acid from the underlying white marble.

20. Organic Materials

Amber

Amber has a specific gravity from 1.04 to 1.10 according to its place of origin. The earliest imitation was known as 'pressed amber' or 'ambroid' and was made by compressing small pieces of natural amber which were too small to be used on their own. The fragments are heated to 200°-250°C and forced through a fine mesh to become a fused mass which closely resembles the natural amber. It may be distinguished by globules seen against a cloudy mass, a flow structure and elongated bubbles. The bubbles in natural amber are usually spherical.

Plastic imitations of amber are more easily distinguished: celluloid (cellulose nitrate), safety celluloid (cellulose acetate) and the casein plastics have all been used. Cellulose nitrate is highly inflammable and is rarely seen today (although it may be met in an older piece of jewellery); safety celluloid is more common, as are the casein plastics. All these materials are sectile: i.e. they can be 'peeled', an action rather like that of sharpening a pencil. Their specific gravities are in the range of 1.32 to 1.34 and their refractive indices are in the range 1.54 to 1.66 (that of natural amber is 1.54). An even better amber imitation is given by the phenol-formaldehyde condensation materials, such as 'Bakelite'. This has a specific gravity of 1.26 to 1.28, and a refractive index of 1.64 to 1.66. A simple test is to make a solution of salt in water – 10 teaspoonful of salt is the measure usually advocated. Most plastics will sink, while amber, pressed amber and copal resin (frequently offered as amber) will float.

The well-known plastics like 'Perspex' (a polymerised acrylic ester) and its relatives, have a specific gravity of 1.18 and refractive index of 1.50. Polystyrene has a specific gravity of 1.05 and a refractive index of 1.58; it is readily sectile and will float in a brine solution. So far it has only been found in a colourless form. The sectility of most plastics can be determined with a penknife blade. When this is applied to true amber, pressed amber or copal resin, the material will splinter. Bakelite is quite resistant to the blade, Perspex very much less so.

It is possible to take a specific gravity reading with an amber necklace because the string makes very little difference to the result. Plastics with their greater density will show their nature at once. If a fragment of a suspected piece can be obtained, it will be found to burn with an aromatic odour if it is genuine (as will pressed amber and copal resin). Plastics will usually give a rank smell and will char; cellulose nitrate will burst into flames.

Some amber, thought to originate in China, is made from a number of shellacs; probably some natural resins are added. It is sometimes known as 'Chinese amber'. Its specific gravity is below that of natural amber.

An amber imitation, known as 'Amberdan' has a specific gravity of 1.23 and a refractive index of around 1.56. Because it is a plastic, it emits a characteristic smell when touched with a hotpoint.

Tortoise-shell
Tortoise-shell is frequently imitated by plastics. An examination with a lens will show that the colour patches on true tortoise-shell are made up of minute dots; whereas the patches are more like swathes in the plastics; the edges are more sharply defined. Casein plastics are most likely to be used in this connection and smell like burnt milk when heat is applied. True tortoise-shell will smell like burnt hair (as it is formed from the protein keratin).

Jet
Jet is sometimes imitated by 'Vulcanite' (a synthetic rubber). This material will smell like burnt rubber when heat is applied; while jet smells like burning coal. Jet has a specific gravity of 1.30: imitations made of black onyx or black glass will have a higher reading.

Coral
Coral is composed of calcium carbonate (calcite) with fibres radiating from the central axis of the branches. It is frequently stained – the dye can be seen concentrated in cracks. It is also imitated by some of the plastics, notably the casein group. True coral will effervesce when touched with a drop of hydrochloric acid, but this will not affect plastics. The specific gravity of coral, at about 2.68, is much higher than that of any of the plastics.

Gilson has recently produced an imitation of coral which is described by Nassau (1979). According to the manufacturer, the coral is made from a natural calcite from a French mine. The specific gravity of this calcite is said to be 2.60 to 2.70 and the refractive index is 1.468 and 1.658. Natural coral has a hardness of about 3½ and the Gilson product matches this; the imitation has a specific gravity of 2.44 compared to 2.6 to 2.7 for the natural material. The refractive index is 1.55 compared to that of 1.49 and 1.65 for the natural coral. Both will effervesce in acids. While the Gilson product shows a brecciated structure, the natural coral has a wood-grain effect. Natural coral also has a dull purplish-red fluorescence, whereas the Gilson coral has a variable fluorescence. The grain-like structure can be detected under 100× magnification.

The chemical composition of the Gilson material was shown by semi-quantitative emission spectrochemical analysis to be rich in silicon, probably in the form of one of the calcium silicates. A small amount of iron could be found which does not appear in natural coral. This would seem to show that the colour must have been derived from some organic pigment. An X-ray powder diffraction spectrum showed the presence of a phase (shown by extra lines) compared to that shown by natural specimens: this could indicate a calcium silicate. Differential thermal analysis showed that both natural and Gilson coral behaved in a similar fashion on heating.

Nassau gives a further note on the Gilson imitation coral in *Lapidary Journal* (1979). Workers at the G.I.A. found that the Gilson product gave both a reddish-brown streak and, after being touched with acid, a reddish-brown wipe. The natural coral gives a white mark in both cases.

Corals have been soaked in a 30 per cent aqueous hydrogen peroxide solution from 12 to 72 hours. The original black improved to golden. Brown (1981) regrets that a line separates black and golden sections in cases of incomplete dye penetration.

Pearls

Real pearls are not often stained but this is a fairly common practice with cultured pearls. The desired colour is black and a very black pearl with an even distribution of colour should be looked at most carefully. Real black pearls are often deep bronze, grey or even bluish in colour.

Silver nitrate is the medium usually chosen for staining pearl. An X-ray photograph will show up traces of this substance between the layers of deposition, because it will appear white on the negative. If the pearls are illuminated by a strong light passed through a blue filter, and then examined through a red filter (the 'crossed filter' technique), stained black pearls will remain black while natural blacks will show a dim reddish glow. Long-wave ultra-violet light will show a similar effect. All black cultured pearls are stained.

From time to time hematite has been used to imitate black pearl. It will give a reddish streak and will not show the true pearly lustre. In any case, the specific gravity of 5.1 should give it away.

Ivory

An imitation of ivory is made from a microcrystalline cellulose polymer made from ground-up wood. The cellulose particles obtained by the grinding are dispersed in water to form a cellulose gel. Acid treatment breaks up the fibres into microcrystals and the water is removed to leave a compact residual product. Dyeing can give different colours. One trade-name for this product is 'Avory'.

21. Glass

Glass is still the commonest gemstone simulant, whether or not it merits the name 'synthetic'. Despite its marked tendency to fracture, thus leaving shell-like (conchoidal) markings, and the 'glassiness' of its lustre, glass (or paste) is still rather more deceptive on occasion than gemmologists might imagine. The refractometer will generally show readings lower than those which the stone simulated would show. However, glass is not always carefully fashioned and a slightly dome-like table will prevent a satisfactory reading, although this is significant in itself. A good general guide is that scarcely any singly refractive stones will show a refractive index between 1.50 and 1.70, although most glasses will give readings in this area. Pollucite and rhodizite are the only natural gemstones in this range; to encounter either in cut form would make a gemmologist's day!

Before using the 10× lens, notice that glass feels warm to the tongue when compared to a crystalline substance. This is because glass con-ducts heat poorly. Clearly it is better to carry out this basic test with a control stone. Notice also that glass fractures easily and conchoidally; although many gemstones also fracture in this way, the fracture marks will be much less prominent.

Bubbles in stones give students a great deal of trouble; somehow they are led to believe that any bubble in a stone means that that stone is a glass, whereas almost all natural minerals show some kinds of bubbles. Those in glass, however, are large, randomly arranged, often spheroid and will reflect the light back to the observer. In some stones, the bubbles appear in sheets and it is necessary to look carefully at the shape of the individual bubbles to be certain that a piece of glass is involved. While most bubbles in glass are spherical, a torpedo shape can be seen on occasion and seems to be confined to glass. Striae (swirls from

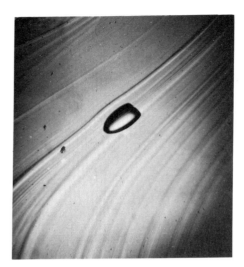

Fig. 21.1. A bullet-shaped bubble in a paste. 25x

imperfect mixing) are also characteristic of glass. They could be confused with the curved growth lines seen in some synthetic corundum, but the striae are generally less regular (see Plates 50, 54).

If a glass is examined between crossed polars, an anomalous double refraction will be seen. There will be no sign of double refraction nor of dichroism. Because the methods of manufacture and the composition of glasses vary so greatly, the student may be deceived by a stone with an 'odd' refractive index or specific gravity. A very dense glass, such as that used in the refractometer, has a specific gravity of about 6.33 and a refractive index of 1.962. However this could never pass as a gemstone; the heaviness and tarnish, not to mention the softness, would give it away at once. More deceptive are the calcium glasses which may imitate emerald or aquamarine; these have a specific gravity around 2.4 to 2.5 and a refractive index of 1.51. A borosilicate crown glass, with a specific gravity of 2.35 to 2.37 and refractive index of 1.50 to 1.51, is sometimes known as 'mass aqua' when appropriately coloured.

Glass has quite a high dispersion and this increases with the refractive index. On the glass refractometer, a glass gemstone will give only a short band of colour at the index position when white light is used; this is because glass of the refractometer closely matches that of the stone in refractive index – it is nearly a shadow-edge. When the spinel refractometer is used, a glass will give a much broader band of colour at the refractive index point.

Just as fused beryl has a lower specific gravity and refractive index

**Fig. 21.2. A 'feather' of
small bubbles in a
paste. 25x**

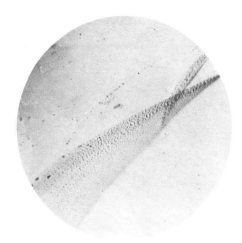

than single crystal beryl, so fused quartz will show lower constants than
natural quartz. Cobalt glass will pass red through the colour filter and
give the cobalt absorption spectrum of three broad bands in the orange,
yellow and green. Some red glasses are coloured by selenium and show
a single broad band in the green. Other glasses may be coloured by rare
earths and show groups of fine lines in the yellow and the green; a lilac
glass coloured by neodymium shows this and the same element will
also give a pink.

Finally, most glasses are not well cut. Some are not cut at all, being
moulded. Poor faceting will often give a clue to the stone's identity.
Rounded facet edges are a clue to moulding.

Reports on Individual Cases from the Literature
Angular inclusions in a green glass with a refractive index of 1.67 and a
very high specific gravity led to the impression of natural emerald. The
G.I.A. Laboratory in Los Angeles found spherical bubbles, single refraction and other pointers to its true nature.

A report on the manufacture of goldstone (a glass simulating the
oligoclase feldspar sunstone) was given by Roscoe (1907). The glass was
a soda-lime product with an excess of alkali, coloured red by cuprous
oxide and with profuse minute spangles of metallic copper, perhaps
obtained from the partial decomposition of cuprous silicate. The
specific gravity was between 2.50 and 2.80 and the refractive index was
about 1.53. Microscopic or lens examination should serve to identify it.
See Plate 51.

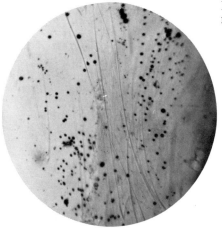

Fig. 21.3. Bubbles and swirl marks in a paste. 22x

A good imitation of chrysoberyl cats-eye, known as 'Cathaystone', is produced by Cathay Corporation of Stamford, Connecticut, U.S.A. It is made from fibre optic faceplates (fused mosaics of several different glasses). Fibres are stacked in cubic or hexagonal bundles. The manufacturers give the hardness as 6, the specific gravity as 4.58 and the refractive index as 1.8. The stones are made in a number of different colours. It will not stand up to sulphuric acid, but will not fade. The stones, with a high coefficient of thermal expansion, can withstand heat up to 538°C (1000°F) if the temperature is raised and lowered in steps of 38°C (100°F) maximum. However they will crack if subjected to a rapid temperature change of 93°C (200°F). Rough material is supplied in the form of blocks with parallel alignment of the eye-producing fibrous structure throughout.

A cheap star stone imitation is made by pressing a white opaque glass into a mould to form a cabochon with six raised edges in the form of a star. The stone is covered with a layer of deep blue glaze, so thin that the edges are only just covered. The star appears to be just below the surface as in the natural stone. The star appears more clear in diffused light than would be expected in the natural material.

A Japanese report discusses 'Reformed' or 'Syberian' jade which is made from dark green translucent to opaque glass. Hardness is 5 to 5.5; the specific gravity is 2.67; and the refractive index is 1.523. Needle-like inclusions are hydroxyl apatite and dendrites are either vapour or liquid phase inclusions, with a lower refractive index than the host. Broad absorption regions extend from 700 to 630nm and from 460 to 400nm.

22. Doublets and Triplets

Composite stones are better known by the names doublets and triplets. Opal doublets with some pretence to respectability are probably encountered more than any other type, although the garnet-topped doublet is still very common.

Most doublets are made by fusing two pieces of material. Both can be pieces of the 'real' stone (the material imitated); an opal doublet with precious opal on a base of common opal would be one example. A triplet has three parts and could consist of the crown and pavilion from the real stone plus a layer of colour, usually a coloured glass. Green glass sandwiched between a crown and pavilion of colourless or pale beryl would form a triplet. Again two pieces of quartz, with natural-seeming inclusions, could be fused together with green glass to give an imitation of emerald. The third type of composite is the well-known example where a slice of a hard stone (usually almandine garnet) is fused to a piece of glass. The garnet top consists of the table facet only (it is a common mistake to assume that these stones are joined at the girdle). The idea was to defeat the hardness test given by the jeweller's file, a test which will by now have fallen into disuse. See Plate 56.

Most doublets and triplets can be examined quite easily by immersing them in a liquid; a glass cell placed upon a sheet of white paper serves very well. Water or monobrononaphthalene will be found useful. A garnet-topped doublet, when placed table facet down on a sheet of white paper, will show a red ring near the girdle. On the refractometer, the table will give a reading near 1.79, while a pavilion facet, if one can be tested, will give one near 1.63. The junction between garnet and glass will be marked by a plane of bubbles; look out also for the characteristic garnet inclusions (rutile crystals). See Plate 56.

A diamond-topped doublet with a base of synthetic white corundum,

**Fig. 22.1. Crossed rutile
needles in the garnet top and
gas bubbles in one plane of a
doublet.**

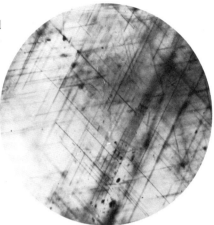

spinel or rock crystal, is still encountered from time to time. When looked at from above, the edges of the table facet can be seen reflected in the junction layer; tilt the stone to see this effect. See Plate 61.

Opal doublets can first be noticed by their characteristic flat or low-domed tops. The reason for the manufacture of such pieces is to use thin slices of good quality opal which would not make a whole stone on their own. If the stone is unmounted, the junction between opal and base can clearly be seen; where the stone is mounted, it is sometimes possible, by examining the table under a strong light, to see bubbles in the junction plane. A powerful beam of light passed through the stone may also show these bubbles which may appear as flattened discs. A careful examination of the edges of a mounted stone may show one or two places where the junction is visible. Opal triplets traditionally had a covering of clear quartz but, in recent years, this has been replaced by plastic or even glass. Where the back of a suspected stone is easily reached, a refractometer test will show up common opal or onyx, which are the most usual backings.

Soudé emerald is a triplet made from a crown of quartz, a layer of green glass and a pavilion of quartz. A refractometer reading will suffice here (1.544 to 1.553 compared to the emerald reading of 1.57 to 1.58). This is the older form of soudé emerald; more recent productions, made from pieces of beryl with a green intermediary, will show natural inclusions. Fortunately the spectroscope will show a broad band in the orange (from the dyestuff); reflected light gives the best results. See Plate 55.

Another type of triplet simulating emerald is made from a crown of synthetic spinel, a green colouring layer and a base of synthetic spinel. The refractometer will show the spinel reading of 1.728 and there should be no problem with identification. Other colours of synthetic spinel have also been used in composites.

Reports on Individual Cases from the Literature

An ingenious composite, in which the colour is given by a colour transparency, has been reported. Any material can be used for crown and pavilion.

An attempt to reproduce star corundum, marketed in the early 1960s in the U.S.A. under the name 'Star of Destiny', consisted of a ceramic back upon which was mounted a thin metallic film; over that was placed a synthetic corundum or spinel top. The top section was transparent. The apparent asterism came from three sets of lines engraved in the base of it. The colour of the whole stone was that of the top section.

A citrine triplet, in which two pieces of rock crystal were cemented together with yellow plastic or resin-type cement, was examined by the G.I.A. The refractive index was normal for quartz and an interference figure could be seen with the polariscope. Immersion showed the true nature of the stone.

A stone with a diamond crown on a base of zircon, showed an arborescent pattern when the cement dried.

A doublet, known as a 'Pavilion Diamond', consisted of a crown of diamond on a base of strontium titanate.

An attractive doublet, to which the name 'Dialite' has been given, consisted of a crown of synthetic white spinel with a pavilion of

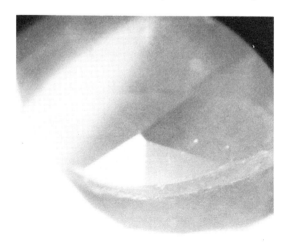

Fig. 22.2. Doublet, consisting of a natural sapphire top and a synthetic ruby base.

strontium titanate. The table gave a refractive index reading of 1.727. At the correct angle, the table facet could be seen reflected in the junction layer as in a diamond doublet.

A doublet imitating emerald and with the trade-name of 'Smaryll' was first described by Webster (1966). Strictly speaking, it was a triplet rather than a doublet, and was made by the firm of Kämmerling of Idar-Oberstein in West Germany. It consisted of two pieces of colourless beryl cemented together with an emerald-coloured duroplastic cement. Poor-quality aquamarine or emerald could also be used for the crown and pavilion. The refractive indices, obtained from two stones, were 1.591 to 1.585 (from the crown) with slightly lower indices from pavilion facets. Another stone gave 1.588 to 1.582 from the table. All the stones showed green through the colour filter and dark between crossed filters. Woolly bands could be seen in the red part of the spectrum. Bubbles could be seen in the cement layer and typical aquamarine-like inclusions in the beryl parts of the stone. No clear-cut extinction could be seen through crossed polars which seemed to indicate that the two parts of the stone had not been crystallographically aligned. As might be expected, immersion revealed the true state of affairs.

Another composite was formed from a single emerald-cut green beryl sawn at the girdle and rejoined with green cement. The inclusions appeared to go right through the stone and, under crossed polars, it appeared to be a single crystal.

In 1966, the G.I.A. reported a long, thin, narrow cabochon consisting of two pieces of translucent jadeite given a rich green by a colouring layer. The join could be seen quite clearly when the stone was examined from the side.

Probably the most dangerous composite are the ingenious stones attempting to masquerade as Imperial jade. They are made by hollowing out a piece of pale jadeite to form a cabochon with thin sides. Another piece of pale jadeite is so fashioned that the two parts will fit together and then they are cemented together. To give the colour, green dyestuff is introduced between the sections. Where the stone is unmounted, a ridge can be seen on the base: this of course gives the game away. But when the stone is mounted, great trouble can arise, because the colour and general appearance is very like that of true jadeite. Fortunately the spectroscope will show a woolly band in the red, rather than the narrow chromium lines which true green jadeite would show. The composite will also show red or pink through the colour filter whereas true green jadeite will remain green.

At least one piece of a so-called 'Mexican jade' proved to be calcite.

This was confirmed by the use of acid. The colour banding suggested that dye had been used.

A composite stone, made to simulate moss agate (why?!), was formed by placing manganese dioxide on a glass plate with gelatine and allowing the 'tree' to form on the gel. The plate was then gently heated to drive off excess water; another clean glass plate was cemented to the top and the whole ground to a cabochon form. The join revealed the deception.

A triplet, with glass between two pieces of synthetic spinel, was intended to resemble peridot. Immersion showed the G.I.A. New York Laboratory the true nature of the stone.

A very interesting composite, reported by the G.I.A. in 1960, consisted of a heat-crackled ruby cabochon which had been drilled at the back. Into the hole thus produced, a natural ruby had been inserted and the whole piece was polished to look as though it were a single stone. The natural part then appeared to be merely a flawed section of a natural stone.

A doublet, consisting of a quartz top on a base of red glass, was reported in Australia. The aim was presumably to imitate ruby.

An interesting doublet reported by Anderson (1972) had a crown of natural Australian sapphire on a base of synthetic sapphire. Another, still more deceitful, had a natural sapphire crown on a base of synthetic ruby. Although there was a bluish tint to the upper layer, it gave the rutile needles necessary for the impression of 'silk'. In any case, the blue-green was swamped by the red in the base. Under crossed filters, the base glowed red while the crown did not. See Plates 58-59.

A star sapphire doublet was produced by joining a natural sapphire top and base (the star was in the top portion, while the colour was in the base). The top was translucent grey and the star very sharp. A cobalt spectrum was detected and there was a bright red through the colour filter. The base had been crackled and the fine blue came from a dye.

Another type of star sapphire doublet was made with two pieces of natural greyish corundum joined with a blue cement which showed arborescent patterns. This stone also contained cobalt.

A doublet of topaz on a seed of beryl was made by Lechleitner. I examined this stone in Germany some years ago. One stone, at least, had refractive indices of 1.609 and 1.620.

An interesting composite is made by cementing a white opal crown to a fire opal pavilion. There is no intent to deceive, because the join, at the girdle, is very easy to see. In addition, the appearance of the stone when viewed from the crown is clearly artificial.

Some corundum, with a good star but indifferent colour, may be improved by utilizing the crown but adding a synthetic back. A triplet can be made by adding a blue cement. A similar use of coloured cement gives imitations of amethyst, emerald, topaz, ruby or sapphire with a crown and pavilion of synthetic spinel or quartz. A low refractive index will give these away in all cases; most examples are quite large. A crown of synthetic sapphire with a pavilion of synthetic rutile is also known.

Sometimes the cement in a composite may fluoresce under short-wave ultra-violet light. In a garnet-topped doublet, the glass back often glows a greenish-yellow (the garnet crown being inert) so that a greenish-yellow powdery glow can be seen surrounding a dark spot indicating the garnet slice.

23. Less Common Synthetics

This chapter summarizes reports on materials which have, for the most part, been produced for industrial and research applications. Some of them, particularly in the United States, have found their way into the hands of the amateur lapidary; others are too small so far to have any ornamental application.

Crystals of the apatite group – silicates rather than phosphates – such as $NaLa_8Si_6O_{24}F_2$, have been grown. With appropriate doping, they can take on a variety of colours.

Barium sodium niobate (sometimes known as 'banana') has the composition $BaNaNb_3O_{15}$ with a refractive index of 2.31. With potassium niobate, $KNbO_3$, which has a refractive index close to diamond, there are two possibilities for simulation. $Gd_{0.15}Y_{0.85}P_5O_{14}$ (gadolinium yttrium phosphate) may also be a possibility for gem use. Yttrium vanadate, YVO_4, is yet another possibility.

Barium titanate, $BaTiO_3$, has a hardness of about 6 to $6\frac{1}{2}$ and a specific gravity of 5.90. The refractive index is 2.40 and it is isotropic.

Bismuth germanium oxide, which can have the composition $Bi_{12}GeO_{20}$ or $Bi_4Ge_3O_{12}$, forms bright orange crystals with a refractive index of 2.55 and a hardness of $4\frac{1}{2}$. Bismuth silicon oxide, $Bi_{12}SiO_{20}$, has been grown by the Czochralski process. Quite large crystals (up to 50mm (1.95 in) in length) have been reported. Some are brown, reddish or orange on removal from the growth apparatus, but a colourless crystal can be produced by annealing.

Bromellite is BeO and crystallizes in the hexagonal system. Growth is by the flux-melt method. As the hardness is 9, it might be considered worth using for ornamental purposes, were it not for the fact that manufacture might be dangerous because of the toxicity of the dust. The specific gravity ranges from 3.00 to 3.02, the refractive indices are 1.720 and 1.735 with a birefringence of 0.015. One specimen at least showed a faint orange fluorescence under long-wave ultra-violet light.

Calcium titanate or perovskite, $CaTiO_3$, is an analogue of strontium and barium titanates. It crystallizes in the orthorhombic system. It is said to have a specific gravity of 4.05 and a mean refractive index of 2.40.

'Catseyte' is the name given to a substance recently produced in the U.S.A. and intended to simulate cat's-eye chrysoberyl. It is made from rare-earth silicates, which are compacted into a mass of linear parallel fibres about 6 to 10mm (0.24 to 0.39 in) in diameter. These are fused with a coloured matrix and coated with a substance of a lower refractive index. The colours available include honey yellow, blue and green.

Some cat's-eye stones have been grown by the floating zone method of crystal growth. Crystals of magnesium titanate showed chatoyancy.

An imitation of cuprite, consisting of almandine with a sputtered surface layer, was reported by the G.I.A. in 1975.

Fluorite, CaF_2, has been grown in a number of colours as part of programmes on doped halides and fluorides. A boule of a vivid green colour was reported by Webster (1970). This had a refractive index of 1.45 and the reported specific gravity was 2.31 (probably a mistake for 3.21). There was a bright blue fluorescence.

Another green fluorite had a refractive index of 1.435 and a specific gravity of 3.186. Absorption bands were seen in the deep red and at about 690nm with a broader band from 630-580nm. Weaker bands also showed at 530 and 490nm. There was no fluorescence except for a weak yellow glow under X-rays. No phosphorescence could be seen.

A colourless fluorite with a refractive index of 1.44 and a specific gravity of 3.197 had a green fluorescence under ultra-violet light with a hint of yellow under long-wave. Under X-rays, there was a brilliant green fluorescence with an exceptionally long green phosphorescence. No significant absorption spectrum could be seen. The fluorescence spectrum showed discrete strong bands in the red, orange and yellow; also in the green with weaker fluorescent bands in the deeper part of this colour. Indium was suggested as the dopant.

A fine, uranium-doped, red fluorite crystal in the author's collection was grown by Bell Laboratories. A similar crystal, reported in the literature, had a refractive index of 1.44 and specific gravity of 3.181. It also showed a rare-earth type spectrum with a sharp line at 365nm with a range of lines from the yellow to the end of the green; the intensity of the lines varied. No luminescence could be seen. The crystal in the author's collection has no discernible absorption spectrum. Stones are also doped with neodymium and show the characteristic fine line absorption spectrum.

Some examples of synthetic fluorite have been reported over the years (Duyk, 1971). In one case, a stone had a refractive index of 1.43 and specific gravity of 3.18. The hardness was 4; the stone showed light red though the colour filter, the body colour of the stone being red. Inside were straight growth planes, crystallites, non-communicating channels on level planes and gaseous cavities.

Forsterite, Mg_2SiO_4, has been grown as clear crystals using the flame-fusion method. Nickel and vanadium, when used as dopants, give green and blue results.

A tablet thought to be intended as an imitation of garnet was reported at the International Gemmological Conference of 1970. It was found to contain ferrosilicon and other materials which showed that it had an artificial origin. The properties fell between andradite and grossular.

Crystals of andradite were grown from solution with lithium molybdate as a flux. From 0.1 to 0.3 per cent chromium was used as a dopant. A light green grossular, also made with a flux of lithium molybdate, had a specific gravity of 3.5 to 3.7. Uvarovite garnet has been grown by the flux-melt method.

Lanthanum indium gallium garnet has the chemical formula $La_3In_2Ga_3O_{12}$. It has been grown, doped with cerium, by Union Carbide. Samarium gallium garnet has also been grown by this firm and I have some small crystals in my own collection. The composition is $Sm_3Ga_5O_{12}$; the refractive index is about 1.9 and the colour is yellow. Neodymium gallium garnet, $Nd_3Ga_5O_{12}$, is close to amethyst in colour and has a refractive index of about 1.9. This is also made by Union Carbide.

A number of germanates have been made which might, at some time in the future, have a gem application. They include scandium and yttrium germanates Sc_2GeO_5, $Sc_2Ge_2O_7$, etc. Erbium germanate forms attractive pink crystals.

The dark orange-red cadmium sulphide greenockite has been made by the vapour-phase method. Greenockite crystallizes in the hexagonal crystal system. The specific gravity was about 4.8. The refractive index for the natural material was 2.505 and 2.529 for the ordinary and extraordinary rays respectively. The double refraction was 0.024. There was a virtually complete absorption below 525nm. There was no diagnostic luminescence, although at least one stone showed a strong orange glow under X-rays but without phosphorescence.

Substitutes for hematite, Fe_2O_3, which is used in carvings, have included a titanium dioxide with a steel-grey colour. It had a specific gravity of about 4, a hardness of about 5½ and yellow-brown streak. It was thought to be man-made. Another substitute appeared to be made from powdered lead sulphide, perhaps with the addition of some silver. The specific gravity was between 6½ and 7 and the hardness about 2½ to 3. It had a black streak and was brittle and easily fusible.

A third substitute had a specific gravity of about 4, a hardness of about 6, a metallic lustre and a reddish-brown streak. Iron and copper were the main metal constituents with some titanium. It was about 81 per cent hematite and may have been either a product of melting from mixed oxides or it may have been sintered.

'Hemetine' is a trade name given to a sintered product consisting of several materials, including the lead sulphide galena. The specific gravity was near 7.0 and the streak was black. More recent material is said to give a reddish-brown streak and to have constants close to those of true hematite.

A material from which good imitations of chatoyant stones could be made was described by Nishiyama (1969). Known as 'Iimori-stone' after its inventor, Dr. S. Iimori of the Physical and Chemical Research Institute of Tokyo, it consisted of a radially developed crystalline mass of fibrous aggregate structure, similar to natural minerals of the amphibole group, particularly nephrite. Iimori-stone was made from the melting of quartz, feldspar, magnesite, calcite, fluorite and other minerals. These are fused at a high temperature to a molten magma and then mineralized to the final state by the addition of other substances. An excess of amphibole particles caused the stone to display a brilliant chatoyancy.

It had a hardness of 5½ to 6 and was made in various colours, including azure blue, deep indigo, lemon yellow, brownish-pink and chocolate brown. It also had a rough texture which made it suitable for carvings of animals and other ornaments. A stone of a yellowish-green colour makes a good imitation of true chrysoberyl cat's-eye. Iimori-stone has been named 'Victoria stone', by which name it is best known. Although the original report was in 1969, recently it appears to have come into prominence again. Other materials have been made in this laboratory including a 'meta-jade' with a brilliant green colour.

KTN is the abbreviation given to the substance potassium niobate tantalate. It is usually colourless as is a specimen in the author's collection. The hardness was just over 6, the specific gravity was reported as 6.43, and the refractive index was 2.27.

A few years ago lanthanum beryllate (some authorities call it beryllium lanthanate) was mentioned in connection with gemstones. It had been doped with neodymium to give $La_2Be_2O_5$:Nd and was sometimes referred to as BEL. Its thermal conductivity was reported as less than half that of YAG.

Lanthanum niobate and neodymium niobate have been grown at Tohoku University, Japan. They are both transparent, while the latter is coloured a darkish purple. Specimens up to 120mm (4.7 in) long were grown by the Czochralski method.

Lithium tantalate has a refractive index of 2.175 and a birefringence of 0.006. The dispersion has been calculated as about twice that of diamond. It has the composition $LiTaO_3$, and can be produced as clear colourless crystals.

Magnesium gallate, $MgGa_2O_4$, is a member of the spinel group, but has better optical properties than spinel itself.

A fine yellow can be obtained with lithium fluoride if chromium is added. The hardness is between 3 and 4, the specific gravity is 2.64 and the refractive index is 1.392.

Manganese fluoride is a dark rose-colour with a hardness of 4, a specific gravity of 3.93 and a refractive index of 1.475 and 1.505. The crystal system is tetragonal.

Rubidium manganese fluoride though soft could make a most attractive gemstone; the colour is pinkish-yellow (peach-colour); specific gravity 4.31 and refractive index 1.428. The hardness is about 4.

Good optical quality crystals of magnesium fluoride have been grown at the M.I.T. The colour produced is pale green.

Magnetite has been synthesized, although it would have little serious ornamental application. The specific gravity for the natural material is 5.17. Its composition is $FeO.Fe_2O_3$.

Another black material which has been made artificially is magnetoplumbite with a composition of $2RO.3R_2O_3$. It is a member of the hexagonal crystal system and the specific gravity of one artificial piece was found to be 5.76. It has a dark brown streak and strong magnetism.

Olivine doped with nickel is the nearest experimenters have come so far to a synthetic peridot.

Periclase is MgO and crystallizes in the cubic crystal system; it is usually colourless. The hardness is about 5, the specific gravity is 3.55 to 3.60. The refractive index has been measured at 1.737. Some stones give a whitish glow under ultra-violet light and a dull purple under X-rays. No phosphorescence has been reported. A dull red was seen between crossed filters. Very faint absorption bands near 540, 485, 467nm, with a cut-off at 416nm, have been seen. Square platelets have been seen in a specimen manufactured in the U.S.A. Some stones were marketed under the name 'Lavernite'.

A green periclase has recently been offered to lapidaries. It has a specific gravity of 3.75 and a refractive index of 1.738. Hardness is about 6. Periclase is MgO; this material contains Cr and Fe.

Phenakite, Be_2SiO_4, has been grown by Bell Laboratories and, with vanadium as the dopant, appears as an attractive blue-green. A crystal in the author's collection was reported some years ago and shown to a London audience. So far there has been no attempt to grow crystals sufficiently large for ornamental use. Natural phenakite has a specific gravity of about 3.00, a refractive index of 1.654 to 1.670, with a hardness of 7½. It crystallizes in the hexagonal system.

Anderson (1972) reported on a cut powellite of 0.42 ct. Powellite is calcium molybdate ($CaMoO_4$) and is a member of the tetragonal system, forming a series with scheelite. The stone was pink, presumably from rare-earth doping, and had a specific gravity of 4.34. The refractive indices were 1.974 (ordinary ray) and 1.984 (extraordinary ray). There was a green fluorescence under both long- and short-wave ultra-violet light. Since powellite has a hardness of 3½, it is not likely to appear on the gem market.

Proustite, which is not of use as a gemstone but is sought by collectors, has been grown by the Czochralski method. Its formula is Ag_3AsS_3 and it has a fine dark red colour which, however, suffers surface alteration on exposure to light. It is used in laser modulator and semiconductor work.

A star rutile has been produced by the National Lead Company of the U.S.A., though it has never caught on commercially. It was grown by the Verneuil process and was named 'Star-Tania'. Another version ('Sapphirized Titania' or 'Sierra Gem') has a sapphire layer deposited on the soft rutile surface. This layer could be up to 2 millimicrons thick.

Scheelite, $CaWO_4$, is sometimes offered as an imitation of diamond although it is anisotropic (crystallizing in the tetragonal system). Some crystals were grown using the Verneuil technique, the manufacturers being Linde Air Products. Various colours of scheelite are achieved by the addition of dopants; neodymium gives purple, while other elements give various shades of green and yellow. The absorption spectra are reproduced by Webster (1970). They show the appropriate fine line absorption spectrum which may occasionally be seen, though very faintly, in the natural material.

Most scheelite today is made by pulling, because it is chiefly required for use for rods for lasers. The hardness is about 5, while the specific gravity is about 6.00. The refractive index for the natural material is given as 1.94 and 1.92 with a birefringence of 0.016. As with much natural scheelite, the synthetic product gives a bright bluish-white fluorescence under short-wave ultra-violet light. One report mentioned a stone which gave a strong orange under both long- and short-wave light and a pink under X-rays; the specific gravity in this case was 6.16. Another report mentioned a scheelite of a peridot green colour which gave a brick or orange colour in one part of the stone only under ultra-violet light (type not specified).

A dark garnet-red stone showed no discernible lines in the absorption spectrum; a stone resembling fine demantoid garnet also had nothing in the visible region. A lavender-coloured synthetic scheelite gave a very strong absorption spectrum from the colouring element neodymium. Such a complex spectrum immediately indicated to the observer that the stone was synthetic, because no natural material ever shows a similar one. The absorption spectrum of some natural brown scheelites also contained a number of fine lines but they are much less pronounced. Another complex line spectrum was seen in a crystal of YGaG coloured pink. Again it was attributable to rare earths.

Silicon carbide, SiC, was described by Mitchell (1962) as 'a rare synthetic'. The author has seen only four or five cut stones, although it is quite easy to obtain the characteristic rough with its many bladed and colourful crystals. Silicon carbide is made in an electric arc furnace and is used as the well-known abrasive 'carborundum'. To make it, a mixture of low-ash coke and glass sand (pure SiO_2) is heated in a brick container with temperatures up to 2600°C obtained by the use of heavy currents. A multicrystalline mass results with iridescent crystals, because a thin film of SiO_2 forms on the crystals when they are heated to 1000°C in air. The cut stones do not show this iridescence but are a green not unlike that shown by some diamonds. The refractive indices are 2.648 and 2.691 with a double refraction of 0.043. The specific gravity is 3.20, and the hardness 9½. Inside the stone reported were hexagonal plates, probably negative, which were oriented parallel to the parent (hexagonal) crystal. Under long-wave ultra-violet light there is a mustard yellow fluorescence. The dispersion is about twice that of diamond, with which it could possibly be confused, although it always has a greenish colour.

A green variety of spodumene, $LiAlSi_2O_6$, was reported by Kuznetsov in the U.S.S.R.; the beta form was prepared by the late Ito at the University of Chicago and was a light blue in colour. Small specimens are in the author's collection. Ito also prepared sodalite, $Na_8Cl_2Al_6Si_6O_{24}$, forming small dark blue crystals. He has also made nickel olivine (bright green crystals) with the composition $(Ni,Mg)_2SiO_4$ and bright green $Be_2CuPr_2Si_2O_{10}$.

Synthetic azurite and malachite (tiny crystals of the former are in the author's collection) have been prepared by Kostiner at the University of Connecticut.

Tourmaline has been grown by the hydrothermal method. The first growth on a seed is thought to have been in 1949. Taylor and Terrell replaced sodium by calcium and potassium and M was manganese, magnesium, vanadium, chromium, iron, cobalt, nickel, copper or zinc. M in this context refers to the formula $NaM_3Al_6B_3Si_6O_{27}(OH)$.

Topaz can only be made by the hydrothermal method because the hydroxyl group – the composition of topaz is $Al_2(F,OH)_2SiO$ – would be removed by heating in a fluxed melt. Such crystals have been grown, but in sizes too small to cut.

Wurtzite, the hexagonal form of ZnS, gives a most beautiful green when doped with cobalt. Nickel gives a canary yellow and copper a bluish-green. These crystals are grown by chemical vapour transport.

Although $YAlO_3$ (yttrium orthoaluminate) has a number of possible industrial applications as well as a use as a diamond simulant, it was never used in either connection as much as was at first expected (as a possible gem it has now been overtaken by zirconia). It has high conductivity and hardness and can be grown more quickly than YAG. It can be doped successfully with a variety of elements giving colours and possible laser adaptability. However Fe^{3+} was discovered by EPR signals and, after much work, was found to have come from the volatilization from ceramics in the insulation used for the growth mechanism. As iron is a strong inhibitor of fluorescence, this meant that the material had great disadvantages industrially and its gem potential was insufficient to justify large-scale production. A bluish to orange-pink stone examined had been doped with didymium and gave the characteristic fine line spectrum. The maker claimed a refractive index of 1.938 and a specific gravity of 5.35. The hardness is said to be in excess of 8.

Yttrium orthovanadate has a possible gem application. Grown by the Czochralski method, it can be doped with a number of elements including chromium and vanadium.

'Yttralox' is the name given to Y_2O_3, which is a possible diamond simulant. It is hard to grow as the melting point is very high (over 2000°C). Yttralox itself is actually a ceramic material made from heating powdered Y_2O_3 with some thorium oxide and applying high pressure. The refractive index is 1.92 and the dispersion is 0.039 compared to diamond's 0.044. The specific gravity is 4.84; the hardness is 7½ to 8; and it has a cubic crystal system. However, since the advent of zirconia, this and other possible substitutes will now probably not be encountered.

Zincite, ZnO, is very rarely found sufficiently transparent in its natural state (when it is coloured red by manganese) to facet. However it is made artificially in various colours. Stones in the author's collection are small and yellow with a bright yellow fluorescence under ultra-violet light and green under X-rays. The hardness of the natural stone is just under 4, while the specific gravity is about 5.5. The refractive indices are 2.013 and 2.029.

Zircon doped with vanadium to give a purple colour with marked dichroism was made at Bell Laboratories some years ago but no gems were ever marketed. The crystals were well formed showing clear prism and pyramid forms. Because zircon is rather easily soluble in all convenient fluxes, the best method for growth is hydrothermal. In this case, it gave a growth rate of 0.25mm (0.01in) per day. The mineralizer used was a combination of KF–LiF. The infra-red spectrum showed bands at 333, 231, 186, 159 and 151nm. The first of these was thought to be related to the presence of (OH); similar bands have been found in hydrothermally-grown quartz.

From time to time it has been suggested that zircon would be a suitable laser material; crystals grown with a flux of V_2O_5, giving blue stones, have been reported. Other crystals of the zircon group have been grown experimentally at the Clarendon Laboratory, Oxford; they include $ZrSiO_4$, $ThGeO_4$, Zn_2SiO_4 and Mg_2SiO_4. Doping of zircon ($ZrSiO_4$) with Tb gave yellow; $ThGeO_4$ doped with Er gave pink; and $ZrGeO_4$ doped with Tb gave orange-red.

Appendix: Trade-Names

Trade-names have been given to some synthetic materials. All these names are objectionable on mineralogical, if on no other, grounds; their use is strongly to be discouraged.

Doublets

Laser Gem (synthetic corundum on strontium titanate)

Carnegiegem

Diarita (synthetic spinel on strontium titanate)

Ferrolite (proposed for a black iron slag with possible gem use: Webster, Gems (2nd Ed.) 1962)

Kaolite (moulded imitation cameos: Webster, Gems (2nd Ed.) 1962)

Stained Chalcedony (Green)

Emeraldine

Triplitine (emerald-coloured beryl triplet)

Cubic Zirconia

CZ

Cerene

Cubic Z

Cubic Zirconia

Cubic Zirconia II

Cubic Zirconium

Cubic Zirconium Oxide or Dioxide

Diamon-Z

Diamond-QU

Diamonair II

Glass

Royalite

Synthetic Corundum

Diamondite

Crown Jewels

Walderite

Violite

Diamonesque

Diamonique III

Diamonite or Diamondite

Diconia

Djevalite

Fianite

Phianite or Phyanite

Shelby

Singh Kohinoor

Zirconia

Zirconium

Zirconium Yttrium Oxide

Synthetic Rutile

Astryl
Brilliante
Diamothyst
Gava Gem
Jarra Gem
Johannes Gem
Kenya Gem
Kimberlite Gem
Lusterlite
Miridis
Rainbow Diamond
Rainbow Gem
Rainbow Magic Diamond

Rutile
Sapphirized Titania
Star-Titania
Tania-59
Tirum Gem
Titangem
Titania
Titania Brilliante
Titania Midnight Stone
Titanium
Titanium Rutile
Titanstone
Zaba Gem

Synthetic Spinel

Alumag
Magalux
Strongite

Corundolite
Erinide
Rozirdon

Strontium Titanate

Bal de Feu
Diagem
Diamontina
Dynagem
Fabulite
Jewelite
Kenneth Lane Jewel
Lustigem

Marvelite
Pauline Trigere
Rossini Jewel
Sorella
Symant
Wellington
Zeathite
Zenithite

YAG

Alexite
Amatite
Astrilite
Circolite
Dia-Bud
Diamite
Diamogen
Diamonair
Diamone
Diamonique
Diamonite

Diamondite
Diamonte
Di'Yag
Geminair
Kimberly
Linde Simulated Diamond
Nier-Gem
Regalair
Replique
Somerset
Triamond
Yttrogarnet

Bibliography

Journals

The following is a list of journals abstracted, which are likely to be encountered and are in constant use. Many historical references were abstracted from journals now extinct. In a number of cases only one reference from each journal appears.

Acta Crystallographica	Munksgaard, Noerre Soegade 35, DK 1370 Copenhagen K, Denmark. (Published in two sections, A (bi-monthly) and B (monthly)
Acta Metallurgica	Pergamon Press, Headington Hill Hall, Oxford OX3 0BW. (Monthly)
American Mineralogist	Mineralogical Society of America, 1707 L Street N.W., Washington, D.C. 20036, U.S.A. (Bi-monthly)
Analytical Chemistry	American Chemical Society, 1155 16th Street, Washington, D.C. 20036, U.S.A. (Monthly)
Angewandte Chemie	Postfach 129/149, 6940 Weinheim, West Germany. (Semi-monthly)
Applied Optics	Optical Society of America, 2100 Pennsylvania Avenue, Washington, D.C. 20037, U.S.A. (Monthly)
Applied Physics Letters	American Institute of Physics, 335 East 45th Street, New York, N.Y. 10017, U.S.A. (Twice monthly)
Australian Gemmologist	The official organ of the Gemmological Association of Australia, Box 149 GPO, Sydney, N.S.W. 2001, Australia. (Irregular)
Bell Laboratories Record	Bell Laboratories, 600 Mountain Avenue, Murray Hill, N.J. 07974, U.S.A. (Monthly)
Berichte, Deutsche Keramische Gesellschaft	5340Bad Honnef, West Germany. (Monthly)

Bulletin of the American Ceramic Society	American Ceramic Society, 65 Ceramic Drive, Columbus, Ohio 43214, U.S.A. (Monthly)
Bulletin of the American Physical Society	American Physical Society, 335 East 45th Street, New York, N.Y. 10017 U.S.A.(Monthly)
Bulletin de l'Association Française de Gemmologie	The official organ of the Association Française de Gemmologie, 163 Rue St. Honoré, 75001 Paris, France. (Irregular)
Bulletin, Société Française de Minéralogie et Cristallographie	120 Boulevard Saint-Germain, Paris 6, France. (Monthly)
Carbon	Pergamon Press, Headington Hill Hall, Oxford OX3 0BW. (Bi-monthly)
Central Glass & Ceramics Research Institute Bulletin	Central Glass & Ceramics Research Institute, Jadavpur, Calcutta 700032, India. (Quarterly)
Ceramic Age	2800 Euclid Avenue, Cleveland, Ohio 44115,U.S.A.(Monthly)
Chemie der Erde	VEB G. Fischer Verlag, Postfach 176, 69 Jena,East Germany. (Four per year)
Czechoslovak Journal of Physics	Artia ve Smekach 30, 11127 Prague, Czechoslovakia. (Monthly)
Doklady — Earth Science Sections	American Geological Institute, 2201 M Street, Washington, D.C. 20037, U.S.A.(Translations of Doklady Akademii Nauk S.S.S.R.) (Bi-monthly)
Fortschritte der Mineralogie	E.Schweizerbartsche Verlagsbuchhandlung, Stuttgart, West Germany. (One per year)
Gemmological Newsletter	7 Hillingdon Avenue, Sevenoaks, Kent TN13 3RB. (A weekly bulletin published during the academic year and including details of new materials, book reviews and abstracts)
Gems and Gemology	The official organ of the Gemological Institute of America, 1660 Stewart St, Santa Monica, California 90404, U.S.A. (Quarterly)
Indian Journal of Pure and Applied Physics	C.S.I.R., Hillside Road, New Delhi 12, India. (Monthly)

Indian Journal of Technology	C.S.I.R, Hillside Road, New Delhi 12, India. (Monthly)
Inorganic Chemistry	American Chemical Society, 1155 16th Street, Washington, D.C. 20036, U.S.A.(Monthly)
Japanese Journal of Applied Physics	2ndToyo Kaiji Building, 4-24-8, Shinbashi, Minato-ku, Tokyo 105, Japan. (Monthly)
Journal of the American Ceramic Society	American Ceramic Society, 65 Ceramic Drive, Columbus, Ohio 43214, U.S.A. (Monthly)
Journal of the American Chemical Society	American Chemical Society, 1155 16th Street, Washington, D.C. 20036, U.S.A. (Fortnightly)
Journal of Applied Physics	Argonne National Laboratory, Argonne, Illinois 60479, U.S.A. (Monthly)
Journal of Chemical Education	Division of Chemical Education, American Chemical Society, Easton, Pa18042,U.S.A.(Monthly)
Journal of Chemical Physics	American Institute of Physics, 335 East 45th Street, New York, N.Y. 10017, U.S.A.(Twice monthly)
Journal of Crystal Growth	North-Holland Publishing Company, Box 211, Amsterdam, Netherlands. (Monthly)
Journal of the Electrochemical Society	215 Canal Street, Manchester, New Hampshire, U.S.A. (Monthly)
Journal of Gemmology	The official organ of the Gemmological Association of Great Britain, St. Dunstan's House, Carey Lane, London EC2V8AB.(Quarterly)
Journal of the Gemmological Society of Japan	The official organ of the Gemmological Society of Japan, c/o Institute of Mineralogy, Petrology and Economic Geology, Tohoku University, Aoba, Sendai, Japan 980. (Articles are in Japanese, but include abstracts in English; specializes in reports of synthetic materials. Period not established)
Journal of Geophysical Research	American Geographical Union, 1707 L Street, Washington, D.C. 20036, U.S.A.(Three per month)

Journal of Materials Science	Chapman & Hall, 11 New Fetter Lane, London EC4P 4EE. (Monthly)
Journal of Nuclear Physics	North-Holland Publishing Company, Box 211, Amsterdam, Netherlands. (Monthly)
Journal of the Optical Society of America	American Institute of Physics, 335 East 45th Street, New York, N.Y. 10017, U.S.A.(Monthly)
Journal of Physical Chemistry	American Chemical Society, 1155 16th Street, Washington, D.C. 20036, U.S.A.(Monthly)
Journal of Physics	Institute of Physics, Netheston House, Marsh Street, Bristol BS1 4BT. (Monthly)
Journal of the Physics and Chemistry of Solids	Pergamon Press, Headington Hill Hall, Oxford OX3 0BW. (Monthly)
Kogyo Kagaku Zasshi (Journal of the Chemical Society of Japan)	5,1-chome, Kanda-Surugadai, Chiyoda-ku,Tokyo, Japan. (Monthly – in Japanese)
Kristall und Technik	Akademie-Verlag, Leipzig, East Germany. (Twelve per year – not necessarily monthly)
Kristallografija	Mezhdunarodnaya Kniga, Moscow G 200,U.S.S.R.(Bi-monthly)
Lapidary Journal	P.O. Box 80937, San Diego, California 92138, U.S.A. (Monthly. The largest magazine extant catering for the mineral collector and amateur faceter, but also including up-to-date accounts of new synthetic materials)
Materials Research Bulletin	Pergamon Press, Headington Hill Hall, Oxford OX3 0BW. (Monthly)
Mineralogical Abstracts	Published jointly by the Mineralogical Society of Great Britain and the Mineralogical Society of America, 41 Queen's Gate, London SW7 5HP. (Quarterly. Contains a section on gemstones which includes synthetic materials)
Mineralogical Magazine	The official organ of the Mineralogical Society of Great Britain, 41 Queen's Gate, London SW7 5HR. (Quarterly.

	Includes the list of new mineral names in which most trade names for synthetic products are included)
Neues Jahrbuch für Mineralogie (Mönatshefte)	E.Schweizerbartsche Verlagsbuchhandlung, Stuttgart, West Germany. (Monthly)
Philosophical Magazine	Taylor & Francis, 10-14 Macklin Street, London WC2B 5NF. (Monthly)
Physica	North-Holland Publishing Company, Box 211, Amsterdam, Netherlands. (Monthly)
Physics Letters	North-Holland Publishing Company, Box 211, Amsterdam, Netherlands. (Weekly)
Physics Status Solidi	Akademie-Verlag, Leipzig, East Germany. (Six per year)
Proceedings of the Royal Society of London	6 Carlton House Terrace, London SW1Y 5AG. (Irregular)
Proceedings of the Second [etc.] International Conference on Crystal Growth	c/o Journal of Crystal Growth, North-Holland Publishing Company, Box 211, Amsterdam, Netherlands.
Retail Jeweller	International Thomson Publishing, 19 Soho Square, London W1. (Fortnightly)
Review of Physical Chemistry of Japan	Kyoto University, Kyoto, Japan.
Review of Scientific Instruments	American Institute of Physics, 335 East 45th Street, New York, N.Y. 10017, U.S.A. (Monthly)
Roczniki Chemii	Ul. Miodowa 10, Warsaw, Poland. (Monthly)
Science	American Association for the Advancement of Science, 1515 Massachusetts Avenue N.W., Washington, D.C. 20005, U.S.A. (Weekly)
Scientific American	415 Madison Avenue, New York, N.Y. 10017, U.S.A. (Monthly)
Solid State Communications	Pergamon Press, Headington Hill Hall, Oxford OX3 0BW. (24 per year)
Synthetic Crystals Newsletter	(Issued irregularly and including detailed reports of man-made crystals)

Yogyo Kyokai Shi (Journal of the Ceramic Society in Japan)	22-17, 2-chome, Hyakunincho, Shinjuku-ku, Tokyo 160, Japan. (Monthly – in Japanese)
Zapiski Vsesoiuznogo Mineralogischeskogo Obshchestva	Mendeleevskaya Lin, Leningrad V 164, U.S.S.R. (Bi-monthly)
Zeitschrift für Anorganische und Allgemeine Chemie	Johann Ambrosius Barth Verlag, Salomonstrasse 188, 701 Leipzig, East Germany. (Eight per year)
Zeitschrift der Deutschen Gemmologischen Gesellschaft	The official organ of the Deutsche Gemmologische Gesellschaft, Postfach 2260, D 6580, Idar-Oberstein, West Germany. (Quarterly)
Zeitschrift für Kristallographie	Akademische Verlagsgesellschaft, Falkensteiner Str. 75-77, Frankfurt/Main, West Germany. (Twice yearly)
Zeitschrift für Naturforschung Ausgabe A	Uhlandstrasse 11, Tübingen, West Germany. (Monthly)

Monographs

Anderson, B.W.: Gem testing (9th ed.); Butterworths, London, 1971

Arem, Joel E.: Man-made crystals; Smithsonian Institution Press, Washington, 1973

Boleszny, I.: Manufacture of artificial gemstones (Research Service Bibliographies, series 4. No. 119.); State Library of South Australia, Adelaide, 1969

Bond, W.L.: Crystal technology; John Wiley & Sons, New York, 1976

Cockayne, B. & Jones, D.W.: Modern oxide materials; Academic Press, London, 1972

Connolly, T.F.: Compilation of crystal growers and crystal growth projects; Research Materials Information Center, Oak Ridge, Tennessee, U.S.A., 1972

—— Solid State physics literature guides, (vols. 2 and 3); IFI/Plenum, New York & London, 1972

Elwell, D.: Man-made gemstones; Horwood, Chichester, 1979

Elwell, D. & Scheel, H.J.: Crystal growth from high-temperature solutions; Academic Press, London, 1975

Galasso, F.S.: Structure and properties of inorganic solids; Pergamon Press, Oxford, 1970

Gilman, J.J.: The art and science of growing crystals; John Wiley & Sons, New York & London, 1963

Laudise, R.A.: *The growth of single crystals;* Prentice-Hall, New Jersey, U.S.A., 1970

Liddicoat, R.T.: *Handbook of gem identification* (10th ed.); Gemological Institute of America, 1975

Lobachev, A.N.: *Crystallization processes under hydrothermal conditions;* Consultants Bureau, New York & London

MacInnes, D: *Synthetic gem and allied crystal manufacture;* Noyes Data Corporation, New Jersey, U.S.A. & London, 1973. (Gives details of a number of patent specifications.)

Milek, J.T. & Neuberger, M.: 'Linear electrooptic modular materials'. *Handbook of electronic materials* (Vol. 8); IFI/Plenum, New York & London, 1972

Mullin, J.W.: *Crystallization;* Butterworths, London, 1961 (A later edition has been published.)

Nassau, K.: *Gems made by man,* Chilton, Radnor, Pa., 1980

Sahagian, C.S.: *Growth of single crystals* (Physical Sciences Research Papers No. 186); Office of Aerospace Research, U.S.A.F. Massachusetts, U.S.A., 1966

Ueda, R. & Mullin, J.B.: *Crystal growth and characterization;* Proceedings of the I.S.S.C.G. Springschool, Japan, 1974 – North-Holland Publishing Company, Amsterdam, 1975

Webster, R.: *Gems* (3rd ed.); Newnes-Butterworths, London, 1975

Winchell, A.N. & Winchell, H.: *The microscopical characters of artificial inorganic solid substances;* Academic Press, New York & London, 1964

Yaverbaum, L. H.: *Synthetic gem production techniques,* Noyes Data Corpn., Park Ridge, 1980

International list of available electronic materials, (2nd ed.); Defence Research Group, Panel on Physics and Electronics, Document AC/243 (Panel III) D/67 (Revised), OTAN/NATO, 1974

Synthèses Cristallines (3rd ed.); published as a series by the Centre d'Études Nucléaires de Saclay (Nos. 1-4) and by the Centre de Documentation sur les Synthèses Cristallines de Montpellier (No. 5)

Index

Note: Numbers in italic refer to illustrations